CREATING A SHARED MORAL COMMUNITY

This book explores the religious, educational, and social practice of a Muslim congregation and the moral world it generated within a mosque in the UK.

The life of the mosque is described through religious practice, communal activities and informal encounters, and the history and ideas that shaped the moral world and thinking of the Indo-Guyanese who built it. Marked by a double diaspora experience with its implication of loss and re-imagining, the congregation's conception of living a Muslim life is embodied in both rituals and in styles of comportment and socialising while religious concerns are voiced in sermons, in religious classes, and in responses to everyday situations. Links are made between anthropology and developmental and psychoanalytic understandings of embodied experience and the emergence of ethical capacity.

This account contributes to the literature on Muslim communities in Europe and 'ordinary ethics'. As such, the book will be of interest to sociologists and anthropologists, to those involved in religious and psycho-social studies, and to clinicians working with Muslim communities.

Judy Shuttleworth has worked as a Consultant Child and Adolescent Psychoanalytic Psychotherapist in community and hospital settings in the National Health Service in the UK. Her previous publications are in the field of clinical work and infant observation. Her interest in the social and cultural context of mental health services led to an MSc in medical anthropology (University College London) and a PhD from the London School of Economics on which this book is based.

Routledge Advances in Sociology

For more information about this series, please visit: https://www.routledge.com/Routledge-Advances-in-Sociology/book-series/SE0511

CREATING A SHARED MORAL COMMUNITY

The Building of a Mosque Congregation in London

Judy Shuttleworth

Routledge
Taylor & Francis Group

LONDON AND NEW YORK

First published 2023
by Routledge
4 Park Square, Milton Park, Abingdon, Oxon OX14 4RN

and by Routledge
605 Third Avenue, New York, NY 10158

Routledge is an imprint of the Taylor & Francis Group, an informa business

British Library Cataloguing-in-Publication Data
A catalogue record for this book is available from the British Library

Library of Congress Cataloging-in-Publication Data
Names: Shuttleworth, Judy, author.
Title: Creating a shared moral community : the building of a mosque
congregation in London / Judy Shuttleworth.
Description: Abingdon, Oxon ; New York : Routledge, 2023. |
Series: Routledge advances in sociology | Includes bibliographical
references and index.
Identifiers: LCCN 2022036611 (print) | LCCN 2022036612 (ebook) |
ISBN 9780367529826 (hardback) | ISBN 9780367529857 (paperback) |
ISBN 9781003080008 (ebook)
Subjects: LCSH: Muslims--Religious life--England--London |
Guyanese--Religious life--England--London | Mosques--England--
London | Mosques as community centers | Communities--Religious
aspects--Islam | London (England)--Religious life and customs
Classification: LCC BP65.G72 S58 2023 (print) | LCC BP65.G72
(ebook) | DDC 297.09421--dc23/eng/20221026
LC record available at https://lccn.loc.gov/2022036611
LC ebook record available at https://lccn.loc.gov/2022036612

ISBN: 978-0-367-52982-6 (hbk)
ISBN: 978-0-367-52985-7 (pbk)
ISBN: 978-1-003-08000-8 (ebk)

DOI: 10.4324/9781003080008

Typeset in Bembo
by KnowledgeWorks Global Ltd.

In memory of my husband Alan Shuttleworth

Alan was a source of support and encouragement
throughout this research though sadly he
did not live to see this book published.

CONTENTS

ACKNOWLEDGEMENTS

I would like to thank the Trustees of the mosque in which I did my fieldwork and those in the congregation who generously allowed me to attend prayers, classes, and social events alongside them.

I also wish to express my gratitude to Michael Lambek, Charles Stafford, and Mathijs Pelkmans, who supervised and encouraged me at various stages in this research, and to Magnus Marsden, who was the examiner of my PhD thesis.

1

INTRODUCTION

Introduction

The mosque described in this book was built by Muslims from Guyana who migrated to London in the 1960s. Building the mosque, which took place over many years, was a communal project through which this group expressed their continuing commitment to living and practicing as both Muslims and as Guyanese. In time other Muslims from the local community joined the congregation, but this is a study of the Guyanese – a particular group of Muslims at a particular moment in time[1] and their religious and communal lives within the mosque.[2]

Two contrasting perspectives on Muslim lives have been prominent in the last 20 years within the anthropology of Islam. Studies of religious revivalist movements describe the cultivation of self-conscious religious subjectivities through study and attentive practice and the challenges this poses to Western secular conceptions of agency (Mahmood 2005; Deeb 2006; Hirschkind 2006; Jouili 2015). Another body of work has focused on Islam as present within the texture and flow of the everyday lives of those who happen to be Muslim and attempts 'to do justice to the full complexity of the worlds that people create and inhabit' (Marsden and Retsikas 2013: 2). This latter perspective has been challenged as suggesting an opposition between piety and everyday lives and for an implication, as Fadil and Fernando put it, that the pious are too exceptional to count as real (Fadil and Fernando 2015). Yet this split is not solely the result of the conceptual frame of 'everyday religion' and the lives of 'ordinary Muslims', it also reflects the numerous internal tensions felt by those who see themselves as following different interpretations of Islam or between different generations who hold different views as to the living of a good Muslim life, as well as arising from the many choices that have had to be made by individuals in the course of adapting to life within European societies.[3] Though the congregation on a Friday is now large and diverse, it is the Guyanese

DOI: 10.4324/9781003080008-1

and those closest to them who are the focus of my study – how they lived out their commitment to their own way of being Muslim, the difficulties this sometimes created with some within the wider congregation, and the efforts of a Guyanese imam to encourage, through sermons, lectures, and classes, both a greater knowledge of the Quran and a capacity to think for oneself rather than depend solely on others for religious understanding. In so far as the Guyanese adopted a stance that differed from others, this might be regarded by some as indicating a less religiously committed position, but I came to see being Guyanese Muslims as involving an interconnection of the religious and the social (Marsden 2005: 26) that required an active, creative engagement with experience. It is this moral engagement and the life it generated within the mosque that I explore through the different activities and events that I observed and participated in.

While Muslim communities across Europe have many experiences in common – the rebuilding of post-migration diaspora communities, becoming a minority group and the focus of the anxieties of the majority and the impact of a new de-territorialised globalised Islamic perspective – different contexts are created by the different history and traditions with respect to religious affiliation, citizenship, and education within European countries (Werbner 2002; Mandel 2008; Bowen 2010; de Koning 2013; Fadil 2013; Jouili 2015). In Britain, the circumstances in which ethnic minority groups find themselves have been influenced by a discourse of 'multi-culturalism' fostered at a local borough level, such as the one in which the mosque is located.[4] Studies of small-scale local situations create an increasingly differentiated picture of the social contexts in which Muslim communities in Europe have settled[5] and the mosque and its congregation constitute one such small-scale world in which individuals participate, both collectively and as individuals, in worship, study, and social relationships, against the background of an ethnically mixed local community.

Though there were core religious rituals in which all who attended the mosque took part, the diversity of practice and thinking within the congregation became visible when, from time to time, some individuals challenged the Guyanese and their way of being Muslim. Rasanayagam (2018) recounts giving a talk in a university department in the USA on the process whereby an Uzbek becomes Muslim. He described this not only in terms of rituals and religious practices but also as emerging through participation in the social life of the community and in its own Muslim traditions with respect to illness and spirit possession. He was challenged by a Muslim member of his audience as 'misrepresenting Islam' by including traditions that the questioner did not consider to be part of the religion at all. This raises issues as to how Islam is defined and who is authorised to do so. The Guyanese who built the mosque might be included in this questioner's challenge. For them being Muslim and being Guyanese were interwoven in a way that was sometimes contested by others. Their commitment to the mosque and to their own conception of the life within it was expressed through the 'moral work' (Mattingly 2012) involved in living out their conception of a Muslim life that held together these different elements. Moral work carries a more on-going quality than is often conveyed in accounts of ethical interventions, but perhaps for the same reason, 'moral labour' might still better convey its repetitive life-reproducing aspect (see Lambek 2010: 15, on Hannah Arendt).

The mosque was an opportunity to observe a sustained communal world in which something serious was unambiguously at stake. Here the need to keep alive the moral commitments of that world and to act with respect to the values of a shared inheritance, was apparent both in adherence to the rituals of Islam and in the style in which sociality was conducted. However I take the effort to maintain these commitments and values as being of relevance to our understanding of the life of other kinds of communal worlds. From the perspective of 'ordinary ethics', the ethical is a quality of 'life lived for itself' expressed in 'everyday comportment and understanding' rather than in special cases or authoritative disputes (Lambek 2010: 3). Though this living is in the face of mortality and the uncertainties and sufferings of life, it also entails the presence of hope. This assumes a mature capacity for experience in the face of reality. On the other hand, Keane (2010, 2016) and Rumsey (2010), building on research by developmentalists, explore the origins of the ethical in relation to the forms of communication that immediately precede speech.[6] I will return later in this chapter to the ethical implications of the infants' participation in a social world through a consideration of research into the still earlier bodily experiences of 'being with others' among neonates and the light this sheds on the beginning of an awareness of the human through attunement to adults' states of relatedness within an expanding social and moral world. I use the term 'moral' to refer to these qualities of relatedness and attunement that form the largely unconscious background to our species mode of 'being in the world' (Zigon 2007; Zigon and Throop 2014) out of which the emotional, imaginative, and intellectual capacities emerge that underpin the exercise of conscious ethical judgement that participation in a moral world requires.

My informants were not all equally religiously observant, but as Pelkmans suggests, 'catching doubt in midair is ... [a] far from a straightforward task' (2013: 5). In describing the life of the mosque, I have sought a balance between the 'making and doing' of religious practice[7], that all could participate in, and the thoughts of those who could, and did, articulate religious views, including the women in a Saturday class who claimed a space for their doubts and failures.

My background and its link to the research

The research into the life of a mosque congregation on which this book is based began as a very general question about the impact of the social and moral worlds within which people live that arose in relation to my work in the National Health Service (NHS). How to consider the experience of an individual or family and the resources they bring to bear on the difficulties they encounter and the help they are offered in relation to the moral qualities of the larger social context in which they live? The same question applies to the clinician they seek help from – what shared resources can be drawn on by the clinician in their practice. I had been wondering about how this interest could be taken forward when the opportunity to study the communal life of a Muslim congregation and the moral world created through religious practice presented itself rather by chance.

The background I brought to this research was different from that of a postgraduate at the start of a career as an anthropologist. After an undergraduate degree in anthropology at Manchester University, I trained as a psychoanalytic psychotherapist working with children, adolescents, and their parents, and I went on to work as a clinician and teacher in the NHS. By the time I thought about undertaking this research, I was working in the paediatric department of a district general hospital. Though an individual young person or their family is the focus of attention, clinical work, of necessity, takes place within the conditions of a local community and the preoccupations of a society at a particular time and this poses questions as to the material and moral resources that are available to patient and clinician alike. One of the elements of the external social and moral context that I became conscious of was the impact on mental health services of the growth of an instrumental audit culture that gradually overtook and replaced an earlier approach that, whatever its shortcomings, had its roots in the value placed on the potentially meaningful nature of the encounter between a clinician and a patient. Timimi (2015), a child and adolescent psychiatrist, writes about the impact of a 'medico-technical' model of symptom-based problem-solving interventions that leaves no space for 'relationships, contexts and values'.[8] It was out of a consciousness of this change in the background to my professional life that I began to think about the question that lies behind this research as to what it was that had been lost, the pervasiveness of what had once been present, and how it is that something so intangible and elusive as a moral world is ever sustained.[9] While working at the hospital, I did a part-time MSc in medical anthropology intending to do the dissertation in an area related to my clinical work, but NHS ethical procedures made this impossible in the timescale required. Then, at the last moment, I had a chance introduction to the secretary of a local mosque and used the opportunity this offered for an observational study of a girls' after-school religious class that took place within the mosque, though independently of it (Shuttleworth 2008). As a result of this experience, I went on to undertake an ethnographic study of the mosque's adult congregation as a way of exploring the life of a group committed to sustaining and handing on a shared moral context.

Though anthropology and psychoanalysis have had a complicated century long relationship, there is an overlap in methodology between the researcher's relationship to interlocutors in the ethnographic method and the clinical relationship. In a paper delivered at a Festschrift for the anthropologist Ronald Frankenberg, the first person to undertake fieldwork within the UK, Elizabeth Bott Spillius, an anthropologist who became a psychoanalyst, examined the complementary relationship between the approaches of the two disciplines to their respective fields of study (Spillius 2005). Though the configuration of the social world and the internal world of the individual remain the distinctive areas of enquiry of the two disciplines, the relationship between the social and the individual, 'the indissoluble relation between minds, bodies and environment', as Marchand (2010) puts it, has itself become a subject of interest. The life of the mosque took place across these domains and registers of experience. In seeking a framework that could encompass this, I took as my starting point Hirschkind's (2006) work on the ethical impact of taped sermons among young men in Cairo with its focus on the bodily affective registers of human experience and communication rather than the conscious, the symbolic, and the discursive. This work creates a bridge to understandings of bodily affective processes within social, religious, and moral worlds beyond the context of Muslim religious revival – a bridge between the perspectives of anthropology and child development, albeit a different aspect of it from the link suggested by Keane (2010) and Rumsey (2010). The importance of the musicality of relatedness in the social environment of our species and non-symbolic bodily experience in the precursors of language in infant communication have emerged through developmental research over the past half-century. This picture of infancy derived from experimental research and its implications for our understanding of adult experience overlaps with that of Klein's psychoanalytic model of the development of the mind. In this model bodily and emotional experience of others, the growth in awareness of both dependence on and separateness from needed others, and the emergence of a nascent moral sensibility in the first year of life are key elements (Klein 1959). There are important links between anthropology, developmental research, Klein's elaboration of Freud's thinking, and subsequent (post-Kleinian) developments of this psychoanalytic model of mental growth with respect to the awareness of moral qualities and the exercise of ethical capacities within ordinary generative human functioning. This area of overlap illuminates the question at the heart of my research as to how a shared moral world is generated, inhabited, and maintained, and I will draw on this in my analysis and elaborate on developmental and psychoanalytic perspectives in footnotes.

Keane (2014) suggests that it is the stance of the ethnographer towards the particularity of experience that renders visible the space of freedom and reflection that lies between natural laws and the norms of a culture. Clinical work in the public sector is often framed in terms of 'the referral problem', the need for a diagnosis that will indicate an evidence-based intervention or the demands of a wider social system that something be done. However, it is also possible to see the task as primarily a collaborative attempt to think with a family or young person about the particular details of their experience and, though it may take time, through that effort itself, for a new perspective to emerge from which the situation can be seen and lived afresh. In this light, the task of clinical work is to attempt to open for the individual or family a space for reflection, for creativity and freedom, between an organic generalising account and the expectations and demands of a social world, neither of which determines a life. This is a study of a mosque congregation that describes how a group of people created and maintained such a space and the capacity it engendered to think about and act on what they valued.

The mosque as a research site

The mosque stands at the corner of a residential road just off a busy high street in an inner London borough.[10] From the outside, with its dome and minaret, it is clearly a mosque, but internally it is a complicated physical space that retains its history and the stages of its transformation from a single-story light industrial building through its use as a synagogue to becoming an all-purpose hall for Muslim prayer and congregational activities. Over a period of about 20 years, the congregation outgrew this space and by the time of my fieldwork a new purpose-built domed building linked to the old hall was complete.[11] Though the creation of the mosque began as the work of one migrant group, the Guyanese, they were joined by Mauritians of similar south Asian descent and double migration experience and by others from a variety of backgrounds who together formed a group with an apparently shared outlook on religious practice and socialising, particularly with respect to gender mixing. The chair of the mosque often referred to this group within the congregation as 'Guyanese oriented'. This designation is significant in relation to the increasing ethnic and religious diversity of the congregation that now includes Muslims from the surrounding area who were originally from north Africa, Uganda, Somalia, and Eastern Europe, each with different Muslim traditions. Though many from these communities used the mosque mainly for congregational prayer and Quran recitations during Ramadan, some individuals of different ethnicities, particularly women, also attended other communal events.

Following my initial period of fieldwork at the girls' after-school class, I kept in contact with the mosque secretary and approached her again for the Trustees' permission to undertake research on the adult congregation. It was agreed that I could come regularly to the mosque, but beyond that, I was left to find my own way as best I could. Because I was doing my research part-time, I built my visits around a series of regular events so that I could plan my time in relation to my work but also because there were times when the mosque was largely empty or closed. Though, at first, I followed up various leads to external gatherings and visited some other mosques and classes, after a few months, I made the decision to concentrate on the Guyanese mosque and the 'Guyanese oriented' group within it. During the two years of my fieldwork, I regularly attended Friday prayers and the rituals of Ramadan, a group for women that met once a month for religious self-education; a weekly gender-mixed study group that one of the visiting preachers started at his home, a weekly women's class led by another visiting preacher that was held at the mosque, a women's keep fit group led by a non-Muslim Guyanese and an assortment of other life cycle events. In addition, there were more peripheral rituals, occasional lectures, and other events.

Maintaining a focus on the mosque and committing my time to regular attendance at the same repeated events created a structure within which to slowly accustom myself to what at the start had been a wholly unknown environment, to compare small changes against the background of repeated events, and to develop my understanding of the mosque as a site of overlapping activities. It was also consonant with an observational approach to the study of infancy with which I was familiar from my clinical background.[12] I explained the nature of my research to each new group I encountered and to any new person who enquired and for some I became a familiar and predictable presence. I participated when I could – helping to serve meals, to clean the mosque for Ramadan, and to mind the shop – and observed when participation was impossible, as in prayer. In the religious classes, I joined in along with everyone else, doing the homework and answering questions about theology and practice about which I knew nothing at the start. However, I could read and understand modern standard Arabic, and this gave me a place within the class as I could help explain the grammar. Some of the conversations I quote took on the character of an unstructured interview, but for the most part, they were remarks made in the ordinary course of events that had a structure and significance of their own.

My encounter with the mosque and its congregation was at first a confusing experience, and, as an outsider, I felt conspicuous and vulnerable. Over a period of months, I began to feel more familiar with the surface structure of the repeated events that I witnessed – how this followed that. Though the chapters describe the different kinds of activity that took place – religious ritual, sociality, and the efforts of some within the congregation to develop greater scriptural knowledge of Islam – my attention was drawn to the overlap and transitions between those areas and to the qualities that were present across the life of the mosque. The mosque encompassed both the differences within the congregation and the vicissitudes of individual practice; the continuing growth of the congregation reflected, among other things, the religious and social background that was shared among the core group of Guyanese, Mauritians, and others. The different chapters trace aspects of this background, starting in Chapter 2 with the history of the Guyanese. Chapters 3 and 4 describe the idea of a Muslim community as it was manifested in the practice of collective prayer and as it was invoked in many of the sermons. Chapters 5 and 6 describe the way the religious and the social were interwoven and lived through a mode of sociability and how that was reflected upon in conversation. Chapters 7 and 8 describe a local manifestation of the search for greater religious knowledge that is widespread among Muslims living in Europe. Chapter 9 describes the relationship between a Bangladeshi imam, who had been appointed by the Trustees, and the children's class he took in which aspects of the religious and social world of the Guyanese were carried forward to a new generation.

I was, and still am, very grateful to the Trustees and to those I met subsequently for allowing me to be present at a time when the media interest in Islam was generally in terms of terrorism and reports of Islamophobia. My consciousness of their trust in me contributed to my wish to observe rather than actively ask questions. The fact that I was approaching retirement and that I worked with children in a local hospital no doubt helped me to present my research and my presence as something that was not too contentious, though my age has also meant that my material is skewed towards the parental and grandparental generation within the congregation. From time to time, I would suddenly be pounced on by the chair of the mosque and asked to say a few words at a meeting and although I felt generally welcomed, I came to realise later that some of the Trustees had needed to field questions that arose from the anxieties of others about me. While many of the Guyanese may have felt they could welcome an outsider's interest in their community and were used to relationships with non-Muslims, for some, it was puzzling that I was interested in the practice of ordinary Muslims rather than seeking what was 'correct'. Although I dressed at the mosque in a way that was not dissimilar to Guyanese women of my age, I know I did not look Muslim, but there was only one occasion when I was openly challenged, and this was because a woman took exception to the fact that while I was on the prayer balcony, I was not joining others in prayer. A Ugandan woman I knew from the monthly Sunday meetings explained who I was and managed to diffuse the situation, but the woman who had challenged me was obviously not pleased. This was at a time when *hizb-ut-tahrir* leaflets were being distributed outside the mosque, and, on leaving, I noticed the woman in conversation with one of the men who were leafleting.

Over and above these tensions with respect to Islam, there is a special difficulty in relation to observing religious practice and the expectations of conversion that it may arouse (Clarke 2013). I was aware that those who allowed me to be present may have been doing so out of a sense of religious obligation. This was most obviously the case in the classes, but in that setting, there were opportunities for others, especially Azzim, the freelance imam who took the class, to comment on the ambiguity of my studying Islam for an intention other than conversion. In this setting, it was helpful that I could explain that I had been brought up within a religious tradition. However, my position as a non-Muslim observing religious practice was nonetheless problematic. One person explained this quite simply as related to a fear of gossip, while others may have felt I would expect them to explain their religious practice and that they would then be judged as incorrect or failing. But being an outsider also allowed yet others to volunteer information that they were not necessarily comfortable to make known to other Muslims.

I have changed the names of everyone who appears in the text and amalgamated some encounters where this did not affect the understanding of the material. However, I am very aware that even with the passage of time since my fieldwork, some people's identity cannot be disguised from those who know the mosque, but they are the individuals who most explicitly gave their consent to my study.

And finally, the issue that Azzim taxed me with during his classes, as to the use I would make of the experience if I did not use my knowledge to become Muslim. I can only say that, within the limits of my capacity, I have used the experience that he and others at the mosque generously offered me in that I have been changed by it and for this I am grateful to all those I got to know, their acceptance of my presence and the chance this gave me to learn and develop. Rasanayagam suggests that such an encounter with the faith of others should be undertaken not as a representative of some other position but as an individual who 'must visit as a guest' (Rasanayagam 2018). I hope that this was the spirit in which I became a regular visitor to the mosque.

The life of the congregation as the life of a moral community

In his exploration of the nature of the ethical, Keane (2016) asks what gives ethics its apparent coherence given that 'the phenomena we might call "ethical" cannot be identified with a single unifying basis in organic structures, cognitive functions, or cultural content' (ibid: 72). He goes on to suggest that this 'apparent coherence' of the ethical has something to do with the interactions between persons and the long-term ethical projects that social life generates and adds that the vulnerability of face-to-face interactions and the limitations they place on individual control 'may even be one condition for ethics' (ibid: 100). Building a mosque and the sustaining of a congregation is just such a long-term ethical project born of collective commitment to a religious tradition and the moral values shaped by a communal history, but it also involves an acceptance of the vulnerability of dependence on the uncertain commitment of the others in an inherently fragile endeavour.

Collective prayer conducted in Arabic and performed in a universal form is at the heart of the shared religious traditions of Islam. Participants in such a ritual event can have differing intentions and understandings and the performance of collective prayer at the mosque was a potentially complicated and, at times, a contested matter in terms of the details of its correct form and the material and organisational practicalities that surrounded it. Yet Rappaport (1999) argues that ritual establishes a religious reality that is not dependent on the inner state of individual participants, a reality that may nonetheless be felt by the individual to be central to their religious life. Rappaport roots ritual's formal, given, and, from the perspective of any individual participant, unchanging structure in both the illocutionary power of ritual speech and in the unifying bodily impact of ritual. I will build on the latter argument in which the musicality of the words of prayer and the accompanying bodily movements forms an expressive, aesthetic element in a familiar collective performance that is open to all. In suggesting the bodily rather than symbolic impact of ritual, Rappaport cites the work of Victor Turner (1969) on the ritually induced transformational state of 'communitas'. Rappaport elaborates Turner's account of this state in terms of the alignment of neurophysiological responses within a group such that the distinctions between persons that pertain in ordinary time dissolve, discursive logic is over-ridden by primary process thinking and strong emotional states predominate. This, Rappaport argues, is both a social phenomenon that transforms a collection of individuals into something like 'a single organism' and a quality of individual experience in which 'developmentally earlier [forms of] functioning' come to the fore, creating a mode of being that is 'more participatory and less de-centred than conceptual thought' (Laughlin et al 1990: 277 cited by Rappaport 1999: 227). Thus, ritual can be understood not only as producing special collective experiences but as a form of sociality that can be linked to human functioning early in development.

Keane (2010, 2016) and Rumsey (2010) have turned to developmental research to consider the origins of ethical capacity, chiefly the work of Tomasello (1999) but also that of Trevarthen (1979, 1998), Trevarthen and Aitkins (2001), and Hobson (1998, 2002). Trevarthen makes a distinction between the immediacy of the face-to-face relationship between infant and mother (parent/carer) as a communicative partner in the first months of life and that which emerges later in the first year that he calls primary and secondary intersubjectivity respectively. Keane and Rumsey explore the implications for the origins of ethical capacity of the stage of 'secondary intersubjectivity' when the infant starts to share objects of interest with a responsive companion. It is out of this dawning awareness of being in the presence of another person's mind through the coming into being of a 'third object' of mutual interest that the possibility of multiple perspectives and self-awareness emerges and, with it, the experience of inhabiting a world held in common. However, Rappaport's description of ritual is referring to something earlier – the world of the neonate and the bodily experience of others created out of the immediacy of attunement to the sounds and movements of 'primary intersubjectivity' through which the infant first participates in the musicality and movements of a social world of 'song and dance' (Condon and Sander 1974; Trevarthen 1998; Malloch and Trevarthen 2009; Caper 2020).[13]

The work of Condon and Sander (1974) and its development in later studies of communicative musicality across the life span by Malloch and Trevarthen (2009) illuminates the foundations of the social in the bodily nature of neonatal experience and the mutual responses of mothers and infants Trevarthen (1979: 98). Condon and Sander (1974) see the synchronisation through which infants join in the sounds and movements of adult communication, aligning their bodily and emotional states, as suggesting that the bond between human beings lies in 'participation within shared organisational forms rather than [as] isolated entities sending discrete messages'. This 'shared organisational form' into which the neonate is absorbed is a social formation of attuned bodily experience that transcends the boundaries of the individual akin to Rappaport's description of ritual states. While infants are able from birth to dance to the music of human speech and join in the movements of a human presence, this collaborative musicality generates a profound sense of relatedness to others that continues throughout life not only in language but also in the need for participation in communal life. Thus, as Keane (2016) maintains, development does not start with an 'individual self-contained biological organism … genetically predisposed to ethics or morality' but with an infant absorbed from the beginning into a world of others. Yet, as another strand of developmental research from the 1970s showed, from two months, infants are aware of failures of attunement and capable of participating in mutually regulated reparative processes (Tronick 2007: 10–11).

That this world of others that the infant is absorbed into is potentially a moral world is apparent in this experimental work, but this was explicitly the focus of an earlier model of development that Klein based on observation and psychotherapy with young children between the two world wars (1937, 1952, 1959). This model envisaged a gradual transition from the second quarter of the first year of life as ushering in a crucial developmental transformation that constituted the infant's entry into a shared moral world. Klein suggested that the infant's relationship to the mother is first built out of the intense bodily sensations of feeding and the physical comfort of a human presence, initially experienced as quite separate from the equally intense threats posed at other times by bodily experiences of hunger, discomfort, and panic. Though this stage would equate in time with the period that Trevarthen called primary intersubjectivity it includes a greater range of naturally occurring infant states than could be the focus of an experimental design. Klein described this primary form of relatedness as slowly giving way to a more complex relationship with others in which the presence of both pleasurable and distressing kinds of experience can be increasingly tolerated within a more integrated perception and with this development the anxieties attendant on the beginnings of a sense of vulnerability and ambivalence towards this more complicated world start to emerge. Developing the capacity to cope with having mixed feelings and yet maintaining contact with others who are only partly, and intermittently, felt to be a source of good experiences, becomes, in this model, the task of the infant from the second quarter of the first year onwards, along with the capacities that emerge in secondary intersubjectivity. Coping with ambivalence, disappointment, and anger while keeping hope and love alive is a never finished task of adult life; the pain and anxiety of responsi-bility, failure and mortality are experiences which the individual only manages to hold in mind *through* relationships to others and *within* a shared moral world. It is '[I]n the infant's repeated encounters with loss and recovery in relation to those they depend on, [that] Klein sees the foundations of the human capacity to mourn and to recover trust and hope in the goodness of life. In the years when Fascism was gaining ground in Europe, Klein explored the fragility of love and goodness and the human capacity to feel responsible for the preserving and restoring of this quality of the human world' (Shuttleworth 2017).[14]

In this light, the mosque and the rituals and social events that take place there provide a space that can contain, to some extent, the vicissitudes of individual com-mitment and the anxieties felt about failure that ethnographies of everyday religious practice depict (Schielke 2009; Simon 2009, 2014; Schielke and Debevec 2012), while the mosque is sustained in this function through its continuing use by the congregation. Though many of the sermons sought to address this complex inter-relationship and concerns about the state of the community, the *umma*, through explicit theological statements, I will explore the many varied and on-going uses of the mosque, both ritual and social, as generating the medium in which a shared world was carried and communicated both within and beyond the prayer hall.

Hirschkind (2006) describes the ethical impact of the soundscape of a particu-lar moral world. His ethnography of religious practice in Cairo concerns a loosely connected group of young men going about their daily life for whom listening to taped sermons as the continuous, often unattended to, background soundscape of their lives, was a way of developing their religious sensibilities. While the impact of these sermons is described in the same bodily affective registers that Rappaport cites with respect to ritual, Hirschkind places them in relation to an Islamic account of the psychophysiology of preaching and a view of the bodily affective processes of social life based on the work of two social theorists, Jousse ([1925] 1990) and Massumi (2002).[15] The nature of the relationship between embodied experience and conscious feelings and thoughts, between non-conscious visceral states and a mind capable of reflection, was described by the neuroscientist Antonio Damasio (1999) as a continuous two-way process between the brain and the constantly changing states of body and mind as they register shifts in the internal and external environment. For Damasio the visceral, the embodied and the subjective shape, and are shaped by, this process. This implies the permeability of different registers as opposed to a cutting off the somato-affective, pre-reflective registers from language on the one hand or the prioritising of the cognitive on the other; as Eisenlohr puts it 'the bodily-affective, conceptual, and deliberative registers of experience are mutually constituting' (Eisenlohr 2006: 263). This is consonant with Jousse's view of 'the indivisible unity of body and mind' in whom 'language and consciousness are constructed upon … the mnemonic faculties of the senses and the dynamics of bodily rhythms (respiration, pulse, heartbeat and so on)' (Hirschkind 2006: 77). Yet developmental research suggests that these are not only the rhythmic qualities of an individual's experience but the qualities of an enveloping social background of continuous bodily affective communication into which the individual is always being drawn as a participant.

If the social environment that characterises our species is first encountered by the infant as an enveloping context of synchronised sounds and movements, a 'shared organisational form' as Condon and Sander (1974) put it, this is an image that also evokes the idea of a living organism with its own internal rhythms. Though with a very different object of study in mind, Pelkmans describes the trajectories of collective ideas within a group in terms of 'the swelling of momentum, the flash of intensity, the release of energy' that he calls 'pulsations' (2017: 3). Unlike the more mechanical image of 'cycles' of doubt and hope in an earlier work (Pelkmans 2013), he uses here the physiological image of 'pulsations' to describe the way energy and enthusiasm builds to states of effervescence as a group of Muslims in Kyrgyzstan gathers to offer religious proselytising only for it to eventually fade out in detachment, disappointment, and doubt as the task ends and individuals peel off and return to their former lives (2017: 182). Pelkmans' reference to the pulsating of moral life within the group, that he links to the work of Victor Turner on the special states created by ritual, echoes both the dynamics of musicality (cf the 'pulse, quality and narrative' in Malloch and Trevarthen 2009: 4) and the bodily nature of social experience, in which a group find themselves drawn 'automatically, regularly, and irresistibly into each other's mental and emotional spheres' (Caper 2020) and function, for a time, as a single organism.[16] To the adult mind, this is a mental image, a metaphor, that helps one to think afresh about the nature of social processes, but for the neonate, such an encompassing environment of sound and movement must initially have been experienced as a bodily process, something direct and concrete. Only later in development will such bodily experiences be grasped through a mental image as an idea and become something to think and speak about but at the cost of being divorced from its bodily origins.[17]

In cultivating pious states of feeling Hirschkind's interlocutors were attending not only to the verbal content of the sermons and their implications for religious practice but experiencing their impact as transmitted directly to the hearer through the musical dynamics of the delivery, prompting bodily, affective, and imaginative responses. A recurrent image, both in the sermons they listened to and in the way the young men expressed the nature of their impact, was that of 'opening the heart', which Hirschkind renders as 'states of emotional receptivity and response' (Hirschkind 2006: 75). This was sometimes spoken of by individuals in terms of a directly calming effect but also as the 'taking in' of that capacity for 'moral discrimination' that they felt was necessary for proper conduct. The experience of this 'opening of the heart' to affective currents of sound is, as Hirschkind puts it, one in which the 'body registers its involvement with its sensory surroundings' (ibid: 77) and becomes able to discern, and attend to, an ethically appropriate focus. Hirschkind's descriptions evoke not the boundedness of an individual consciousness or the body as the ground for conscious self-fashioning but the body as receiving and responding to the affective-imaginative currents flowing within the environment as part of the on-going, naturally occurring life of human beings.[18] Though the young men listening to sermons are intentionally using this dynamic to develop a religious sensibility, Hirschkind stresses that human beings are *naturally* attuned to one another and imaginatively responsive to the musical qualities of their sound world, the relational states carried within it and its potential to bring moral feelings of relatedness to life within, and between, individuals. It is this view of the musicality of early pre-symbolic, pre-reflective bodily experience, it's receptive, attuning, and communicative potential that may be said to constitute the medium in which 'the moral life of the mosque' is carried across the range of religious, social, and individual activities. Though I will describe discrete acts of conscious ethical reflection and interventions which emerged from this moral background, it is a background in which ethical potential is present in 'nonvolitional currents of affective and psychic force not amenable to wilful control' (Pandian and Ali 2010: 6).

In the chapters that follow, I describe the way life was lived within the mosque as constituting a shared world and I draw attention to the expression of moral sensibility and ethical capacity that takes place within ordinary experiences of relatedness – 'the transcendent quality of experience itself' as Rasanayagam puts it (2011: 164). Worship, preaching, and teaching have an explicit religious focus yet this focus finds its meaning not as a free-standing pre-existing system of thought but within the complex relationships and obligations of on-going lives lived alongside others in which it is embedded. Sociability embodies and enacts aspects of communal life and locates individuals within a larger context of values, but in the mosque it also brought into focus the differences within the congregation, the passage of time, and the anxieties associated with both external challenges and internal threats to a sense of hope, confidence, and continuity. The idea of Guyana and the multi-ethnic religiously syncretic form of life experienced there by those who built the mosque was explicitly invoked as a moral resource when difficult situations arose in the present and shaped what was being handed on into the future. It is this potential of on-going experience to contain and develop a moral sensibility that I will explore.

Notes

1 My fieldwork took place between 2009 and 2012 with occasional visits to the mosque until 2017.
2 Despite the tendency in the media to homogenise Muslim experience 'no one is Muslim in general' (Lewis and Hamid 2018: 18). Not only are there different ethnic and religious traditions but individuals who seek to find their own way in a complex and often contested sphere (Bowen 2015; Hamid 2018).
3 Living within complex modern societies may include not only adaptations of Muslim practice but also non-practice and the adoption of other forms of spirituality (Fadil 2011, 2013; Jeldtoft 2011; Shively 2014).
4 If the decentralised system of local government in Britain created opportunities for pragmatic local accommodations through a discourse of multi-culturalism, in contrast to ideas of the nation, citizenship, and secularism in France (Bowen 2007), an unwritten constitution, an established church and a legal system that recognises discrimination on the grounds of race but not religion has created other obstacles (Hellyer 2009). Sovik (2015) compares the position of Muslims within the public school system in France and Germany against the background of historic differences with respect to the relationship between religion and state and the greater emphasis on community rather than the nation in German.
5 For example, the building of a local mosque in a Dutch town (Verkaaik 2012), the passing on of religious practice and commitment within families in provincial Denmark (Pedersen 2015) and Islamic education in a Helsinki comprehensive secondary school (Rissanen 2015).
6 Keane and Rumsey mainly cite the developmental researcher Tomasello (1999) but also mention Trevarthen (1979, 1998), Stern (1985), and Hobson (2002), a body of work that began in the 1970s at a time when technological development in videotaping made possible fine-grained research into the relationship between mothers and new-borns.
7 A phrase used by Lambek for which I have been unable to locate a source.
8 For a further account of these changes Shuttleworth et al (2017).
9 In this example, the loss was of a context that sustained the meaning of a professional activity but more broadly, what is at stake are the moral goods carried internally within a tradition of practice (MacIntyre 1981).
10 I have used substitute names for those individuals who appear in the book and although it isn't possible to disguise the mosque itself, I have not specifically identified its location.
11 At this point, the new building was still being paid for, but after about five years, it was clear that yet more space was needed, and the second stage of rebuilding was undertaken on the same site, this time replacing the original hall.
12 In contrast to experimental studies of infancy, Infant Observation is the naturalistic study of an infant growing up within a family over the first two years of life through weekly unstructured observation visits to the infant at home in which the observer seeks to establish a way of being present, without actively shaping events – an observer but not a participant. It creates a framework within which to observe the emergence of different registers of experience as the infant develops within an environment of intimate relationships and the changing impact of the observer's presence on the family. The significance of the patterns that form and change over time are discussed

within a small seminar group (Miller et al 1989; Waddell 2006). As a preparation for clinical work, it aims to foster a sensitivity to the impact of bodily states within familiar relationships, the way adult care supports the development from pre-verbal to verbal communication and the dawning of symbolic experience in the infant and entry into a cultural world. As well as laying the foundation for clinical work, it has also been used as a research methodology (Rustin 2006; Urwin and Sternberg 2012).

13 Drawing on the work of developmentalists Condon and Sander (1974) and Malloch and Trevarthen (2009), Caper, a psychoanalyst, suggests the ground of sociality lies in bodily processes whereby 'Human animals draw each other automatically, regularly, and irresistibly into each other's mental and emotional spheres. Spontaneously forming communities marked by shared mental organisation. This recruitment activity constitutes a substantial part of everyday life … transcends the boundaries of the individual and gives rise to a rapport in which disagreements and discriminations that might occur on the basis of a verbal discussion are suppressed in favour of sharing a "co-ordinated, embodied space and time"' (Caper 2020: 5). Caper links this developmental work to that of earlier psychoanalysts on the emergence of the mind out of bodily experience and the nature of relationships within groups (Bion 1961, 1962; Meltzer 1986).

14 For a summary of this theoretical model and its relationship to developmental research at that time, see Shuttleworth (1989); for an extended account of Klein's contribution to current psychoanalytic thinking, see Rustin and Rustin (2017).

15 Martin (2013) argues that Massumi's position, and that of the 'affective turn' within anthropology more generally, creates a gap between affect as a brain event and the conscious experience of an individual. I suggest that Damasio is offering an intrinsically 'joined up' account of the mutually affecting relationship between mind, body, and brain.

16 Wilfred Bion (1962), a psychoanalyst, described the mind as coming into being through the infant's experience of being taken into the receptive space of the mother's (parents/carers) mind. The micro responses through which the mother comes to know the infant's state, an experience with which the infant, in turn, comes to identify, is framed in terms of the image of a functioning digestive system. Bion's (1961) experience as a psychiatrist working with groups both in the army during WW2 and later in the NHS led to his interest in the mental life of groups (Hinshelwood 2003; Caper 2020).

17 It was to capture the on-going impact of such bodily experiences and their transformation into thought within the mind that Klein postulated a continuing process taking place on the boundary between the somatic and the mental – phantasy (Isaacs 1952). This spelling was to distinguish it from conscious daydreaming.

18 Mahmood (2005: 32) writes that 'the women are summoned [in the classes] to recognise themselves in terms of the virtues and codes of these [Islamic] traditions, and they come to measure themselves against the ideals furnished by these traditions', and she argues that in doing so the women are exercising ethical freedom through this conscious effort to re-make themselves.

References

Bion, W. (1961) *Experiences in Groups.* New York: Basic Books.

Bion, W. (1962) *Learning from Experience.* London: Heinemann.

Bowen, I. (2015) *Medina in Birmingham, Najaf in Brent.* London: Hurst and company.

Bowen, J. (2007) *Why the French Don't Like Headscarves: Islam, the State, and Public Space.* Princeton: Princeton University Press.

Bowen, J. (2010) *Can Islam be French? Pluralism and Pragmatism in a Secularist State.* Princeton: Princeton University Press.

Caper, R. (2020) *Bion and Thought Too Deep for Words.* Abingdon: Routledge.

Clarke, M. (2013) 'Integrity and Commitment in the Anthropology of Islam', in Marsden, M. and Retsikas, K. (eds) *Articulating Islam: Anthropological Approaches to Muslim Worlds.* London: Springer.

Condon, W. S. and Sander, L. W. (1974) 'Synchrony demonstrated between movements of the neonate and adult speech', *Child Development* 45(2): 456–462.

Damasio, A. (1999) *The Feeling of What Happens*. London: Heinemann.

Deeb, L. (2006) *An Enchanted Modern: Gender and Public Piety in Shi'a Lebanon*. Princeton: Princeton University Press.

de Koning, M. (2013) 'The moral maze: Dutch Salafis and the construction of a moral community of the faithful', *Contemporary Islam* 7: 71–84.

Eisenlohr, P. (2006) *Little India: Diaspora, Time and Ethnolinguistic Belonging in Hindu Mauritius*. London: University of California Press.

Fadil, N. (2011) 'Not-/unveiling as an ethical practice', *Feminist Review* 98: 83–109.

Fadil, N. (2013) 'Performing the salat at work: Secular and pious Muslims negotiating the contours of the public in Belgium', *Ethnicities* 13(6): 729–750.

Fadil, N. and Fernando, M. (2015) 'Rediscovering the "everyday" Muslim: Notes on an anthropological divide', *Journal of Ethnographic Theory* 5(2): 59–88.

Hamid, S. (2018) *Sufis, Salafis and Islamists*. London: I.B. Tauris.

Hellyer, H. A. (2009) *Muslims of Europe: The 'Other' Europeans*. Edinburgh: Edinburgh University Press.

Hinshelwood, R. (2003) 'Group Mentality and "Having a Mind"', in Lipgar, R. M. and Pines, M. (eds) *Building on Bion: Roots*. London: Jessica Kingsley.

Hirschkind, C. (2006) *Ethical Soundscapes*. New York: Columbia University Press.

Hobson, P. (1998) 'The Inter-Subjective Foundations of Thought', in Braten, S. (ed) *Intersubjective Communication and Emotion in Early Ontogeny*. Cambridge: Cambridge University Press.

Hobson, P. (2002) *The Cradle of Thought*. London: Pan Macmillan.

Isaacs, S. (1952) 'The nature and function of phantasy', *International Journal of Psychoanalysis* 29(2): 558–566.

Jeldtoft, N. (2011) 'Lived Islam: Religious identity with "non-organized" Muslim minorities', *Ethnic and Racial Studies* 34(7): 1134–1151.

Jouili, J. S. (2015) *Pious Practice and Secular Constraints*. Stanford: Stanford University Press.

Jousse, M. ([1925] 1990) *The Oral Style*. New York: Garland Publishing Inc.

Keane, W. (2010) 'Minds, Surfaces and Reasons in the Anthropology of Ethics', in Lambek, M. (ed) *Ordinary Ethics*. New York: Fordham University Press.

Keane, W. (2014) 'Affordances and reflexivity in ethical life: An ethnographic stance', *Anthropological Theory* 14(1): 3–26.

Keane, W. (2016) *Ethical Life: Its Natural and Social Histories*. Princeton: Princeton University Press.

Klein, M. (1937) 'Love Guilt and Reparation', in Money-Kyrle, R. (ed) *The Writings of Melanie Klein* 1975 Volume 1 | International Psychoanalytical Library, No. 104. London: Hogarth [Reprinted London: Vintage 1988].

Klein, M. (1952) 'On Observing the Behaviour of Young Children', in Money-Kyrle, R *The Writings of Melanie Klein* 1975 Volume 3, No. 104. London: Hogarth [Reprinted London: Vintage 1997].

Klein, M. (1959) 'Our Adult World and Its Roots in Infancy', in Money-Kyrle, R. (ed) *The Writings of Melanie Klein* 1975 Volume 3 | International Psychoanalytical Library, No. 104. London: Hogarth [Reprinted London: Vintage 1997].

Lambek, M. (2010) 'Introduction', in Lambek, M. (ed) *Ordinary Ethics*. New York: Fordham University Press.

Laughlin, C., McManus, J. and d'Aquili, E. (1990) *Brain, Symbol and Experience: Towards a Neuro-Phenomenology of Human Consciousness*. Boston: New Science Library.

Lewis, P. and Hamid, S. (2018) *British Muslims: New Directions in Islamic Thought, Creativity and Activism*. Edinburgh: Edinburgh University Press.

MacIntyre, A. (1981) *After Virtue*. London: Duckworth.

Mahmood, S. (2005) *The Politics of Piety*. Princeton: Princeton University Press.

Malloch, S. and Trevarthen, C. (2009) *Communicative Musicality*. Oxford: Oxford University Press.

Mandel, R. (2008) *Cosmopolitan Anxieties: Turkish Challenges to Citizenship and Belonging in Germany*. London: Duke University Press.

Marchand, T. (2010) 'Making knowledge: Explorations of the indissoluble relation between minds bodies and environment', *Journal of the Royal Anthropological Institute*: 16(special issue): 1–21.

Marsden, M. (2005) *Living Islam: Muslim Religious Experience in Pakistan's North-West Frontier*. Cambridge: Cambridge University Press.

Marsden, M. and Retsikas, K. (eds) (2013) *Articulating Islam: Anthropological Approaches to Muslim Worlds*. London: Springer.

Martin, E. (2013) 'The potentiality of ethnography and the limits of affect theory', *Current Anthropology* 54(S7): S149–S158.

Massumi, B. (2002) *Parables of the Virtual*. London: Duke University.

Mattingly, C. (2012) 'Two virtue ethics and the anthropology of morality', *Anthropology Theory* 12(12): 161–184.

Meltzer, D. (1986) *Studies in Extended Metapsychology: Clinical Applications of Bion's Ideas*. Perthshire: Clunie Press.

Miller, L., Rustin, M. E., Rustin, M. J. and Shuttleworth, J. (1989) *Closely Observed Infants*. London: Duckworth.

Pandian, A. and Ali, D. (2010) *Ethical Life in South Asia*. Indianapolis: Indiana University Press.

Pedersen, M. H. (2015) 'Islam in the Family: The Religious Socialisation of Children in a Danish Provincial Town', in Sedgwick M. (ed) *Making European Muslims*. Abingdon: Routledge.

Pelkmans, M. E. (2013) *Ethnographies of Doubt*. New York: I.B. Tauris and Co Ltd.

Pelkmans, M. E. (2017) *Fragile Convictions*. New York: Cornell University Press.

Rappaport, R. (1999) *Ritual and Religion in the Making of Humanity*. Cambridge: Cambridge University Press.

Rasanayagam, J. (2011) *Islam in Post-Soviet Uzbekistan: the morality of experience*. Cambridge: Cambridge University Press.

Rasanayagam, J. (2018) 'Anthropology in conversation with an Islamic tradition: Emmanuel Levinas and the practice of critique', *Journal of the Royal Anthropological Institute* 24(1): 90–106.

Rissanen, I. (2015) 'Negotiating Identity, Difference and Citizenship in Finnish Islamic Education', in Sedgwick, M. (ed) *Making European Muslims*. Abingdon: Routledge.

Rumsey, A. (2010) 'Ethics, Language and Human Sociality', in Lambek, M. (ed) *Ordinary Ethics*. New York: Fordham University Press.

Rustin, M. J. (2006) 'Infant observation research. What have we learnt so far?', *Infant Observation* 9(1): 35–52.

Rustin, M. J. (2012) 'Infant Observation as a Method of Research', in Urwin, C. and Sternberg, J. (eds) *Infant Observation and Research*. Hove: Routledge.

Rustin, M. E. and Rustin M. J. (2017) *Reading Klein*. New York: Routledge.

Schielke, S. (2009) 'Ambivalent commitments: Troubles of morality, religiosity and aspiration among young Egyptians', *Journal of Religion in Africa* 39(2): 158–185.

Schielke, S. and Debevec, L. (2012) 'Introduction', in Schielke, S. and Debevec, L. (eds) *Ordinary Lives and Grand Schemas: an Anthropology of Everyday Religion*. Oxford: Berghahn Books.

Shively, K. (2014) 'Entangled ethics: Piety and agency in Turkey', *Anthropological Theory* 14(4): 462–480.

Shuttleworth, J. (1989) 'Psychoanalytic Theory and Infant Development', in Miller, L. Rustin, M. E., Rustin, M. J. and Shuttleworth, J. *Closely Observed Infants*. London: Routledge.

Shuttleworth, J. (2008) 'Creating religious experience in contemporary society', *Infant Observation* 11(1): 17–28.

Shuttleworth, J. (2017) 'Reading Klein; Review article', *Infant Observation* 20(2–3): 196–198.

Shuttleworth, J., Britton, J., Keenan, A. and Thomaidis-Zades, K. (2017) 'Thinking Psychoanalytically about Mental Health Services for Children, Adolescents and Their Parents', in Vaspe, A. (ed) *Psychoanalysis, the NHS, and Mental Health Work Today*. London: Karnac.

Simon, G. M. (2009) 'The soul freed of cares', *American Ethnologist* 36(2): 258–275.

Simon, G. M. (2014) *Caged in on the Outside: Moral Subjectivity, Selfhood, and Islam in Minangkabau, Indonesia*. Honolulu: University of Hawai'i Press.

Sovik, M. (2015) 'Religion and Citizenship in France and Germany: Models of Integration and the Presence of Islam in Public Schools', in Sedgwick, M. (ed) *Making European Muslims*. Abingdon: Routledge.

Spillius, E. B. (2005) 'Anthropology and psychoanalysis: A personal concordance', *The Sociological Review* 53(4): 658–671.

Stern, D. (1985) *The Interpersonal World of the Infant: A View from Psychoanalysis and Developmental Psychology*. New York: Basic Books.

Timimi, S. (2015) 'Children and young people's improving access to psychological therapies: Inspiring innovation or more of the same?', *British Journal of Psychiatry Bulletin* 39: 57–60.

Tomasello, M. (1999) *The Cultural Origins of Human Cognition*. Cambridge: Cambridge University Press.

Trevarthen, C. (1979) 'Communication and Co-Operation in Early Infancy: The Origins of Primary Inter-Subjectivity', in Bullowa, M. (ed) *Before Speech*. Cambridge: Cambridge University Press.

Trevarthen, C. (1998) 'The Concept and Foundations of Infant Intersubjectivity', in Braten, S. (ed) *Intersubjective Communication and Emotion in Early Ontogeny*. Cambridge: Cambridge University Press.

Trevarthen, C. and Aitkins, K.. (2001) 'Infant intersubjectivity: Research, theory and clinical applications', *Journal of Child Psychology and Psychiatry* 42: 3–48.

Tronick, E. (2007) *The Neurobehavioural and Social-Emotional Developments of Infants and Children*. London: W.W. Norton.

Turner, V. (1969) *The Ritual Process*. Chicago: Aldine.

Urwin, C. and Sternberg, J. (eds) (2012) *Infant Observation and Research*. Hove: Routledge.

Verkaaik, O. (2012) 'Designing the "anti-mosque": Identity, religion, and affect in contemporary European mosque design', *Social Anthropology* 20(2): 161–176.

Waddell, M. (2006) 'Infant observation in Britain: A Tavistock approach', *International Journal of Psychoanalysis* 87(4): 4–22.

Werbner, P. (2002) *Imagined Diasporas among Manchester Muslims*. Santa Fe: School of American Research Press.

Zigon, J. (2007) 'Moral breakdown and the ethical demand', *Anthropological Theory* 7 (1): 131–150.

Zigon, J. and Throop, J. (2014) 'Moral experience: Introduction', *Ethos* 42(1): 1–15.

2

THE MOSQUE, ITS CONGREGATION, AND ITS HISTORY

British Guiana/Guyana

The history of the mosque itself and the presence of a diverse congregation at the time of my fieldwork reflects the complex history that the Guyanese brought to the endeavour. The Guyanese have a double migration history. They are the descendants of an Indian diaspora who travelled from the Indian sub-continent to the Caribbean and British Guiana (now Guyana), Mauritius, Fiji, and South Africa as indentured workers, a migration that began after the abolition of slavery in 1834, driven by the demand for labour in the sugar plantations, and continued until 1917.[1] Though single men were in the majority, women were also part of this migration both as part of families and as individuals (Lal 2018). The grandparents and great-grandparents of some of the Guyanese I got to know at the mosque had been part of the last period of migration in the late 19th and early 20th centuries, but no one seemed to know many details of their family history and little material evidence has survived.[2]

Reflecting the demography of those areas of the Indian sub-continent from which they were drawn, this diaspora population was mainly Hindu but also included Muslims (approximately 16 per cent) and Christians (1 per cent), the latter had risen to 10 per cent by the 1960s through religious conversion (Jayawardena 1966). Though Islam had first entered the country in the 16th century it was only re-established with the arrival of this Indian workforce in the 19th century (de Kruijf 2007).[3] Today Guyana is a multi-ethnic society of indigenous South American people and those of African and Indian descent, with Muslims making up 15 per cent of the total population (Chickrie 2007). As well as the gradual loss of local Indian languages and their replacement by English, the religious traditions of both Hindus and Muslims were subject to syncretising pressures. Lal (2018) suggests that indenture may have been 'simultaneously

DOI: 10.4324/9781003080008-2

an enslaving and liberating experience for many' particularly women (ibid: 90) and writes 'The fact that women were prepared to leave a life of drudgery lived on the sufferance of others for distant unknown places across the ocean would suggest that these were women of pride and determination, and enterprise and self-respect. These were certainly the values they inculcated in the children and grandchildren' (ibid: 88). Chickrie (1999) suggests that women's involvement in the workforce militated against *purdah* and gender segregation. He argues that because migration took place before the out-break of inter-religious tensions in the sub-continent and that all were subject to the same conditions of indenture, the Indo-Guyanese could come together as a community, stressing their Indian past and their common interests *vis-à-vis* Guyana's other ethnic groups. This, de Kruijf (2007) argues, diminished the importance of caste distinctions and led to a more egalitarian ethos, intermarriage, and fictive kinship ties between Hindus and Muslims of Indian descent. Shared public participation in syncretic forms of religious rituals emerged, expressive of their common situation of economic and political restriction (Khan 1997, 2004; Mohapatra 2006; Khanam and Chickrie 2009; Chickrie and Khanam 2016; Leonard 2018). Based on a study in the 1950s, Jayawardena (1963: 23) writes that 'Hinduism and Islam are regarded as alternative ways of being Indian. A close study of their customs reveals a considerable degree of convergence and syncretism has developed'. Under the colonial government, education was left to plantation owners and European evangelists and only Christian holidays were officially recognised, so that Christian creole culture became influential in the lives of all, including Muslims (de Kruijf 2007).

The dynamic potential of diaspora encounters with difference is described by eyewitnesses to the public celebration of Muharram in British Guiana and Trinidad during the 19th century. A festival of Shi'a Islam, it was immensely popular with Hindu and Sunni Muslims in which members of the Christian creole and Afro-Caribbean population also participated (Mohapatra 2006). Khan describes being Muslim in Trinidad as based in the following of customs, the freedom to participate sincerely in the ceremonies of other religious traditions, such as Catholic rituals to the Virgin Mary, as well as in the emergence of forms of superstition that were recognised by those involved as different in kind from the three main religious traditions (Khan 2004). By the early decades of the 20th century, Hindu missionary activity in British Guiana, Suriname, and Trinidad sought to bring the homogeneity of an 'official' Brahminised form of Hinduism to bear on folk traditions and to limit the mixing of Hindu and Muslim forms of religious activity, creating a sharper boundary between their adherents (Vertovec 1994; Khan 2004). Despite this, studies of more recent social formations suggest that inter-faith marriage, generalised social reciprocity and participation in syncretic, religiously based community events continued to be a feature of Guyanese life (Rauf 1974; Williams 1991). The fact that all had suffered the experience of indentured labour has been described as giving rise to an attitude of egalitarianism across castes. This was described in Trinidad as the valuing of a capacity to 'live good with people' (Khan 1997) and in British Guiana/Guyana as the acceptance of others as being 'people like us', a social disposition called *mati* (Jayawardena 1968; Williams 1991; Robinson 2006; Halstead 2008).[4]

Over time, however, this inclusiveness, born of having been, perhaps quite literally, in the same boat, gave way in the face of three currents of change. Firstly, an indentured workforce tied to plantations began to live as free labourers within village communities or as part of a more diverse workforce in urban settlements (Mohapatra 2006; Halstead 2008). Secondly, at the end of the 1950s, in the run-up to independence, inter-ethnic tensions between Afro-and Indo-Guyanese, fostered and exploited for political purposes, especially in urban centres, led to racialised identities, challenging and replacing the social inclusiveness of *mati* (Halstead 2008). At this time, there was a split in the main multi-ethnic political party in Guyana, the People's Progressive Party of Guyana (PPP), which both groups had previously supported.[5] The violence continued for several decades, contributing to the Indo-Guyanese diaspora in the UK, Canada, and the US, while these globalised connections fed the economic disparities that further undermined social cohesion. Thirdly, from the 1970s, the social and religious accommodations between Indo-Guyanese Muslims, Hindus, and Christians came under attack by Muslim preachers from West Africa and Saudi Arabia who emphasised the importance of the 'correct' form of Islam, a process similar to that of 'Brahminisation' within the Hindu population. Khan (2004) describes the paradox that, as both Hindu and Muslim religious traditions became subject to external influences, becoming in a sense more global, so the focus of both religious groups became narrower, limiting the perspective of the Indian population that had formerly participated in local forms of creolised culture and shared religiosity. Moreover, this wave of Muslim proselytising activity led to multiple religious factions within the Indian Muslim community, each taking a different stance towards the tension between 'purified' Islam and cultural traditions, respectively (Chickrie 2007; de Kruijf 2007). Though the first generation of Guyanese who eventually built the mosque in London had left for the UK by then, these same currents of globalised movements within Islam were flowing through the UK and felt within the mosque. Yet so too was the legacy of an earlier multi-ethnic and multi-faith Guyanese Islam that was carried in imagination into a second migration and found expression in the building of a mosque and in the forms of communal life within it.

Research on migration from the Indian sub-continent to the Caribbean, Mauritius, and Fiji has fed into the larger literature on the experience of migration and the shift towards a view of culture as fluid and situational – a live object rather than a piece of 'tied and tagged baggage that belongs with one national ethnic or religious group' even while it may also be represented by those involved as fixed and unchanging (Baumann 1999: 95). Baumann argues that culture exists in both forms, that 'rhetoric is essentialised, yet the activity is processual' (ibid: 91). The place of 'Guyana' in the experience of the Guyanese in London is as both an idealised imagined object and a live resource used creatively in difficult moments, though often through the idiom of a joke. Though the Caribbean and Mauritian literature mainly concerns the larger Hindu Indian populations in both places, it is relevant to the Muslim Guyanese, not only because of the shared the experience of migration and indenture but also because of its focus on the processes by which a new sense of belonging is generated (Jayawardena 1963, 1980; Vertovec 1994; Khan 2004; Eisenlohr 2006; Mohapatra 2006; Halstead 2008). Post migration experience and the emergence of new diasporic cultural and religious forms are seen as generated not by replication but in actively creative engagements with the material, relational and imaginative possibilities available within a new context through which Werbner (2018: 319) suggests ritual finds a new power to 'reconcile the past and present'.

For this reason, before moving on to this second migration, I will use the way two Guyanese men talked about what they felt had been the impact of this past on their way of thinking about being Muslim to suggest the complexity of possible responses to this diaspora experience and the active process by which this past was carried into the present. These were not formal interviews, but they were both individuals I had opportunities to talk to from time to time and who were comfortable doing so. Although overall, I had more contact with women at the mosque, these conversations tended to be addressed to others in a group and were not explicitly intended to explain their thinking to me. However, for this very reason, it was largely through my contact with women that I was able to think about how individuals express themselves, physically and verbally, in the moment. Though these exchanges may have been passed over at the time without a noticeable response, they fed into a social world a sense of a shared way of understanding or raised a contested perspective that others rejected. I will turn to these exchanges later and begin with the accounts of two men talking about their Guyanese past.

The past as a resource in building a future

Mr Rahman was the president of the mosque at the time of my fieldwork; Azzim was a visiting preacher, a generation-and-a-half younger than Mr Rahman, who taught a class for women and gave occasional lectures. These two Guyanese men gave very different accounts of their responses to their apparently, rather similar religious upbringings in rural Guyana, responses that sustained the different forms in which they lived out their religious commitments in London. Growing up in British Guiana in the 1930s and Guyana in the 1970s, respectively, neither of these men had access to a well-established system of religious education, though both reported attending classes where the Quran was memorised without explanation or understanding (Eickelman 1978). For English speakers like them, the barrier to understanding was particularly hard to overcome. Moreover, Azzim referred to the low level of general education available in rural areas. Nonetheless, it seems likely that the beginnings of a transformation in Islamic understanding were underway during the period in which Azzim was growing up that would have sustained his wish to develop his understanding of

Arabic while still in Guyana. Mr Rahman only undertook a course of religious study some years after his move to London. Yet it seemed that for both the transformation of Islam from something absorbed through imitation to something that could be understood (Eickelman 1992) fed into the capacity to think and act independently that both Mr Rahman and Azzim displayed when I knew them. However, at this point, I want to draw attention to their different responses to the religious world in which they found themselves when they were young as reflecting contrasting stances towards Islam and the nature of the link between the human and the divine (Keane 2013).

When I first met him, Mr Rahman was an energetic man in his late seventies. By then, he had been involved in the Guyanese Muslim community in north London for fifty years. He had not originally meant to settle in the UK, nor had religion figured in his plans. As a child in rural Guyana, taught to read Arabic by rote – 'we understood nothing, so we always questioned why we were doing things we don't understand'. The result, as he put it, was that 'I didn't used to be so serious about religion and, when I married, I only had knowledge of the formalities'. He said that his father had tried to learn Arabic and that he used to write to 'somewhere in Egypt and to the Woking Mosque in the UK for literature. When the first English Quran came over, we started to have a picture of more understanding ... but we still had this backward ... we were backward people'.[6] He conveyed a sense of having felt on the outer periphery of the Muslim world and that religious knowledge and understanding were somewhere else.[7]

He said, 'I could see the flaws in what we had been told when we were young ... but you can't blame them [the parental and grandparental generation] for that because they were following custom as well. In my estimation, it was like this – they had the lamp and they just kept the light going by pouring a bit of oil but another generation comes up and we must move on a bit more from that ... but it's not easy because you always have a fight with other people ... even up to today. Different cultures have a different understanding of things. Some culture becomes part of religion. You can't take it out because we are living, practising for hundreds of years, thousands of years, maybe ... '

From the standpoint of his adult experience of attending religious classes in London, Mr Rahman was aware of the shortcomings of a religious education that had lacked access to expert knowledge and was transmitted by the rote memorising of a text without understanding. Yet whatever he may have felt at the time, in later life he had found a perspective from which its moral value as a human experience and as social resource could be appreciated. His later religious education at the Central Mosque, not at that time in Regent's Park, though based on knowledge of the Quran had not, apparently, created an idea of religious understanding that fundamentally altered his stance. He presented the situation in terms of a valuing of the commitments of past generations and the wisdom accrued piecemeal through time and experience.[8] Mr Rahman spoke as if he took Muslim cultural traditions, not as the encroachment of human imperfection on the divine revelation but as the valued and valuable consequence of generations of human living as Muslims. 'Keeping the lamp burning' was, then, not just the best that could be managed by a community on the edge of the Muslim world. Rather, he presented it as a vital sign of something alive within the tradition of Guyanese Islam that continued to animate and motivate him – something of value to be handed on into the future, as it had been handed down to him. It is this appreciation of the lives and efforts of earlier generations of Muslims that allows what might have been regarded as errors to be seen in a different light – something to be accepted and valued. Such a moral object suggests the active and creative processes of imagination such as Marsden (2005) describes in his account of the capacity of Muslims in North-West Pakistan to manage religious plurality. He draws attention to the Chitrali villagers nuanced creative styles of thinking and ethical decision making '[that] is strikingly at odds with conventional under-standings of Islam that see it as a book centred faith that provides believers with a coherent set of doctrines and rules by which to live their lives' (ibid: 23). For Mr Rahman, Islam as a lamp kept alight by others, was an idea that could be turned to in moments of challenge, but I also understood it as indicative of some more continuous presence in his mind – a live and enlivening moral thread that linked his life to those of earlier generations and sustained the effort to build the mosque with all its attendant challenges.

Azzim, probably in his mid-forties at the time of my fieldwork, was also born in rural Guyana, a generation or so later than Mr Rahman. He often talked about his own deficient schooling and his long struggle to gain a religious education. He had to teach himself Arabic from whatever books happened to be available before he could go on to read the Quran. In the process of this self-study, he became aware of the low level of religious knowledge and practice among the other English-speaking Guyanese Muslims around him. He once described how he lost his job in a sugar factory because of his insistence on taking time for reli-gious practice. He then sought help in finding another job from a local sheikh who gave him something with writing on it that he was to bury in a ditch. He said he did not feel comfortable about doing it, as he did not think that such a practice was in the Quran, but he did it nonetheless. Nothing happened. When he spoke to the sheikh about this, he was told it had not worked because he had not believed in it; Azzim agreed that this was true. He decided instead that he would get another job when Allah willed it. The object of the story, as I heard Azzim explain it in a class, was, on the one hand, the pointlessness of such a 'reli-gious' practice as a remedy for his unemployed state, for which the sheikh was willing to take money and, on the other, the grave religious error it constituted. Over time Azzim came to see the sheikh's way of thinking and acting as embed-ded within a proliferation of Muslim practices that were culturally transmitted misunderstandings that altered the original message of Islam – God's word as revealed to the Prophet, to which humankind could have nothing to add.[9]

Azzim responded to the inadequacy of his religious upbringing by actively seeking a direct knowledge of the text for himself while still a young man in Guyana. That this seemed to be more open to Azzim than it had been for

Mr Rahman may have been not only due to his determination but also the emergence by then of a more self-conscious climate of religious proselytising in Guyana. As a result, Azzim became committed to a new perspective on Islam: a textual revelation that could be grasped intellectually as well as embodied through the imitation of the form of practice of the Prophet. In contrast to Mr Rahman's valuing of the accretions of human efforts in the past, Azzim orientates himself to a divine object located outside human culture. For him, God is accessible *only* through direct knowledge of the meaning of Quran not through memorisation without understanding.[10] Nor is there a legitimate place for either a relationship with the divinity based on the model of human intimacy or the absorbing of Islam as a way of life inherited from and shaped by earlier generations. His approach privileges the conscious and rational capacities of the human mind over emotions and unreflective human attachments to tradition through the proper practice of prayer does allow a place for the impact of bodily experience. Such separation of thought and feeling is at odds with our human understanding of imaginative and ethical capacity as based in processes of integration, to which Azzim might reply that this is precisely a human understanding appropriate to human things but not to the divine revelation of the Quran.

However, while Azzim was consistent in his criticism of cultural additions to Islam, he could also be accepting of human realities. Though he often spoke scornfully of the tendency in Guyana for the richest person in the village, rather than the most knowledgeable or the most pious, to take the role of religious leader, he also used his experiences of growing up on what he, like Mr Rahman, felt was the edge of the Islamic world as the basis for understanding those ordinary Muslims he encountered in the UK. He saw them as similarly stuck in error and misconception, but he reserved his criticism for the sheikhs and teachers whom he thought misled them. He described the difficulties of being a reforming teacher and of learning, early on, and from bitter experience, that telling others, especially those older than himself, that they were wrong, was not productive. It was this very engagement with his own experience of learning and teaching that I noticed in the classes could draw him back into a consideration of the complexities of human living.

These two men espoused different religious views that reflected larger theological differences within Islam. Yet hearing their accounts and seeing their thinking at work in response to the unfolding demands of particular situations in the mosque made me aware of the qualities they had in common – a shared Guyanese past, an on-going involvement with the Guyanese community in the UK, an acceptance of gender mixing and a willingness to actively engage with non-Muslim society in London. Both men had sustained a relationship to the object of their commitments over a long period, and, for both, this had involved engaging with others and with the demands of material reality – whether in the building and maintaining of a mosque or in the establishing of classes as part of a larger proselytising endeavour. Their religious commitments, as I observed them lived out in concrete situations, brought to the fore the complexity, contradictions, and failures that are the outcome of an engagement with others and the inevitable reality of any life. For Mr Rahman and Azzim, both the congregation and the class were full of difficulties that had to be struggled with if a sufficient measure of communal solidarity or religious understanding and development were to be achieved and for the mosque and the classes, respectively, to survive. However, while Mr Rahman's perspective was explicitly informed by the recognition of these complications and built out of the value he placed on them, Azzim's stated view remained that of a commitment to an unchanging divine revelation outside the vicissitudes of the human. Yet both men brought their formative experiences of Guyana into the new post-migration situation in which they found themselves and in which they both actively worked to realise their respective projects in London.

Engaging with new realities in London

In the 1950s and 1960s, the Indo-Guyanese began a second migration, this time to the UK and North America. The Muslim Indo-Guyanese were a small minority within this diaspora among whom were those who settled in London and eventually built the mosque.

Mr Rahman's account of the early days of his involvement with the Guyanese in London was related mainly during conversations in his office at the mosque amid many interruptions. He first travelled to the UK in 1959 to do a course in tailoring and dry cleaning, but, as he related it, he had no thoughts of staying until political unrest in Guyana led his father to tell him he should not return, at which point he sent for his family to join him. Mr Rahman described himself at that time as 'practising [Islam] but not very involved'. He prayed solely with other Guyanese 'in private homes and basements' in a way that that was reminiscent of the description by Muslim architect Gulzar Haidar of 'prayer in makeshift settings' when he first reached London (Haidar 1996). Though Haidar refers to the relief of performing a familiar religious practice in the company of other Muslims, the vulnerability of such informal gatherings of religiously unsophisticated individuals from the periphery of the Muslim world was apparent in a story Mr Rahman told of being caught up in a new religious movement in the early 1970s. Some of the leaders of the North London Islamic Group, which he referred to under the rubric 'Guyanese-oriented', heard about a sheikh in Manchester and 'they became convinced that this man was a prophet or something'. The reference to 'Guyanese oriented' implied that there were already other non-Guyanese attaching themselves to this group, whether through marriage or individual choice or perhaps simply because it was a local Muslim group. Werbner (2018) describes continuing allegiance to external religious leaders and to religious movements originating in the subcontinent as a pattern of diaspora religious practice among the Indian and Pakistani Muslim communities in the industrial areas of the North of England. As a result, she suggests, the response among these communities was less innovative and responsive to local context.

Instead, 'the wide variety of streams, denominations and movements evident in South Asia has been transposed into Britain almost wholesale' and often associated with acrimonious splits so that by the 1970s, most religious groups also had their own mosques (ibid: 325). It seems likely that at this point, the Guyanese felt the need for an already established religious leadership and a place within a larger organisation and a more charismatic, effervescent style of religiosity.[11] Mr Rahman became for a while part of this group. He moved his family to a city near Manchester and spent some years involved with this sheikh before becoming disillusioned and returning to London. However, many stayed on, only abandoning the Manchester project much later. During these years, those in London (including Mr Rahman) had formed a new group, the United Islamic Association (UIA). Mr Rahman had also met an older Pakistani Muslim in London who had encouraged him to undertake a course of study at the Central Mosque, not at that time on the Regent's Park site. This absorbed much of his time and attention for several years. It led not only to his developing his knowledge of Islam but to his becoming committed to an enduring project, the building of a mosque, and eventually to leading the group that would achieve that.

A leadership challenge was mounted within the UIA by one of the late returners from Manchester through what Mr Rahman felt were rigged elections and the signing up of large numbers of new members. He described this challenge as motivated more by personal ambition than theological differences, though he said that there were accusations at the time about people belonging to different sects and added, laughing, that 'this (dispute) was when we first realised that we were Sunni'.[12] As a result of the dispute among the Muslim Guyanese in London, those who would eventually go on to build the mosque left the UIA to pursue their own path. Mr. Rahman's account of these various organisations echoes Vertovec's description of the formal and informal associations that helped to sustain social networks and meet religious needs among the Hindu Indo-Guyanese community in London (Vertovec 2000: 118). Certainly, the life of the Muslim Guyanese at this time seemed to revolve around the forming of organisations and disputes about who ran them (cf Werbner 2018). There is a striking absence in Mr Rahman's account of references to the theological aspects of the split from the group in Manchester or that within the UIA.[13] While theological disputes among Muslims in Guyana at that time had led to a proliferation of different groups (Chickrie 2007; de Kruijf 2007) that may have contributed to the surfacing of various rifts within the Muslim Guyanese community in London, this situation was not mentioned. The splits in London in the 1970s and 1980s were presented to me as driven by personalities rather than theological differences, yet it seems likely that they also expressed the emergence of a variety of doubts and differences among a group who had not yet found a collective home and put down roots. Mr Rahman felt that finding such a communal home, somewhere to use as a mosque, was essential – a vision that was shared by some within the group but not all. Though doubts and differences would inevitably remain, the mosque as I encountered it gave an enduring material form to the memories and aspirations of this group of Guyanese. More recent tensions at the mosque, which I refer to below, were more clearly recognised as linked directly to the impact on British Muslims of globalised theological and political movements within Islam, and though this was rarely spoken about except by the Trustees of the mosque, it seemed that they felt sufficient confidence in the value of their own project to resist.

'Guyana' was a recurrent theme during my fieldwork – whether recalled as a memory, as sustaining a religious stance that could be made explicit under challenge or as embodied in the way individuals conducted themselves and engaged in social relationships. It was referred to as an idea that had sustained the group and the building of the mosque as a new communal home for Muslim Indo-Guyanese in London. It was an idea that carried associations of difficulties surmounted (indenture and migration), of the divisions of caste, religion, and gender replaced by an inclusive, egalitarian idea, *mati*, and, despite the later political upheavals, a robust feeling of agency and political competence. Though there is some historical evidence for this picture, its external veracity is not the main point; rather, it was an imagined Guyana and an image of being Guyanese that sustained a feeling of effectiveness and hope. If this idea of Guyana as a place where differences were tolerated and the capacity to do so was valued, was an idealised, essentialised imaginary, Mr Rahman's account of 'being Guyanese' also involved a robust willingness to engage in the complicated processes of disputes, forming into factions, standing one's ground, and if need be, allowing splits to take their course.[14] Though my fieldwork took place during a less tempestuous period within the congregation it was nonetheless clear that the exercise of constant vigilance was still required to defend a Guyanese conception of being Muslim within the mosque.

After the split with the UIA, the new grouping, led by Mr Rahman, began informal prayer gatherings in private homes. This developed by stages, through the acquisition of a house and then, in the mid-1980s, a local hall that had been used first for light industry and then as a synagogue. For 15 years, this anonymous-looking building was both a prayer hall and a place for social events until the new architect-designed mosque with a tiled and carpeted prayer space for men, and a similarly decorated balcony area for women was built on the adjacent site in 2000. This new build had been paid off by 2005, but by the end of my fieldwork in 2012, the congregation had outgrown this space and another three-storey structure was about to be built on the site of the old hall. The overseeing of the building works and the setting up and managing of the Charitable Trust that runs the mosque bespeaks a considerable level of organisational and financial ability, not only among the immediate group of Trustees but also within the wider Guyanese community whose financial contributions in the form of interest free loans, gifts, and legacies have supported the venture in addition to contributions from the wider congregation. Among the Trustees was an accountant and someone who had been a successful local businessman and there were a number who worked in professional and semi-professional capacities in public sector service.

Seventy per cent of Britain's 3 million Muslims are of South Asian heritage (Hamid 2018). Though originally also from South Asia, the Guyanese felt marginal to these much larger Muslim communities, the diversity of beliefs and practices within them (Vertovec 2002), and their continuing links with religious centres in the subcontinent (Werbner 2002, 2018). However, while they could not call on the resources of a large pre-migration 'home' community it appeared that the Guyanese felt that this has been helpful to them in developing their own mosque in a new context. At the same time, as English speakers from a former British colony, they had a greater access to the local community in London, while their lack of ties to a Muslim religious leadership located elsewhere left them free to make their own way (once they had severed ties with the group in Manchester). This has echoes of the situation described by Mandel (2008) with respect to the Turkish Alevi community in Germany who were marginalised in Turkey, but found themselves freer and more successful in adapting to new circumstances than their Sunni compatriots.

At the time of my fieldwork, the register of members of the mosque, mainly Guyanese and Mauritian, who paid a nominal sum to be on the mailing list, stood at 500.[15] This would indicate the number of households rather than individuals. Yet despite this small number, the mosque is financially and theologically independent of the direct influence of the transnational religious groups based in Pakistan and Saudi Arabia that are involved in the financing of many UK mosques. Mr Rahman described how, in the early days, he had written to other Muslim organisations for loans. Only a Saudi Arabian organisation replied, offering money, but an agent they sent made it clear that they would want control over what happened within the mosque. This offer was refused and those seeking to build the mosque sought to safeguard its independence by funding the venture themselves, initially through an interest-free loan from a Guyanese businessman in South London. Contributions from the Guyanese and the wider congregation and small-scale fundraising events were used to pay off what they could from the loan each month. The commitment to having a place of worship was one of the elements that distinguished this group from the one they had left (UIA), whose members did not want or perhaps were not able to move away from the use of private homes. Money continues to be raised from within the Guyanese community through bequests, fundraising events, and a collection from the congregation on Fridays. Five years after the end of my fieldwork the new (second) extension was complete and fundraising to pay it off was underway. Though this involved constant effort – Mr Rahman's favourite phrase on such occasions was 'put the money in the box before you go in the box [coffin]' – it also reflected the economic success of some Guyanese in the UK and their willingness to put some of their wealth at the disposal of the mosque and their community. Beyond this, the Trustees also made interest-free loans to other mosques in need of funds and the mosque actively supported Palestinian charities as well as responding to emergency causes as they arose.

Like other migrant communities in Europe, the Guyanese found themselves in a particular and changing context with opportunities and obstacles shaped by the history of the wider society (Fadil 2019). The need to find a building to use as a mosque if they were to be able to stop meeting in private homes involved engaging in protracted struggles with other sections of the local community. Despite the racialised conflict that broke out in Guyana in 1962 between those of Indian and African descent and a continuing political struggle for dominance between the two groups in Guyana, the success of the Afro-Guyanese within local borough politics that came to be associated in the 1970s and 1980s with a discourse of multi-culturalism and the support it offered to local ethnic groups enabled the Guyanese to successfully pursue their interests within the community. Some Guyanese would use this idiom to joke to me that 'we were multi-cultural before you were'. I understood this as indicative not so much of a discourse of ethnic identity as expressive of an ironic familiarity with a pragmatic way of conceiving relationships to other ethnic and religious groups within the local community that Baumann (1996) calls 'demotic discursive praxis'. In the early days of the mosque's development, this practical mode of ordinary day-to-day living with others and the confidence and comfort with difference it sustained encountered a form of local politics in which, as Eade (1996: 230) describes in relation to a neighbouring borough, activism was oriented to securing 'community needs defined in secular and class terms'. The Guyanese felt able to participate successfully in these struggles in a way that secured their position and sense of belonging in a new social context.[16]

Despite some religious groups only being willing to sell their redundant buildings for non-religious use, while other ethnic communities, including other Muslims (Mr Rahman cited a Bengali group) were also competing for space in the same locality, Mr Rahman saw the familiarity of the Guyanese with the idea of multi-culturalism as contributing to their eventual success in the search for a building to use as a mosque (Vertovec 2002: 21). Mr Rahman described losing a property they wanted to a Greek Women's organisation because, he said, the mayor at that time was Greek. He said that he had threatened to complain to the council about this. Whether he did or not, it is indicative of the capacity to see the opportunities for engagement with local ethno-politics that Baumann (1996, 1999) describes in Southall. Many years later, a building adjacent to the one that became the original hall-mosque that was owned by the council came up for sale. Mr Rahman described how the Community Relations officer he had brought to the site asked, 'What do you want me to do?' Mr Rahman told him, 'Sell us this land', and it seemed that a deal was done whereby the land alone, rather than the unwanted building was sold. He said triumphantly 'and that was the last thing that happened before the closing of the Community Relations Council!'.

The mosque at the time of my fieldwork

If their identification with 'being Guyanese' facilitated dealings with the formal structures of local government and local public services and continued to animate their way of being Muslim within the mosque, the situation was becoming more complicated with respect to the struggles with the diverse religious traditions within the congregation as a sense of the primacy of religious identity among Muslims came to the fore.

The arrival of other migrant groups from Muslim majority countries and the global currents of renewal within Islam available on the internet brought fresh challenges, this time more obviously and unavoidably theological. Mr Rahman referred in passing to a period in which the serious and well-publicised difficulties in nearby mosques had spilled over into their congregation. However, neither he nor others were willing to speak in any detail about the impact of the disputes at Finsbury Park Mosque during the 1990s, when Abu Hamza al Masri was the imam, or the influence locally of Omar Bakri Mohammad, the founder of *Hizb ut-tahrir*. This group still leafleted outside the gates together with those offering classes, publicising marches, or championing Muslim victims of injustice at home and abroad. The mosque had also had its own internal religious difficulties. When the first generation of Guyanese imams, who were felt to have had insufficient religious training, were replaced by two Saudi-trained Guyanese in the 1990s, it became clear that though they were Guyanese, they had a very different idea of Islam and were not willing to undertake the kinds of rituals and prayers for family members that the community had become accustomed to. Eventually, these two imams were replaced first by one part-time Bangladeshi imam and then by a second who had trained in the UK. Perhaps because of his greater workload and family commitments, it was difficult to make opportunities to talk to the senior imam separate from observing him carrying out his duties but the younger of the two, Bilal, was willing to talk to me at length and also allowed me to observe the classes he ran for children. Because of the size of the congregation, there are two Friday prayers, so a rota of visiting preachers took turns to give the sermon and lead the prayers. Both the vice-president and the mosque secretary made it clear that they needed to maintain constant vigilance with respect to the many visiting preachers and lecturers who spoke at the mosque and referred to the risk that, if ever one of the official imams did not arrive to take prayers, there were always men waiting their chance to take over.

When the congregation moved from meeting in a private house to the mosque as a public space, this carried the implication that it was open to all Muslims. This was a source of considerable anxiety among the Guyanese at the time, and for this reason, while the mosque is open to all for worship, the terms of the Charitable Trust under which the mosque operates specifically limits the Board of Trustees and the voting membership of the Mosque Society to the Guyanese and those married to Guyanese. However, my focus was not on the high-profile disputes of the past but on the life of the congregation as it appeared during the time of my fieldwork and on the more routine form in which different ways of practicing and speaking about Islam surfaced within the mosque. While the Guyanese continued to run the mosque, there was also a larger group around them that included both Mauritians and others from Pakistan and Bangladesh, who regularly attended the additional rituals, and lectures while Hindu and Christian Guyanese and Mauritian relatives and friends were also invited to Ramadan meals and to social occasions at the mosque.[17] This group contrasted with those within the congregation who attended mainly on Fridays and for core rituals during Ramadan but were not generally present at the more peripheral ritual and social events, though some attended the adult religious classes and lectures that took place at the mosque. While the mosque is open to all even the congregation that gathers at Friday prayers may be said to be self-selecting and the mosque continues to be led by and associated with, the Guyanese.

The material, financial, and moral tasks the Guyanese took on in building the mosque as a new physical space in which to reconstitute a sense of belonging after the losses of migration was complicated by the context in which it was undertaken. For the most part, the differences in religious traditions and levels of commitment within the congregation were treated by the Guyanese as something to be accepted and accommodated, but the congregation brought into the mosque perspectives from which the Guyanese knew they might be judged by others as being in error. These included not only those who belonged to different traditional ways of being Muslim but also those who had found a new sense of Muslim belonging within the virtual currents of a de-territorialised Islam and the new individualised forms of religiosity that Roy describes as offering an alternative experience of post-migration Muslim community (Roy 2004, 2007). The containing of these differences was an on-going preoccupation that drew on the resources which the Guyanese spoke of as based in their experience of, and an attachment to, a religiously and ethnically diverse society, British Guiana/ Guyana. Now lost in external reality, through both migration and the passage of time, Guyana lived on in their way of orienting to Islam and as a mode of sociability within the mosque. The Guyanese referred explicitly to their complex history as contributing to their sense of how they have lived their lives in London and as underlying the difference they felt to exist between themselves and other Muslim groups in the UK. Though only a few among those I got to know outside of the religious classes seemed to feel they could, or needed to, voice their position on religious matters, all those I got to know were giving time of their lives to the mosque and to the rituals of Islam that took place within it, while many were engaged with the practical functions which maintained both the fabric of the building and the life of the community.

Notes

1 Though the indenture system ended in 1917, there was a further period of immigration between 1921 and 1928.
2 One person I met had only the luggage label from the trunk of a great-uncle who had migrated to Guiana.
3 Though Chickrie and Khanam (2016) suggest the majority of Muslim Guyanese were Barelvi Sunnis with a very small Shi'a presence and claim a considerable degree of knowledge among the religious leaders prior to independence, this was absent from the accounts given by Mr Rahman and Azzim later in this chapter.
4 However, Williams' ethnography includes an account of the tensions surrounding a Hindu-Muslim-Christian wedding she observed in the 1970s which suggests a more complicated picture.

5 The People's Progressive Party was originally a multi-ethnic party formed in 1950 out of a merger between the British Guiana Labour Party led by Forbes Burnham and the Political Affairs Committee led by Cheddi Jagan. Concerns in the US and the UK about the communist sympathies of PPP suggest outside interference contributed to a subsequent split, with the Indo-Guyanese continuing to support the PPP under Jagan and the Afro-Guyanese population voting in the first post-independence government under Forbes Burnham and the Peoples National Congress.

6 This was a recurring reference in reports on the Indo-Caribbean diaspora, particularly from the perspective of the second migration of Hindu-Guyanese to the US (Halstead 2008).

7 I use this designation because that was how Mr Rahman seemed to have experienced the matter, but as Kresse (2013) points out, this does not mean that engaged forms of religious thinking do not take place at a distance from Arab or Muslim majority countries.

8 This reflects the encounter between Islamic learning and indigenous forms of knowledge on the East African coast (Parkin 2007).

9 As Azzim explained in the classes, with respect to worship everything permitted was specified while in relation to living a Muslim life only those things that were forbidden were specified.

10 This would run counter to an interpretation of rote learning as the embodiment of the divine revelation (Boyle 2006).

11 Pelkmans (2017) links the attraction of such leadership style to the experience of living in frontier situations (ibid: 182).

12 Mr Rahman linked this new perception of where he stood to this dispute as if it took place prior to his religious training.

13 From the timing, it is possible that the group in Manchester was Deobandi. In the early 1970s, a sheikh arrived in Bury in Greater Manchester and founded a Deobandi College. However, Mr Rahman's account implied that his disaffection with the group arose from a feeling of being manipulated financially and emotionally by individuals who may not have been central to this organisation.

14 Mr Rahman often moved between an idealised and more complicated, realistic way of speaking about being Guyanese. As Baumann puts it, he was able, like many ordinary people, to command a 'double discursive competence' switching between an essentialised and a processural rhetoric as the need arose, an ability developed through exposure to everyday multicultural practice (Baumann 1999: 92).

15 Muslim Guyanese have always been a minority within a minority and their absolute numbers are small. From the 1991 census, Vertovec (2000) estimated the total Guyanese-born population in the UK as 20,400 and within this the Indo-Guyanese as 5,400. Assuming the ratio of Hindus to Muslims reflected that in Guyana, the Muslim Guyanese would have numbered only about 1,000 in 1991.

16 Counsellors and local MPs attended events at the mosque and the Trustees and one of the imams took part in a local wreath laying on Remembrance Sunday along with other religious and civic groups.

17 This was the group that the chair of the mosque referred to in chapter 1 as 'Guyanese oriented'.

References

Baumann, G. (1996) *Contesting Cultures: Discourses of Identity in Multi-Ethnic London.* Cambridge: Cambridge University Press.

Baumann, G. (1999) *The Multicultural Riddle.* London: Routledge.

Boyle, H. (2006) 'Memorization and learning in Islamic schools', *Comparative Education Review* 50(3): 478–495.

Chickrie, R. (1999) 'Muslims in Guyana: History, traditions, conflict and change', *Journal of Muslim Minority Affairs* 19(2): 181–195.

Chickrie, R. (2007) 'Islamic organisations in Guyana: Seventy years of history and politics, 1936–2006', *Journal of Muslim Minority Affairs* 27(3): 401–428.

Chickrie, R. and Khanam, B. (2016) 'Hindustani Muslims in Guyana: Tradition, Conflict and Change, 1838 to the Present', in Hassankhan, M. S. and Goolam, V. (eds) *Indentured Muslims in the Diaspora*. New Delhi: Manhar.

de Kruijf, J. (2007) 'Muslim transnationalism in Indo-Guyana: Localized globalization and battles over a cultural Islam', *European Journal of Anthropology* 50: 102–124.

Eade, J. (1996) 'Nationalism, Community, the Islamization of Space in London' in Metcalf, B. D. (ed) *Making Muslim Space in North America and Europe*. Berkeley: University of California.

Eickelman, D. F. (1978) 'The art of memory: Islamic education and its social reproduction', *Comparative Studies in Society and History* 20(4): 485–516.

Eickelman, D. F. (1992) 'Mass higher education and the religious imagination in contemporary Arab societies', *American Ethnologist* 19(4): 643–655.

Eisenlohr, P. (2006) *Little India: Diaspora, Time and Ethnolinguistic Belonging in Hindu Mauritius*. London: University of California Press.

Fadil, N. (2019) 'The anthropology of Islam in Europe. A double epistemological impasse', *Annual Review of Anthropology* 48: 117–132.

Haidar, G. (1996) 'Muslim Space and the Practice of Architecture: A Personal Odyssey', in Metcalf, B. D. (ed) *Making Muslim Space in North America and Europe*. Berkeley: University of California.

Halstead, N. (2008) 'Violence, past and present: "Mati" and "non-Mati" people', *History and Anthropology* 19(2): 115–129.

Hamid, S. (2018) *Sufis, Salafis and Islamists*. London: I.B. Tauris.

Jayawardena, C. (1963) *Conflict and Solidarity on a Guyanese Plantation*. London: Athlone Press.

Jayawardena, C. (1966) 'Religious belief and social change: Aspects of the development of Hinduism in British Guiana', *Comparative Studies in Society and History* 8: 211–240.

Jayawardena, C. (1968) 'Ideology and conflict in lower class communities', *Comparative Studies in Society and History* 10: 413–446.

Jayawardena, C. (1980) 'Culture and ethnicity in Guyana and Fiji', *Man* (NS) 15(3): 430–450.

Keane, W. (2013) 'On spirit writing: Materialities of language and the religious work of transduction', *Journal of the Royal Anthropological Institute* 19: 1–17.

Khan, A. (1997) 'Migration narratives and moral imperatives: Local and global in the Muslim Caribbean', *Comparative Studies of South Asia, Africa and the Middle East* 17(1): 127–144.

Khan, A. (2004) 'Sacred subversions? Syncretic Creoles, the Indo-Caribbean, and "Cultures in-between"', *Radical History Review* 89: 165–184.

Khanam, B. and Chickrie, R. (2009) '170th anniversary of the arrival of the first Hindustani Muslims from India to British Guiana', *Journal of Muslim Minority Affairs* 29(2): 195–222.

Kresse, K. (2013) 'On the Skills to Navigate the World, and Religion, for Coastal Muslims in Kenya', in Marsden, M. and Retsikas, K (eds) *Articulating Islam: Anthropological Approaches to Muslim Worlds*. London: Springer.

Lal, B. V. (2018) 'Indian Indenture: Experiment and Experience', in Chatterji, J. and Washbrook, D. (eds) *Routledge Handbook of the South Asian Diaspora*. London: Routledge.

Leonard, K. (2018) 'Indians Abroad: Mixing It up', in Chatterji, J. and Washbrook, D. (eds) *Routledge Handbook of the South Asian Diaspora*. London: Routledge.

Mandel, R. (2008) *Cosmopolitan Anxieties: Turkish Challenges to citizenship and belonging in Germany*. London: Duke University.

Marsden, M. (2005) *Living Islam: Muslim Religious Experience in Pakistan's North-West Frontier.* Cambridge: Cambridge University Press.

Mohapatra, P. (2006) '"Following custom?" Representations of community among Indian labour in the West Indies, 1880–1920', *International Review of Social History* 51: 173–202.

Parkin, D. 2007. The Accidental in Religious Instruction. In Berliner, D. and Sarro, R. (eds) *Learning Religion.* Oxford: Berghahn Books.

Pelkmans, M. E. (2017) *Fragile Convictions.* New York: Cornell University Press.

Rauf, M. A. (1974) *Indian Village in Guiana: A Study of Cultural Change and Ethnic Identity.* Leiden: Brill.

Robinson, K. (2006) 'Idioms of vernacular humanism: The West and the East', *Anthropological Forum* 16(3): 241–255.

Roy, O. (2004) *Globalised Islam: The Search for a New Ummah.* London: Hurst and Co.

Roy, O. (2007) *Secularism Confronts Islam.* New York: Columbia University Press.

Vertovec, S. (1994) '"Official" and "popular" Hinduism in diaspora: Historical and contemporary trends in Surinam, Trinidad and Guyana', *Contributions to Indian Sociology* 28(1): 123–147.

Vertovec, S. (2000) *The Hindu Diaspora.* London: Routledge.

Vertovec, S. (2002) 'Islamophobia and Muslim Recognition in Britain', in Haddad, Y. (ed) *Muslims in the West: From Sojourners to Citizens.* Oxford: Oxford University Press.

Werbner, P. (2002) *Imagined Diasporas among Manchester Muslims.* Santa Fe: School of American Research Press.

Werbner, P. (2018) 'Ritual, Religion and Aesthetics in the Pakistani and South Asian Diaspora', in Chatterji, J. and Washbrook, D. (eds) *Routledge Handbook of the South Asian Diaspora.* London: Routledge.

Williams, B. F. (1991) *Stains on My Name, War in My Veins: Guyana and the Politics of the Cultural Struggle.* London: Duke University Press.

3

PRAYING TOGETHER

Collective prayer around mid-day on Fridays[1] brings together in the mosque a diverse group of Muslims. It is a ritual that can contain, at least while it lasts, the differences in tradition, knowledge, piety, and commitment and instantiate instead an idea of the universal and unchanging unity of Islam. The power of ritual to bring about such a transformation – from human diversity to an ideal moral entity, the community of believers (the *umma*), in submission to the will of God[2] – has occupied a special place in the history of anthropology (Rappaport 1999). Yet collective prayer was a fragile moment of unity and communality in the face of the reality of diversity and the confusion of the mundane world beyond the mosque out of which the congregation emerged and to which it returned afterwards.

Gathering for prayer

The mosque was open every day, and people came and went in small numbers for prayer, classes, and other events throughout the week, but it was around mid-day on Friday that the central ritual of the Muslim world was performed here as in mosques across the globe. This local gathering in of individuals to form a congregation in preparation for acting together in prayer takes place at a specific and predictable, though slowly shifting, point in time.[3] The times of prayer move steadily each day following the changing time of sunrise and sunset in the different seasons and would be known by those who pray daily. Calendars were also sold as part of fundraising. Yet many people I came across did not know when prayer was due, indicating that many were not so observant, or at least in any systematic way. The Central London Mosque in Regent's Park sets the exact timing for Muslims in the UK. This became apparent when there was a delay in the printing of the special Ramadan calendars because the mosque secretary was still

DOI: 10.4324/9781003080008-3

waiting for the timings from Regent's Park. By contrast, the sighting of the new moon at the start and end of Ramadan is determined in Saudi Arabia though this practice is open to debate in some quarters. In the class I attended, there was a discussion as to whether the timing should be set by a local sighting; in the kitchen, during the preparation of the meal that breaks the fast, the likely timing of the end of Ramadan as between a Friday and a Saturday in that year was thought, with some irony, to be a matter that would be settled in Saudi Arabia in accordance with their own social convenience. While the liturgical timing of the rituals of Muslim practice links this local congregation to Islam as a global religion, it also creates a new context of difference and the awareness of a hierarchy and of power as located elsewhere. The intrusion of the secular comes as something of a shock when, at the end of congregational prayer, in Spring and Autumn, there was an announcement of clocks going forward or back in line with the switch to and from British Summer Time.

This process of gathering, from which the Arabic name of Friday prayer derives,[4] starts outside as people move towards the mosque in increasing concentrations from the surrounding streets, emerging from houses, buses, and parked cars, a process that is mirrored in the dispersal afterwards. One of the imams rendered this experience through a visual image of angels simultaneously gathering over the mosque. While there is a hadith that records the Prophet speaking of angels standing at the gates of every mosque on Fridays to write down the names of those who attend, and there were frequent references to God's judgement in the sermons, this image of gathering angels evoked a different idea to that of record-keeping and judgement passed on individuals-one in which a congregation is formed in a responsive mirroring of angelic activity. There is a contrast between the idea of a congregation gathered in by a conscious fear of judgement and one in which both human beings and angels act in a natural, synchronous response to God. The mirroring of the material and spiritual domains and the spanning of the divide between them suggests a link which is imperceptible to physical senses and beyond human control (Keane 2013). The imam's image also directs our attention, as no doubt he intended, to the public and collective nature of Friday prayer and to the individual's dependence on the presence and prayerful dispositions of others rather than prayer as being an individual act of choice and agency.

Rappaport (1999) argues that it is through the nature of ritual itself that such diversity is transformed, albeit temporarily, into a kind of unity. For any individual, a ritual event can appear as given and unchanging within a larger enduring canon; its performance includes all who attend, regardless of private states of conflict, ambivalence, or doubt. All who join the prayer lines at the mosque are therefore acknowledging Islam publicly, affirming its account of divine reality and in doing so, realising that ordering of the world that the Quran proclaims.[5] Rappaport also suggests that out of the physical proximity and the aligning of individual worshippers to one another, an embodied experience of unity emerges that he describes as 'more intimate and binding' (ibid: 118) and that, like the image of the invisible angelic gathering, takes place outside human awareness.[6]

Yet, on closer inspection, this gathering is not unproblematic. The congregation contained numerous ethnic and religious distinctions and differences that held the potential for conflict. Minor disruptions and disputes within the congregation that carried the potential for more major problems occurred regularly outside prayer itself. However, the fact that collective prayer takes place each week reinstates a shared reality that is of continuing significance for those involved but beyond the individual's capacity to instantiate. It is this transcendent moral reality to which the imam's words gave visual form.

The internal diversity of the congregation

Friday prayer is open to all, and women as well as men from all the local Muslim communities attended the mosque in large numbers. Unlike in many UK mosques, the provision for women was comparable to that for men, and, for the most part, women seemed to feel welcome (Shannahan 2014). There is a separate balcony area for women, adjoining toilet and ablution facilities, and an additional space beyond the balcony that are all integrated into the architecture and decorative style of the building. Women stewarded the balcony and took part alongside men in the cleaning and maintenance of the building. However, the crush on Fridays often meant that men took over extra space on one side of the balcony, separating it off with moveable screens. This competition for space continued at the end of prayers, as the women were often forced to wait with small children and buggies near the main double doors while the men surged out. Leaving together would not have been acceptable to some of the men, and, in this situation, that view took precedence. Aware of the difficulty this created for the women, who sometimes complained about it, the Guyanese male stewards would every so often hold the men back for a short while, asking them to 'allow the sisters to pass'.

While the Guyanese accept the need for segregated prayer, there is gender mixing in all other areas of the mosque. If women were provided with a prayer balcony, their presence was not uncontested by some sections of the congregation, and, as Shannahan (2014) suggests, space in both its material and immaterial aspects expressed deep feelings about gender relations. There are accounts of men and women attending prayer together, though physically separated, in early Islam (Makris 2007) but many within the congregation have come from societies in which women pray only within the home and this continues in the many mosques established by Pakistani and Bangladeshi communities in the UK that have minimal, or no accommodation for women (Werbner 2018).

However, the congregation contained other indicators of ethnic and religious difference, the most visible of which were the great variety of forms and degrees of Muslim dress among both men and women.[7] Some wore ordinary Western clothes with long sleeves, longer length skirts, and headscarves for the women; others dressed in the traditional styles of the Somali and other African communities; and a few were in explicitly global rather than ethnic 'Islamic' dress. Though this self-consciously Islamic group included men of all ages, clad in long white garments and white crochet caps, among the women, it was mainly the young who dressed Islamically in either a black or carefully colour co-ordinated *jilbab*, and an elaborately wound *hijab*. Some created scarf ensembles with long biased-cut skirts in subtle colours, combining the Islamic with a highly personalised style – as Tarlo puts it 'a new form of Muslim personal art' (Tarlo 2010: 1). Only a very few wore the complete black covering garment, the *niqab*.[8] When prayer starts, all will pray side by side, but the differences of dress that marked out this latter group do not always go unremarked. One Guyanese woman, apparently assuming I was wondering why a woman who had passed between us was dressed in the *niqab* and, perhaps, wishing to reassure me, said, 'probably it was the way they dressed in her country'. If prayer gathers everyone into a common ritual, dress marks out the difference. Her suggestion that this was a cultural form rather than a religious choice may have been her understanding or may have been a tactful way to explain the situation to me, but it calls attention to the interpretive adjustments through which differences and perturbations in the fabric of social life need to be continuously managed (Zigon 2007, Zigon and Throop 2014). However, among those I met who wore the *niqab*, it was always a conscious personal religious choice rather than part of the traditions into which they had been born. Some women unfastened their face covering while on the balcony, but others remained completely covered. A woman standing near the door to the balcony asked of another, in an irritated tone of voice, why she was covered since there were only women in that part of the mosque; the woman pointed silently to a closed-circuit TV camera in the corner (there was a monitor in the shop covering different areas of the mosque). The questioner shrugged and the moment passed, but it briefly brought to the surface the uncomfortable gap created by overt signs of individualised religiosity in contrast to the overwhelmingly communal nature of the ritual and the forms of religious dress and conduct among the Guyanese who, though not in the majority on Fridays, nonetheless set a particular benchmark for what constituted ordinary Muslim practice in the mosque. Whatever the actual motivation of the woman in the *niqab*, her form of dress is a marker for the political and religious challenges of groups like *hizb ut-tahrir* that, by implication, pass judgement on other Muslims through the stereotyping of dress as indicative of piety and may stir in others the kind of discomfort and unease that Tarlo (2005) describes herself as feeling. Women wearing the *niqab* or more formal Islamic dress did not attend the events where there was gender mixing. Hence, it was mainly on Fridays and during the prayers and recitations of Ramadan that such encounters occurred. The potential for more substantial disputes at the mosque was avoided through the self-selected attendance at other events and the availability of other mosques, though the sense of contestation was present in many of the leaflets distributed outside.

As I walked in the same direction as those gathering for Friday prayers, I often became conscious of the ambiguity of my position and my own feelings of ambivalence at the point at which I put on my headscarf and became part of this flow of people. The moral complexity of this situation for the researcher has been a matter of concern among anthropologists working in Muslim countries

(Lukens-Bull 2007; Clarke 2013). As many of my visits involved prayer, the female secretary of the mosque had made it clear that I should wear a headscarf. Apart from that, provided I wore loose trousers and took a long-sleeved, high-necked top with me if I was wearing summer clothes, I managed with items from my ordinary wardrobe that were not dissimilar to those worn by older Guyanese women. This allowed me to feel I was not dressing up and trying to 'pass', and if asked, I always described myself as non-Muslim. During my fieldwork, I became increasingly aware that something of my dilemmas were shared by others. There were Muslim women who dress for the mosque in a style they did not generally adopt – one Mauritian woman described herself as wearing a 'part-time hijab' – a problem that men who wore ordinary Western clothing did not encounter. One of the female Trustees gave a witty account of how, realising she had arrived at the mosque straight from work in an outfit that was a bit too short to pass muster, she had had to shimmy her skirt down over her hips so that it would cover her legs. This story vividly encapsulated the gap she experienced between the secular world in which she worked and her participation in the mosque. The degree of diversity in lifestyle and practice within the congregation was thus even greater than the range of mosque attire might suggest. Moreover, the underlying motivations may be difficult to determine. Fadil (2011) suggests non-veiling should not be understood only as indicating the impact of a liberal secular world but also as expressing, for some women, their own disagreements with, and freedom to think about, what others interpreted as religious obligations.

On Fridays, I would enter through the door used mainly, but not exclusively, by women.[9] Having taken off my shoes and left them in the rack reserved for women, I went upstairs to the balcony above the male prayer hall. Whether due to an oversight by the architect or the emergence of stricter sensibilities among some in the congregation since the drawing up of the plans, 'hospital' screens were always placed around two of the three sides of the balcony so that if men looked up, they could not see the women praying. On one side of the balcony that faced the direction of prayer, the open railing allowed women at the front to look down at the imam while otherwise remaining concealed.[10] As if to answer a question I had not actually voiced as to why this segregation was maintained when gender mixing was generally the norm elsewhere in the mosque, one Guyanese woman explained the need in terms of the physical nature of Muslim prayer. In all the domestic circumstances in which I observed prayer where both men and women were present, the men prostrated in front of the women, as if this is a less disturbing and arousing experience for a woman than the other way around; or perhaps, as Mahmood explains, it is rather that the responsibility for maintaining order in the domain of sexual relations falls to women (Mahmood 2005: 110).

The rituals of prayer

Two modes of congregational activity, the sermon and collective prayer, together make up the core ritual on Fridays, but I will consider prayer first and then the sermon. In comparison with the lengthy rituals of transition through the life stages or rituals of healing that have shaped anthropological thinking, the core act of worship in Islam is strikingly plain – a brief but 'dramatic gesture of submission', as Henkel (2005) puts it. It is an act composed of repeated cycles of simple bodily movements – standing, bowing from the waist with the hands on the knees, prostrating with the forehead and nose on the ground, and sitting back with the heels under the body – accompanied by brief recitations in Arabic – the phrase 'God is greatest' (the *takbir*), the short opening *sura* of the Quran (*al fatiha*) and other short verses and supplications. The ritualised nature of the five obligatory *(fard)* daily prayers *(salah)*, whether performed collectively or individually, distinguishes them both from the freedom that is accorded to private supernumerary prayer, which may be undertaken in one's mother tongue and composed in whatever manner meets the needs of the moment, and from other ritual activities at the mosque which owe their form to particular cultural traditions or to ad hoc initiatives – for example, the celebration of the Prophet's Birthday, or an event to pray for a sick person. These latter activities, the subject of later chapters, were not a unifying point across the congregation but rather refracted the differences within it; yet for the Guyanese and those who identified with them, they gave form to their communal life and collective commitments to their way of being Muslim.

Within Islam, the form of ritual worship is understood as that which was established by the practice *(sunnah)* of the Prophet, and the main elements of Friday prayer are held in common by Muslims. However, accounts of the Prophet's practice and teaching (the *hadith*) are accorded varying degrees of authenticity, interpreted in different ways by different schools *(mathab)*, and have been elaborated over time in the practice of the different traditions derived from them, allowing a degree of legitimate difference in practice.[11] In the class I describe in Chapter 8, there was little awareness of these interpretive traditions, while for others, different forms of practice often prompted references to the Prophet having said there would be 73 forms of Islam only one of which was correct. Though the Guyanese did not seem to see their practice in this light, the awareness of a widespread concern with error among some sections of the congregation gave a sharp edge of anxiety to disagreements about the practice at the mosque when they did arise. In the two imam-led study groups I attended, news about new forms of religious practice that had been encountered in the neighbourhood brought criticism and ascribed to the activity of a local sheik in one group and were often referred to somewhat humorously in the other as 'a South Asian thing'. One of these imams, Azzim, who took the Saturday women's group, opposed all innovations of practice as a grave error, while the other, a Bangladeshi preacher, who held a mixed gathering in his home, thought a 'one-off' event such as meeting for a meal on the Prophet's birthday or to read some chapters *(suras)* of the Quran on the anniversary of a death was permissible. For him, it was in seeking to repeat such events, in specifying how many, or which, *suras* were to be recited and in formalising a way in which they should be performed that such events became ritual innovation *(bid'a)*.[12] Since the form of worship has been fixed by the Quran and the Sunnah, such innovation constitutes idolatry *(shirk)* through the explicit or implicit, denial of the unity, integrity, and completeness of the Divine revelation to the Prophet.

Many of the disagreements at the mosque were, in fact, between different cultural traditions within Muslim societies rather than disputes about recognised differences in theological interpretations of Islamic practice. The myriad and often hidden forms of *shirk* were an issue that particularly concerned Azzim. He felt that resisting the slide towards increased ritualisation required constant vigilance.

In the sermons and the classes, there was an emphasis on the correct forms of practice without which, some insisted, prayer would not be accepted by God. When one woman in the class asked about praying in her own language, Azzim made it clear that whatever obligatory prayer was due had to be performed first in Arabic and that only then could one pray in a non-ritualised vernacular form. Thus, even when undertaken in private, ritualised prayer brings the individual into conformity with the obligations laid on all. Transformative power is invested in the correct form of words such that the pronouncement of the statement of witness (*shahada*) to the oneness of God and to Mohammed as God's messenger creates the individual as a Muslim.[13]

I was initially rather shocked to witness the taking of the *shahada* by people who were not able to recite it as a whole or even to do so phrase by phrase, and instead repeated the words after the imam, syllable by syllable. On one occasion, a middle-aged woman in a black *jilbab* and *hijab,* whom none of us had seen before, came into the Saturday class with a young Portuguese man who, she said, wanted to make the *shahada*. Though he spoke virtually no English and no Arabic, Azzim helped him to do so, and the pair left immediately afterwards. No questions were asked as to who they were and why they had come at this point. Azzim told the young man that he would now have to learn about the religion, but it was the stumbled, broken phrases requiring many corrections and repetitions that had transformed him into a Muslim. In saying the words, he had entered into the obligations they entailed, whether or not he fulfilled them. Though Azzim was strict in his insistence on the correct language of prayer, he would not have seen agency as invested in the words as such.[14] Seeking to bring about an outcome by writing the words of an *ayah* on an amulet was, for him, the fetishising of a material object and, therefore, *shirk* and it seems clear that locating efficacy and power in human speech acts, as such, would also constitute *shirk*. For Azzim only God had such power, and to speak God's words aloud, as the Prophet did, is to acknowledge that divine locus of power and no other.

Henkel (2005) puts the issue more pragmatically – that the 'limited and sharply defined commitment' of the *shahada* is easy to fulfil in speech, while an 'unreserved commitment to the divine rules laid out in the Quran and the *sunnah* of the Prophet, as variously interpreted by Muslim scholars and ideally as encompassing and shaping the entirety of the believer's existence' is scarcely achievable by an individual and its form and requirements are 'hardly possible for a large community to agree'. From this perspective, the *shahada*, incorporated and repeated in numerous prayers, may be said to transform a range of internal states, shifting feelings of ambivalence and doubt as well as the hard to fulfil aspirations of piety into something binary that either is or is not the case. If the intention of the young man who came to the class was to become Muslim and he said the words correctly, then he was now a Muslim, regardless of his lack of understanding of the words he spoke. Yet this transformation is detached from the living of a life in the light of its implications. It reflects a perspective on Islam – God's revelation as an object that is whole and complete, in contrast to a concern with what it is in human terms to see oneself as being, among other things, Muslim.

Prayer (*salah*) takes only a few minutes and can be performed anywhere, provided the ground is clean or covered and that the required ablutions (*wudu*) have been completed so that one is in a state of ritual purity. Though congregational prayer is often visually impressive because of the size of the gathering, it is essentially the same in form as other prayers during the week, whether conducted alone or with others.[15] Henkel (2005) suggests, in relation to urban life in Turkey, that the simplicity and brevity of this universal Muslim ritual constitutes a 'highly mobile body technique' that can be slotted in as 'a sequence of practice into everyday life'. While this may be so in principle, not all Henkel's informants are in fact managing, or even attempting, to adopt this as a regular practice and, as I will describe in a later chapter, even those sufficiently committed to attend classes encountered difficulty in fulfilling these obligations within the complexity of their lives. Yet, in some of the homes I visited, prayer did indeed take place amid the trappings of everyday life. It required that the usual schedule of activities be put to one side but once commenced, it seemed that the demands of the ritual could create a protected and focused space around the worshipping individual – a mother praying as her young children continued to bounce around on a bed beside her, or a gender-mixed discussion group around a dining table temporarily transformed into segregated prayer lines in the sitting room area with men taking up a position in front of women. This adaptability of the location of prayer to ordinary life led Azzim to refer frequently in the class to the demands of Islam as 'easy' while ignoring the many requirements and interpretations of ritual obligations that preoccupied and troubled the women in the class. Beyond this, many of those I met did not attempt to fulfil these obligations in any systematic way and did not seem to regard them as essential to maintaining some level of religious practice.[16] The shift in focus among anthropologists of Islam from those who systematically sought piety to the lives of ordinary Muslims has been taken by Fadil and Fernando (2015) as characterised largely by accounts of failures of practice – the young men in Cairo who keep Ramadan but revert afterwards to alcohol, music, and pornography (Schielke 2009). Yet even intermittent religious practice involves a level of commitment, and I will explore the vicissitudes of individual practice in this light.

Praying together as an experience of unity

The Friday prayer that replaces the daily noon prayer is performed in unison. Religious distinctions suggested by the visible differences of dress and ethnicity and the variations in the details of ritual performance associated with different Muslim traditions (such as the raising of the index finger during prayer or differences between men and women in the placing of the hands on the body) that were the subject of discussions in the classes and groups I attended, were submerged within the larger pattern of coordinated movement. So were differences in commitment to religious practice. In terms of Rappaport's argument, conforming to the ritual of prayer, and particularly its performance alongside others, creates a temporary state of attunement among those present. Even on days other than Friday, when there might be only a few women present on the balcony and, looking through the window as I arrived, only a handful of men downstairs, when the call to prayer sounded within the mosque those who were there would form a line, ensuring that any children joined them.[17] The two midday prayers on Friday, during Ramadan and the two major festivals,[18] saw the largest congregation and the greatest diversity. At such times, the imam repeatedly called on those present to 'straighten your lines and close the gaps', to make 'space for others and close the gaps in our hearts', and 'pray this prayer as if it were your last'. This addressed the need to establish a concrete order among those present that would visually reflect the acceptance of a single shared religious reality (Bowen 1989) and invoke a perspective that reached beyond the human lifespan. In communal prayer, the individual worshipper is made dependent on the actions of others.[19]

While the performance of ritual may create a high degree of co-ordination among the participants, this is in the face of both the reality of individual differences and currents of change within Islam.[20] The congregation was a complex grouping in a changing religious context whose existence over time and integrity was re-created by this gathering for prayer each Friday – though, of course, the same people might not be present. Indeed, the passage of time and the absence of those who had died since the previous Friday, or last Eid, was a matter to which the congregation's attention was frequently drawn. The centripetal force of prayer and the gathering in of an increasingly disparate and dispersed group as new communities of migrants arrived and others become more involved in the society around them was reflected concretely in the demand that worshippers, who had been scattered around the prayer space in self-chosen arrangements, should form into lines, whether there were few or many individuals present. This generally takes place automatically in response to the call to prayer, but sometimes individuals required direction – 'Sister, you can't pray alone' – and I came to understand during my fieldwork that not everyone on the women's balcony was equally used to collective prayer. Two women I met, one from Somalia and one from Sri Lanka, who had arrived in the UK as adults, told me that they had never prayed in a mosque before coming to London. Most women in the Muslim world do not attend the mosque for prayer, and when they do so in the UK, it is often in marginalised spaces with the imam's voice relayed through a sound system.

The balcony as a space for women and children

My view of Friday prayer was that from the women's balcony and what took place there. In other settings, I mixed freely with men and women, or at least among those who themselves socialised in this way. In order not to call attention to the fact that I did not join in prayer, I generally sat on the row of chairs arranged along the back wall for the use of older women who could no longer make the prostrations. This allowed me to observe congregational prayer while avoiding the ambiguity of participating, but it also gave me a space from which to observe the use the women made of the balcony outside of this ritual.

On one occasion, when I arrived on the women's balcony, an elderly Pakistani woman I knew was sitting at the back fingering her beads and whispering prayers to herself. She nodded at me in recognition. (When I got up to go after the first prayer ended, she remained seated, again in private prayer but looked up to say, 'See you next week'). The women's area was almost empty, about ten women (and just two or three small children). They were mostly sitting alone, but three young women were sitting in a group, chatting. These little groups with their belongings spread out around them had the appearance of a picnic. One woman was standing in solitary prayer. I noticed that an older woman I knew slightly was talking quietly to another further along the back row. A few more women arrived. One of the women who acts as steward brought some mosque calendars and put them on the chair beside me, telling me to sell them for £2 if anyone asked. A very elderly woman struggled in with sticks and an air of vulnerability. She needed help from the steward to find a seat. A woman of about forty in an East African/Somali style dress came in with some shopping bags. Putting them down, she shook her arms before starting to pray in an apparently calm, relaxed manner. It reminded me of the shaking out a tablecloth, a familiar domestic gesture. The woman was someone I knew from the Sunday Sisters' Circle to be coming in her lunch hour. I was aware that despite an appearance of relaxed tranquillity she would be rushing back to work as soon as prayer ended. Her measured movements brought to my mind an occasion when the teacher of a class I attended explained the proper way to pray was by giving to each bodily movement its proper time, relaxing into each posture before moving on.

With the call to prayer, those who were scattered around the balcony in comfortable informality started to transform themselves into a congregation, forming lines with a shared orientation towards Mecca. In contrast to this smoothly choreographed familiar formation, those who arrived at the last minute, during the sermon, or even after the start of prayer caused a disruption, both physically, in requiring others to move, and in bringing the concerns of the street into the midst of a focused ritualised process. Whatever may be said about the nature of ritual itself and its distinctiveness from the mundane, these scenes were a reminder that it takes place within an everyday human context and is not immune to intrusions (Hounet 2012). However, when the scene on the balcony was not dominated by large numbers jostling to fit in or by the conversations of those who had not yet settled themselves, there were times when the space, and the gathering taking place there, had a profound aesthetic impact.

Thus, on a Friday in winter, I noted that it was dark on the balcony until the space was suddenly lit by the large chandelier hanging down from the dome into the men's area so that the light seemed to rise up into the double-height space and disperse through the gloom of the balcony. The visual impact led me to listen more closely to the call to prayer (only audible within the mosque) and the way the sound seemed to fill the space as the light had done. On this occasion, it struck me as a measured and satisfying sound, not insistent or harsh. Perhaps because of the emptiness of the balcony, I was more aware than usual of the musicality of the sound – the lengthening of the first word of the phrase and a sustaining note at the end. The overall effect was of the light and the sound creating a focus that pulled together a random scattering of individuals into a group, creating a state of readiness and expectation for what would follow.

This aesthetic experience of focus and coherence, due in no small measure to the design and furnishing of the building, was in marked contrast to the kind of space provided for women in other local mosques I visited.[21] One North African woman I met sitting on the balcony while I was waiting for a class to start said that she was enjoying the beauty of the space provided for women in this mosque and observed how different it was from one she usually attended nearer her home. Though Qureshi (1996) stresses the impact of an aesthetic of sound and movement rather than the visual in Islamic ritual, care and expense had clearly gone into the internal appearance of the mosque. Qureshi stresses that 'This process of "making Muslim space" for the Muslim diaspora within the larger Western context must take as its starting point one that is community-internal …. Not what outsiders see, but what insiders identify as creating a "space" for Islam' (ibid: 1996). The dome that is a visible external marker of Islam also creates internally an enhanced acoustic. The group planning a new local mosque in the Netherlands in Verkaaik's (2012) study was torn between what was needed and expected internally by those using the building and the desire to send a message to those on the outside by designing a building that would fit in with its surrounding in a small Dutch town and would look open and welcoming. There was thus a tension between the provision of an internal aesthetic space that sustains the congregation in worship and the mosque as representing the presence of Muslims to the secular world outside. This need to face both ways was in play when the second build was planned at the mosque. There was a concern to create a large space that would be kept solely for events other than prayer so that non-Muslims could visit without the need to remove their shoes. But even within the existing prayer space, the unpredictable physical demands of accommodating a large, disparate congregation as they arrived straight from whatever they had just been doing were considerable, while mundane, un-ritualised, reality crowded in as soon as prayer ended.

As prayer started, the women formed into more compact lines than those adopted for the sermon to accommodate those who had continued to arrive, though this was no easy matter if too many had crammed onto the balcony. While the room might be found for those already there, the stewards sometimes had to insist that others must stay in the wide corridor area beyond and pray there. In prayer, this large and disparate gathering of women began to perform the sequences of movements side by side, with sufficient familiarity for their actions to approximate unison. Though an intensely private moment, a woman praying alone is an intimate and humanly affecting sight; the view across the backs of the women prostrated in worship is an impressive and thought-provoking sight that accords with Rappaport's characterisation of ritual as creating a unified whole that is 'more characteristic of the internal dynamics of single organisms than of social groups' (Rappaport 1999: 224). The watching outsider is not part of this organism, except at those moments when the outer surface of this organism is broken by perturbations through which individuals and every day concerns erupt – exchanges with stewards about late arrivals who need chairs, disputes with those who have positioned themselves so that they block the doorways or impede the prostrations of those behind them, and the presence of young children.

Some women were accompanied by children. Women had the responsibility during worship for young children of both genders. After the age of about seven, boys accompanied adult male members of their family or entered the male prayer hall alone. The nine-year-old son of one of my informants, whom I had formerly only seen fooling about at home, was transformed in identification with an adult Muslim male as he detached himself from his mother and sister and set off ahead of us in his white robe and lace cap to pray with the men, while we went to the women's balcony.[22] In accordance with the widely held view that women's attendance at the mosque is not obligatory or even, in the opinion of some men, desirable, if women with children chose to attend they had to find ways to divide their attention between their prayers and their children, ways which lie outside the tight prescriptions of prayer. Some sat back against the walls with their infants in their laps, attending directly to them, and did not appear outwardly to be praying, whether because they were menstruating or because of their baby's needs; others left their babies propped on coats and bags and prayed at some distance from them. One mother managed to soothe a fretful infant while she prayed by laying him beside her while she prostrated herself, repeatedly sweeping him into her arms as she stood up, replacing the child gently on the floor as she returned to her knees. This was a striking example of how an infant might, almost from the beginning, have an experience of the sounds and movements of something they will later understand as prayer. For the most part, those babies who were awake seemed calmly watchful of what was for them, no doubt, a familiar, or a becoming familiar, scene and an experience of the withdrawal of their mother's attention in prayer that they could generally tolerate without protest. Only rarely were the children oblivious to the atmosphere, which seemed to act on their state in a soothing manner allowing their mothers to divide their attention and pray. Women whose babies became upset during prayer would generally take them out into the corridor area, which was always a rather chaotic place, with an atmosphere quite different from that on the balcony. Some people might try and pray there, but others treated the space as somewhere you could talk, walk around, and eat (despite the many notices to the contrary) so that the atmosphere of prayer on the balcony was absent and children of all ages tended to become more fractious and harder to control. Though two-year-olds moved about unhindered between the lines of women on the balcony or explored the space, peeping through the screens that created the temporary overspill area for the men, their behaviour also seemed modulated by what was taking place around them. Some would imitate the adults' prayer movements, sometimes observing and correcting each other. At other times, they were distracted from their 'prayers' when they became absorbed in the pattern on the carpet or in whispering to each other as they 'prostrated' side by side. On one occasion, the sound of a child 'singing' along in imitation of the imam could be heard clearly. For the most part, the children seemed attuned to their surroundings, 'at home' within the atmosphere on the balcony. In contrast to Stafford's (2007) recollections of the enforced immobility of the Christian services of his childhood, Muslim prayer offers the possibility of actively joining in through imitating the movements of prayer, something a young child could do passably well.

Young children and infants seemed to absorb the non-verbal qualities of the atmosphere, the rhythmic activities and enveloping sounds that filled the space and could, in consequence, tolerate the withdrawal of their mother's attention in prayer, as distinct from the chaotic situation that prevailed in the area beyond. During prayer, the infant is taken into a powerful space in which synchronised movement and musicality transform individual participants into a whole, whether one conceives of that whole as a single organism (Rappaport 1999) or as a 'shared organisational form' (Condor and Sander (1974) [see Chapter 1]. Developmental research suggests that this profound bodily and emotional experience of being with others is a source of shared meaning throughout life. 'We can only cooperate in relationships or social groups by sympathetic harmonisation and synchronisation (with a common pulse) … dancing together with its rhythms and respecting the qualities of its tensions and future oriented impulses and melodies which we share' (Malloch and Trevarthen 2009: 8). It is a state suffused with human relatedness and consonant with Zigon's conception of the 'unconscious moral background' out of which conscious reflective ethical capacity emerges. But the music of different social groups will differ and though there is a presumption of continuity in the soundscape and movements of a social world, this is not necessarily the case. As with migration, there may be a sudden loss of the familiar to be replaced externally by the need to adjust to the 'song and dance' of a new situation while the music of a previous world continues to be heard internally.

Attunement to the soundscape of a Muslim world would depend on opportunities for participation.[23] An exposure to religious activity as a familiar part of that world would, in the ordinary course of things, precedes any formal religious teaching of school-aged children or the conscious seeking of piety in adulthood. This has implications for an understanding of later objectified forms of religious knowledge. Those brought up from infancy within Muslim families who were to some extent practicing would have had the opportunity for early pre-reflective bodily internalisation of the sounds and movements of the religious practice of others that precedes conscious thought, while those whose families were not practising, or where an individual only converted (reverted)[24] to Islam in adulthood would be reliant on a conscious linguistically mediated conception of religious experience. Nor is participation in the embodied and affective atmosphere of a religious world, such as that available to the infants on the prayer balcony, likely to be an isolated event but one sustained by multiple experiences of human contact. During prayer, infants can inhabit a space created by the visual proximity of their mother's physical presence, as well as their own bodily sense of being held together by the 'sedimentation'[25] of past experiences of safety in her care. Indeed, it is through ordinary human caregiving that infants become able to respond to the experience of ritual as a space within which they, and their relationship to mother, are contained by the pattern and repetition of familiar sounds and movements. Both present and past embodied experiences of being with others in multiple ways are dimensions of an adult sensibility to the moral qualities of a community. It is in the qualities of ordinary communal living that sociality constitutes itself as a moral resource located within everyday experience (Rasanayagam 2013). At the same time, this ability to absorb the milieu and traditions of a lifeworld and transform it into moral understandings and conscious ethical capacity has its roots in the developmental processes of infancy. It is out of repeated experiences of bodily attunement to others in infancy that a conscious awareness of self in relation to others emerges and, with it, the capacity to tolerate the anxieties and conflict attendant on dependence and separation, to take responsibility for failure and to manage those occasions that Zigon (2007) calls 'moral breakdown'.[26]

Sustaining a shared world

In his study of listening to taped sermons as a religious practice, Hirschkind describes how the coming together of the music and meaning of the Quran within the body of the listener offers a fusion of intellectual and aesthetic dimensions that 'give the text its unity' (Hirschkind 2006: 154). He points to an Islamic understanding of the power of the divine word to 'inshine human souls' as 'a key element in a pre-rational ordering of the self upon which more rational practices depend' (ibid: 152). From an Islamic perspective, such processes and the way they are imaged are the result of divine power. For the young men in his study, it is the heightened awareness of these bodily states that creates their sense of the reality of religious experience, which they seek to extend by keeping the tapes running in the background. This reference to the need for an object (the Quran) that holds together different sensual modalities and enables that integration of thought and feeling necessary to a complex and full religious experience implies that without it a very different state would prevail – perhaps something like the tension between the intellect and the emotion that Chitrali Muslims experienced as posing a threat to a balanced mind (Marsden 2005: 206). McGilchrist (2010) suggests the neurological basis for this tension between rationality and feelings and hence the need for an object that can sustain a degree of integration.[27] In developmental terms, a human object is needed to support integrative processes in infancy – the presence of a parent with an actively responsive mind that helps the infant to regulate their bodily state, to integrate different sensory modalities (Stern 1985) and who acts as a responsive partner in the song and dance of early relatedness.[28] Over time the infant will internalise this parental presence and come to manage these functions to some extent for themselves. Nevertheless, for neither the young men listening to taped sermons nor the infant are these states of bodily focus and coherence permanent achievements. They can and will be repeatedly lost and need to be recovered and re-established.

The reality of change and loss is a recurrent feature of studies of religious experience (Deeb 2006; Simon 2009, 2014). The impact of prayer may be understood as gathering up an individual or a congregation in a way that re-creates a sense of focus and order, but the change is not fixed but rather calls attention to its fragility and transience and the feelings of vulnerability this inevitably engenders. Pelkmans (2017) writes of the ebb and flow of affective states within a shared endeavour as a dynamic that is intrinsic to the life of such collective undertakings. He describes these processes as if they were the *pulsations* of life within an organism, which calls to mind the pulse within the musicality of bodily sociality (Malloch and Trevarthen 2009).

Some of those I met through classes and study groups spoke of the somatic impact of individual prayer such that they felt that they could anticipate when a prayer time was approaching as a felt bodily need to pray. Those who pray regularly speak of its calming and cleansing effect on the individual (Simon 2009), a sense of internal coherence (Hirschkind 2006) and attunement to others (Rappaport 1999). However, there is also an implication that all these states are subject to depletion and that a framework within which they can be sustained or renewed is needed if they are not, as Simon's informants describe, to be lost in a way that is felt to be unrecoverable. The growth of a capacity to recognise this cycle within the moral background and to acknowledge one's place in it can be understood as the source from which a sense of responsibility and the capacity to repair what has been lost emerges. Yet what is lost is never only an individual matter since the moral background that sustains the individual's sense of relatedness derives from participation in a shared world. It is, moreover, a world that is recognised as shared (Elster 1999: 95).

The core ritual of Friday prayer is regularly and predictably performed in accordance with a liturgical calendar and, therefore, available for all to participate in. The continuing presence of Muslim practice at the mosque, the immediate practical responsibility for which is borne by the Trustees, contributes to a sense of the continuity of God's order amidst the unpredictability, dislocations, and failures of life – an intermediate space between the 'messiness of the human world and the perfection of Islam' (Simon 2009: 258). Whether an individual has maintained their own religious practice or not, by praying side by side with others, the unavoidable ebb and flow of personal states of piety and practice are replaced, for a while, by something more tangible and certain, a visible gathering of Muslims, that holds together across the gaps in individual commitment and the inevitable cycles of doubt and hope (Pelkmans 2013). At the level of bodily sociality, one might also see such experience as not only visibly reassuring but inwardly resonant. As one friend, who did not pray regularly put it to me, when she decided to abandon what she was doing at home and accompany me to the mosque for prayer: 'I'll just go and make my peace with God'. Though she was not regular in her religious practice, she was someone whom I knew to pray at the mosque in private and who would ask the mosque Trustees for prayers for herself and her family in times of difficulty. Of a quarrel with a local *halal* butcher about being given less meat than she had paid for, she said she had eventually let the issue drop, adding that 'I may not always pray but I am not going to have a fight with someone on a Friday. So, I came back here and made *wudu* (ablution) and went to the mosque'. This suggests that both collective ritual and the mosque, as a place within which to access Muslim life and liturgy, may be thought of as functioning as a receptacle for the vicissitudes and failures of religious and social commitment. They create a containing space within which fragmentary and problematic religious experience can attain a degree of form and coherence, and the ruptures of failure can be felt to be reparable.[29] For my friend, this was accompanied by a degree of self-awareness, yet saying you are going to 'make your peace with God' surely passes over into something the nature of which is beyond conscious verbal representation. There was a sense in her way of speaking that this was something available and awaiting her, something that she felt she could turn back to after a rupture. Some individuals may stay on to pray in private after the end of collective prayer and amidst the bustle of people leaving. Whatever the motivation, this is a matter of individual choosing and, perhaps, of need. A woman with whom I had had a conversation in the kitchen earlier in the day about the death of a family member some years previously stayed behind to pray. When she eventually got up, she said something to me, implying that her additional moments of prayer were in the hope of finding some way to still her state of disquietude about her loss, of seeking to move from distress towards something less despairing. The familiarity of religious practice and the physical accessibility of the mosque created a moral space that an individual could inhabit, however transiently, in a way that made good one's own shortcomings by gathering in the unpredictable nature of everyday life and re-establishing the sense of divine order and one's place within it.

Soares and Osella ([2009] 2010) have been critical of ethnographies that 'over-privilege the coherence and disciplinary power of Islam' (ibid: 12), and there was a temptation to attend to the beauty of quiet moments on the prayer balcony at the expense of the more fraught and chaotic or even just the mundane and the practical. While the architecture of the mosque created an aesthetic space which was at times filled with the affective qualities of prayer and recitation in the language of the Quran – as in the call to prayer, the sounds of prayer itself, or the background hum of a *hafiz* class that used a room in the building, where children were struggling to recite from memory – much of the time it was the sounds and idioms of English that had to carry alike religious ideas, practical injunctions to worshippers, and the exchanges of social conversation. Over and above this, in school holidays, the mosque is noisier, during Ramadan, it is more crowded, and at festivals, the mood is more that of a social celebration. Yet even in an Arabic speaking Muslim society, prayer comes to an end and the mundane world begins again raising the issue of how a shared world established through collective prayer is to be sustained. It was the rupture in the fabric of experience created in prayer that the sermons sought to address (Chapter 4). The women in Mahmood's classes met this problem by seeking to reshape all aspects of their lives in accordance with strict interpretations of practice (Mahmood 2005: 116), while the young men found it necessary to use the portability of taped sermons to create a continuous religious sound background for their lives (Hirschkind 2006). The Guyanese conveyed a sense of maintaining their orientation through their practical commitment to their mosque, their style of sociality, and their sense that they played a part as Muslims in the fabric of the local community beyond the mosque.

Notes

1 It is *around* mid-day as the time of the five daily prayers moves in relation to timing of dawn and sunset.
2 Within the mosque, the Creator was referred to as both God and Allah. Unless I am quoting someone who refers to Allah, I use the word God.
3 Tied to the local time of sunrise and sunset, it appears to move through the fixity and uniformity of secular time, reflecting the distinction between mundane and liturgical time (Rappaport 1999).
4 The name of this congregational prayer (*Jummah* prayer) is related to the consonants *j-m-'* that form the root from which the words gathering and assembling are also derived.
5 Rappaport cites J L Austin on the nature of speech acts as one element in his understanding of ritual. Lambek (2010) roots his account of ordinary ethics in illocutionary speech.
6 My argument is built on this account of the embodied experience of ritual and links to both Hirschkind (2006) and the work of developmentalists on embodied experience that precedes the development of language.
7 This variety is in contrast to that within the more homogeneous Muslim communities that settled in the northern cities of the UK (Werbner 2002, 2018).
8 This is a black face veil, with a gap for the eyes, worn with a long black dress (*jilbab*) and black gloves covering the hands.
9 Though one can get to the women's balcony by both the main doors, and both are used by women at other times, on Fridays, a gendered arrangement was adopted whereby women entered and exited the mosque by only one door, though this was still shared with the men!
10 Verkaaik (2012) describes a congregation in the Netherlands who were planning a new mosque and the complex negotiations that took place among them as to what features were essential and what elements, it turned out, were more a matter of aesthetic choice.
11 In what follows, I am generally relying on what I learnt from my interlocutors during my fieldwork, so it reflects the views within the mosque rather than that of an external religious authority.
12 The second group was mixed gender and met in the imam's home, but over time the membership changed until the group no longer had any connection with the local area, consisting entirely of young professionals drawn from across London.

13 From a third person perspective, this transformation may be said to be brought about through the public acknowledgement of a conventional order and the properties of the language of a speech act (Austin [1962] 1975) that instantiates a situation – binding one in the taking of an oath or making true the pronouncing of the married state of a couple.

14 That is he would not have seen the transformative power of the shahada as located in a human speech act.

15 The number of cycles varies between two and four according to the prayer. Congregational prayer has only two cycles.

16 There is, of course, a difficulty in enquiring about this, but sometimes it became obvious that individuals were not performing the five daily prayers and it seemed that they either did not regard this as an obligatory or did not feel this failure created an impediment to the practice of other elements in their religious life.

17 The lines are formed facing the *qiblah,* the direction of Meccah. A niche in the wall of the prayer hall marks the direction.

18 *Eid al fitr* (at the end of Ramadan) or *Eid al adha* (the festival that celebrates Ibrahim's willingness to sacrifice his son, Ishmael).

19 This sense of mutual dependence feeds into an experience of inhabiting a shared moral world.

20 Henkel (2005) suggests, with respect to the complexity of religious views and varying degrees of commitment within Turkish society, that the universal form of Muslim prayer 'transcends local particularities' and 'special religious projects', thus countering the centrifugal effects of the many diverse currents, both religious and secular, within modern Turkey.

21 Other mosques I visited with those I had got to know in the Saturday class were all housed in poorly maintained residential or industrial buildings that could offer little in the way of comfort or material beauty and where the provision for women was poor, with access to the imam and the men's prayer hall only via loudspeaker.

22 There is some elasticity in this requirement in that at least one older boy with developmental problems was often brought by his mother to the wide corridor area around the outside of the women's balcony from where she attempted to pray, not always successfully.

23 The soundscape of domestic life would also differ from that within a public space such as a mosque.

24 Since the created condition of all is Muslim, converts are said to 'revert'.

25 A term from Jousse ([1925] 1990) used by Hirschkind to refer to the accumulation of internalised experience.

26 This account of infancy is informed by both psychoanalytic and developmental perspectives (cf Shuttleworth 1989 for an earlier integration of these perspectives).

27 The neuroscientist, McGilchrist (2010) argues that this integration is inherently problematic, always a struggle and never finalised. Because of the hemispheric structure of the brain, there is an intrinsic paradox at the heart of the human need to unify these perspectives. McGilchrist suggests that rational thought produced by left brain activity is experienced as intrinsically self-sufficient and separable from the immediacy and open-endedness of visceral and emotional responses. This predicament is reflected in the split between the rational and the sensual registers of experience within post-Enlightenment European thought (Connolly 2006).

28 Thus, Daniel Stern (1985) writes of the on-going, mutually shaping bodily-affective states of being that are communicated between of the mother and infant as *integrating* different sensory modalities into a dynamic form of experience he terms 'vitality affects'. In later work, Stern (2012) suggests that 'vitality affects' also captures our adult capacity to sense and respond directly to the contours and dynamics of the state of life in those around us.

29 The capacity to tolerate anxiety sufficiently to recognise and repair damage and failure has an important place in the Kleinian account of human development (Klein 1937). Wilfred Bion (1962) developed Klein's model of the capacity to tolerate anx-

iety, as a prerequisite for reparation, as arising from the infant's experience of adult care. If the infant's distress is taken into the mother's (parent/carer's) mind as a space in which it can be accepted and digested, a more manageable state is communicated to the infant through direct bodily affective processes. Ultimately this function of containing and transforming anxiety is taken over by the individual in the course of development through maintaining an internalised relationship to containing others.

References

Austin, J. L. ([1962] 1975) *How to Do Things with Words*. Cambridge: Harvard University Press.

Bion, W. (1962) *Learning from Experience*. London: Heinemann.

Bowen, J. (1989) 'Salat in Indonesia: The social meanings of an Islamic ritual', *Man* NS. 24(4): 600–619.

Clarke, M. (2013) 'Integrity and Commitment in the Anthropology of Islam', in Marsden, M. and Retsikas, K. (eds) *Articulating Islam: Anthropological Approaches to Muslim Worlds*. London: Springer.

Condor, W. S. and Sander, L. W. (1974) 'Synchrony demonstrated between movements of the neonate and adult speech', *Child Development* 45(2): 456–462.

Connolly, W. (2006) 'Europe: A Minor Tradition', in Scott, D. and Hirschkind, C. (eds) *Powers of the Secular Modern*. Stanford: Stanford University Press.

Deeb, L. (2006) *An Enchanted Modern: Gender and Public Piety in Shi'a Lebanon*. Princeton: Princeton University Press.

Elster, J. (1999) *Strong Feelings*. Cambridge, MA: The MIT Press.

Fadil, N. (2011) 'Not-/unveiling as an ethical practice', *Feminist Review* 98: 83–109.

Fadil, N. and Fernando, M. (2015) 'Rediscovering the "everyday" Muslim: Notes on an anthropological divide', *Journal of Ethnographic Theory* 5(2): 59–88.

Henkel, H. (2005) 'Between belief and unbelief lies the performance of *salat*: Meaning and the efficacy of Muslim ritual', *Journal of Royal Anthropological Institute* 11: 487–507.

Hounet, Y. (2012) 'The Ma'ruf: an Ethnography of Ritual (South Algeria)', in Dupret, T, Pierret, B., Pinto, P., Spellman-Poots, K. (eds), *Ethnographies in Islam*. Edinburgh: Edinburgh University Press.

Hirschkind, C. (2006) *Ethical Soundscapes*. New York: Columbia University Press.

Jousse, M. ([1925] 1990) *The Oral Style*. New York: Garland Publishing Inc.

Keane, W. (2013) 'On spirit writing: Materialities of language and the religious work of transduction', *Journal of the Royal Anthropological Institute* 19: 1–17.

Klein, M. (1937). 'Love Guilt and Reparation', in *The Writings of Melanie Klein* 1975 Vol 1. London: Hogarth [Reprinted London: Vintage 1988].

Lambek, M. (ed) (2010) *Ordinary Ethics*. New York: Fordham University Press.

Lukens-Bull, R. (2007) 'Lost in the sea of subjectivity: The subject position of the researcher in the anthropology of Islam', *Contemporary Islam* 1: 173–192.

Mahmood, S. (2005) *The Politics of Piety*. Princeton: Princeton University Press.

Makris, G. P. (2007) *Islam in the Middle East: A Living Tradition*. Oxford: Blackwell.

Malloch, S. and Trevartehn, C. (2009) *Communicative Musicality*. Oxford: Oxford University Press.

Marsden, M. (2005) *Living Islam: Muslim Religious Experience in Pakistan's North West Frontier*. Cambridge: Cambridge University Press.

McGilchrist, I. (2010) *The Master and His Emissary: The Divided Brain and the Making of the Western World*. Yale: Yale University Press.

Pelkmans, M. E. (2013) *Ethnographies of Doubt*. New York: I.B. Tauris and Co Ltd.

Pelkmans, M. E. (2017) *Fragile Convictions*. New York: Cornell University Press.

Qureshi, R. (1996) 'Transcending Space: Recitation and Community among South Asian Muslims in Canada', in Metcalfe, B. D. (ed) *Making Muslim Space in North America and Europe*. Berkeley: University of California.

Rappaport, R. (1999) *Ritual and Religion in the Making of Humanity*. Cambridge: Cambridge University Press.

Rasanayagam, J. (2013) 'Beyond Islam: Tradition and the Intelligibility of Experience', in Marsden, M. and Retsikas, K. (eds) *Articulating Islam: Anthropological Approaches to Muslim Worlds*. London: Springer.

Schielke, S. 2009 'Being good in Ramadan: ambivalence, fragmentation, and the moral self in the lives of young Egyptians' in Journal of the Royal Anthropological Institute. 15 S24–S40

Shannahan, D. S. (2014) 'Gender, inclusivity and UK mosque experience', *Contemporary Islam* 8: 1–16.

Simon, G. M. (2009) 'The soul freed of cares', *American Ethnologist* 36(2): 258–275.

Simon, G. M. (2014) *Caged in on the Outside: Moral Subjectivity, Selfhood, and Islam in Minangkabau, Indonesia*. Honolulu: University of Hawai'i Press.

Stafford, C. (2007) 'What Is Interesting about Chinese Religion', in Berliner, D. and Sarro, R (eds) *Learning Religion*. Oxford: Berghahn.

Stern, D. (1985) *The Interpersonal World of the Infant: A View from Psychoanalysis and Developmental Psychology*. New York: Basic Books.

Stern, D. (2012) *Forms of Vitality*. Oxford: Oxford University Press.

Shuttleworth, J. 1989 'Psychoanalytic Theory and Infant Development' in Miller, L., Rustin, M.E., Rustin, M.J. Shuttleworth, J. (eds) Closely Observed Infants London: [Duckworth] Bloomsbury Publishing.

Tarlo, E. (2005) 'Reconsidering stereotypes: Anthropological reflections on the jilbab controversy', *Anthropology Today* 21(6): 13–17.

Tarlo, E. (2010) *Visibly Muslim: Bodies of Faith: Fashion, Politics, Faith*. Oxford: Berg.

Verkaaik, O. (2012) 'Designing the "anti-mosque": Identity, religion, and affect in contemporary European mosque design', *Social Anthropology* 20(2): 161–176.

Werbner, P. (2002) *Imagined Diasporas among Manchester Muslims*. Santa Fe: School of American Research Press.

Werbner, P. (2018) 'Ritual, Religion and Aesthetics in the Pakistani and South Asian Diaspora', in Chatterji, J. and Washbrook, D. (eds) *Routledge Handbook of the South Asian Diaspora*. London: Routledge.

Zigon, J. (2007) 'Moral breakdown and the ethical demand', *Anthropological Theory* 7(1): 131–150.

Zigon, J. 2014 'Attunement and Fidelity: two Ontological Conditions for Morally Being in the World' in Ethos 42:1

4

CREATING UNITY THROUGH WORDS

Sermons at the mosque

The special linguistic and bodily-affective qualities of ritual are highlighted by the sharp contrast between the two elements of congregational ritual on Friday – prayer in Arabic and the sermons in English that precede it. During prayer, a religious world is realised through the canonical nature of its movements and language (Rappaport 1999); in sermons, a religious reality may be evoked or spoken about, but it cannot be instantiated as it is in ritual. Of necessity, sermons are subject to the variations and vagaries of an individual preacher's capacity and preoccupations, from which ritual is largely protected.[1] In sermons, the imam must choose his own words and speak for himself. Though the senior of the two imams attached to the mosque often preached at one of the two Friday prayers, he was on a rota that included visiting preachers, each bringing their own concerns and ways of speaking. Among the diversity of preachers, there was no consistent theological perspective or attempt to address and integrate the religious differences within the congregation. Nor was there a common, unifying rhetorical tradition of preaching. There could be no assumption of the immediate, divinely ordained accessibility of the language of the Quran, of which Hirschkind writes, since sermons at the mosque were delivered largely, though not entirely, in English to a congregation with different first languages who were now living within the soundscape of a non-Muslim society. Paradoxically, the relevance of Hirschkind's work to the sermons at this mosque lies in the implications of an absence of the soundscape of a canonical tradition and perhaps, for some, the loss of what they had once known – that degree of homogeneity in the soundscape and the continuity of a shared life-world present within a Muslim society despite the encroachments of modernity and the secular. This is not to deny the complexity and fragmentation created by the different and competing commitments that even the religiously committed in Muslim countries find themselves subject to (Schielke 2010; Ghannam 2011; Shively 2014) but to

DOI: 10.4324/9781003080008-4

call attention to the discontinuity between the soundscape that permeated the mosque during the ritual of collective prayer in Arabic and that which prevailed in those activities conducted in English and its implications for different sections within the congregation.

In such circumstances, sermons may use language to bring a religious experience to mind or to talk *about* religious matters as objects of conscious understanding (Eickleman 1992). Unlike the even tones of prayer, the language and manner of delivery often sought to make a particular emotional impact. Preachers might exhort a congregation to attend to their religious duties amid the distractions of life and the difficulties experienced in non-Muslim society; they might urge Muslim commonality and community – the *umma* – in the face of the heterogeneity of a migrant congregation (Cenker 2015); and they might suggest the need for a particular range of feelings; but they cannot bring these things into being as ritual can. This chapter describes the range of perspectives on Islam that was presented to the congregation in sermons. While the manner in which the sermon was delivered was generally in tune with the verbal content of the sermon there were times, as I will describe below, when a strong expression of emotion in the supplications[2] that followed the sermon seemed intended to balance or even compensate for a less emphatic, more inwardly directed sermon.

While most of the sermons I heard were, in different ways, about the need to live in the present in a manner that mirrored the practice of the Prophet and about the problems of living as Muslims in a non-Muslim majority country, there was a contrast between those preachers who sought to maintain clear distinctions and boundaries between Islam and the non-Muslim world, and those who saw being Muslim in terms of living alongside non-Muslim others, within an area of shared, or sharable values, and within which the individual must address their own difficulties.[3] Most of the sermons preached by visiting imams fell into the former category, in which there was a strong feeling of both the individual and the *umma* as under threat from not only the non-Muslim world beyond the mosque but the current state of some Muslim societies. The sense of threat was added to by the fact that mosque sermons occupied a particular position in the UK media at that time and the awareness of being an object of hostile scrutiny as to what others thought constituted a 'good' and 'bad' Muslim was sometimes strongly present. I will give a series of examples of these concerns and the way the anxieties associated with them were framed. However, this chapter begins and ends with preaching that reflects the thinking of the Guyanese.

Just before one sermon, there was an intervention by the younger of the two official imams.[4] The brief intervention by Bilal that I will describe was striking on the one hand for its acceptance of human reality as he found it, and on the other, for his firmness in relation to his own position of knowledge and religious experience despite his youth relative to most of the congregation. It also calls attention to the difference between a congregation 'at prayer' and the same group during a sermon. In ritual prayer, one participates through the collective performance of prescribed actions accompanied by the recitation of formalised speech; being present at a sermon imposes no such requirements, except the convention that, unlike in a lecture, one does not ask questions, but neither does one have to listen. This ambiguity was particularly marked during a crowded and noisy gathering for the festival of *eid al adha*,[5] when large numbers attended the mosque, bringing together the knowledgeable, the devout, and the minimally practising. As the imam who would be giving the sermon and leading the prayer, Bilal quietly explained to the congregation how the ritual on that day would differ in some way from the more usual form of congregational prayer on Fridays. It was clear that he assumed that some of those present would not be familiar with this difference and that he would need to make this announcement if the ritual was not to be disrupted. On the women's balcony, most were dressed in conspicuously new and highly colourful clothes. The young were intent on greeting each other with elaborate hugs and kisses while the older women were exchanging *Eid* cards. The imam went on to ask that people be quiet and listen to the sermon rather than thinking about the food they would be eating later, as this was an opportunity for them to learn something. Again, there was a tacit acknowledgment that many in the congregation would not be inclined to pay much attention. However, some of the women clearly did want to listen to the sermon as, later, a group of young women in pious black dress, sitting in the front surrounded by those in colourful new *eid* attire, held up a hurriedly scrawled notice to those behind them, reading: 'Sisters, please be quiet – we can't hear!'.

Eid al adha is an event in the shared history of the Abrahamic faiths that is marked in Islam through prayer and donations so that the meat of slaughtered animals may be distributed to the poor[6] – but it is also a communal celebration of food and family in the present. Four prayer times, rather than the usual two on Fridays, are laid on to accommodate the level of demand, and the imam's remarks indicated that its status as a joyful family celebration might overwhelm its religious significance: some might attend the mosque only for events such as this. Rather than taking this as an opportunity to indicate explicitly the lack of religious commitment, Bilal addressed the problem in a low-key, practical way that accepted the reality of the situation. This approach was well attuned to a style of thinking and acting among many of the Guyanese and Mauritians, who were present in large numbers at this event, but it was at odds with the manner adopted by many, if not most of the preachers on Fridays, though they varied considerably one from another.

Peripatetic preachers; local sermons

Many of those leading prayer and preaching at the mosque on Fridays were 'freelance', reflecting the decentralisation of religious knowledge and authority within Islam. While there was no immediate sense of crisis within the mosque during the time of my fieldwork as there had been only a few years earlier, there were indications that the Trustees perceived an undercurrent of potential challenge and a need to be vigilant.[7] Given that the preachers were drawn from many different parts of the Muslim world, some educated abroad and others in the UK, this created a great diversity of subject matter and modes of delivery.[8] Visiting preachers at the mosque sometimes made it clear that they could be consulted for advice and seemed to preach around a circuit of mosques and may thus be said to have careers in this field, akin to those whose recorded sermons circulated in what Roy describes as a marketplace of Muslim thinking (Roy 2007).[9] Those preachers for whom English was not their first language, and those whose religious concerns and manner of delivery required it, interspersed the English sections with long quotations in Arabic, making the sermons fragmented and difficult for me, and presumably other non-Arabic speakers, to follow. These preachers generally delivered sermons in a more emotional style than the ordinary, conversational tone of the English-speaking imams. Thus, while some sermons were delivered in idiomatic English, with casual references to familiar local landmarks and a focus on the everyday concerns of Muslims, other preachers, from a variety of Muslim countries, often adopted a perspective that was not at all local and a timeframe that was not that of the present. Here the preoccupation with the early Muslims evinced 'an indifference to the pastness of the past in favour of its exemplary value in the present' (Hirschkind 2006: 162) – or a concern with the concrete details of the events that take place after death and on the Last Day.

While those who spoke of religious concerns as the moral struggles of individuals to live today in accordance with divine revelation might refer to the events of the founding period of Islam and the end of time (Deeb 2009), the purpose tended to be that of illuminating a focus on everyday experience. One such sermon gave a central place to death and the need to live in the light of the eschaton, but did so not by summoning up concrete scenes of the 'torments of the grave' and the awful punishments that await the sinner, but with the telling immediacy of a remark that we were half-way through Ramadan and there were those who were here with us last year who were no longer with us and we have no guarantee that we ourselves will be here next year at this time. The abundance of God's mercy was contrasted with our difficulty in recognising when we have taken a wrong road and 'need to correct and reconnect our lives'. This difficulty, the imam argued, is because we do not want to change. We prefer escape and delusion, such as through alcohol, but sin only increases the error and the addiction to sin grows until 'your heart feels nothing'. He ended by saying: 'So, brothers and sisters, this is the time to come back and correct ourselves, whether this is to do with our relationship with Allah or with other human beings, whether with Muslim or non-Muslim, we should ask Allah for his forgiveness and not despair of mercy'. The sermon contained many references to 'our' sins and what 'we' should do and relationships with non-Muslims were also placed before God. I thought of it as constituting the sort of sermon that might be the implied target of other preachers who were mockingly critical of what they saw as the government's agenda to promote a 'British' Islam.

For all the preachers, the situation of contemporary Muslims across the world was a recurrent theme and if the sermons of those who were 'local' to the area were less obviously emotional, both groups of preachers made use of the short supplicatory prayer *(du'a)* that follows the sermon to give expression to marked states of feeling, with the apparent aim of stirring the listener to a heightened emotional response as the series of supplications to God rose in a crescendo. This was the more striking when it followed a low-key sermon. Thus, a restrained sermon on the theme of not despairing of God's mercy was followed by a supplicatory litany first for the sick, and then the dead ('spare them the pains of the grave, *yer Allah*'), and then for a woman who, it had been announced, had taken the *shahada* that day. After this, the imam became increasingly impassioned as he asked Allah first for Palestine and then for Iraq to be spared *fitna* (chaos)[10] and to be delivered from the occupation. However, in contrast to the work of Mahmood (2005) and Hirschkind (2006) with individuals who actively sought out strong emotional qualities in sermons as a way of enhancing their religious experience, in this London context, it was problematic to some in the congregation. There were indications that some of those I knew found these expressions of emotion excessive, one woman saying, 'Well, perhaps it (the *du'a*) sounds better in Arabic than in English', and someone saying on another occasion that it was like an express train. Though delivered in English, or perhaps precisely because of this, there was something unfamiliar and jarring for some in the mode in which the supplicatory prayer was often delivered – a fragment from a different soundscape.

There is an inevitable contrast between ritual and sermons, between the eternal as manifest in the received canonical structures of ritual and the humanly made, variable messages of the sermon. By comparison with prayer and Quranic recitation or preaching constructed directly out of lengthy quotations of the word of God that may be relying on the impact of the 'music' to carry something of the transformative aesthetic qualities and layered meanings that Hirschkind (2006: 152–153) describes, sermons in English are naked, improvised, human things, undertaken with more or less skill but with any limitations plain to see.[11] Ritual prayer offers the unity of a predictable form; sermons expose individual differences – differences in the stance adopted towards the issues put before the congregation and in the capacity of the preacher to consider them. Matters of theological disagreement were not commented on within the sermons themselves, yet the differences between them implied marked disagreements.

Unlike the young men in Cairo listening to cassette sermons and exercising choice in their tape selection, the London congregation had to hear whichever preacher happened to be acting as imam on that Friday. However, many of the women, and perhaps the men also,[12] did not actually sit through the whole sermon. They would arrive late, right up to the start of prayer (and sometimes during it),[13] as if the sermon was optional and unimportant; they too may, in a sense, have been exercising choice. A woman who had just started to attend the Saturday classes expressed an oblique criticism of one of the more political sermons and went on to ask me if I knew when Azzim, who taught the class, preached. I offered her my best guess based on what seemed to be the rota pattern and she said she would try to come then. Azzim's sermons were the most abstract in their concern with the dangers of substituting material representations for the transcendent nature of God but as his preaching stood out from the rest in this regard, I will discuss his religious position in the chapter on his teaching and lecturing in Chapters 7 and 8. Given that the accents of some preachers were more difficult to follow than others or that they included long sections in Arabic, there is an inevitable bias in my account towards those sermons where I could understand what was being said. There were some that I found impossible to follow and they constitute an interesting phenomenon in themselves since I assumed that many in the congregation might have had difficulty understanding even if they were familiar with the style of sermonising.

All the preachers I heard were faced with a congregation inhabiting an English-speaking European present. Roy suggests a distinction between those groups who 'try to inscribe forms of Muslim communalism in the framework of the host countries', by accepting, as the Guyanese have done, the task of rebuilding a concrete community in a new situation and those who 'endeavour to express their community as an ideal transnational and non-territorial entity' (Roy 2004: 202). While the experience of living within a non-Muslim society and the struggle of the individual to lead a religious life in such circumstances was shared, this had yet to create a new context of 'intelligibility' for the congregation as a whole (Rasanayagam 2013).[14] It was in the absence of such a shared understanding that the freelance preachers gave their sermons. While the mosque imams focused mainly on the internal religious struggles of the individual, visiting preachers addressed in various ways the impact on Muslim experience of living within a non-Muslim majority society. The examples in the next section reflect a recurring theme in the sermons of the visiting preachers – that of the difficulties in living a Muslim life without a proper Muslim context.

Creating and protecting Muslim space

In congregational prayer, the imagined community of Muslims is made visible and placed in accord with God's order through the correct bodily performance of ritual but when prayer ends, the state of *umma* is thrown back on improvised responses to the all-too-observable realities of everyday life. Though the sermons often cited the threat posed by aspects of the non-Muslim society, these realities can be seen within the mosque itself pressing in as soon as prayer ends or intruding around the rituals of Ramadan when families gather on the women's balcony late into the night. The area outside the balcony starts to resemble a campsite as children are managed and given food and drink, despite the many notices to the contrary. On one occasion, the 'night of power' (*laylat al qadr*), when the recitations continue through the night, several men came upstairs at about 11 o'clock, insisting vociferously on contacting their wives, who were somewhere on the balcony. Eventually, the female stewards managed to convince them that there was no way to get a message to these women in the darkness and in such a crowd. I was at this point sitting outside with a Guyanese woman I knew well. Adolescent girls of East African descent thronged the stairs, swathed in black and looking extremely pious, but, in reality, all were talking, either to each other or on their phones. This jarred with my initially stereotyped response to their attire (Tarlo 2005). My companion made several attempts to persuade them to be quiet so that those who were forced, by the crush, to sit outside could still hear the recitations that everyone had come for, but the girls took little or no notice. The Guyanese woman was extremely cross but also wearily assumed it was to be expected, pious appearances notwithstanding. Such intrusions are always present, in that they are part of ordinary life. The more serious incursions that preoccupied some of the preachers are of a different order, and yet not everyone experiences them as equally threatening to the living of a Muslim life.

While ritual can restore, at least transiently, the individual's internal state and the integrity of the *umma* as a moral object, sermons can only present a congregation with its religious shortcomings and proclaim their consequences in this life and the hereafter. In the four sermons that follow the preachers described the threats to the moral and physical state of Muslims and of the *umma* as the outcome of external events and social interactions with the world that required not only individual action but also collective Muslim vigilance and responsibility. The threat to the object of concern, the *umma*, is seen in these four examples through different lenses: that posed by the presence of a non-Muslim world; by the lack of an appropriate and necessary context for a Muslim life, not only in Western societies but also in Muslim majority countries at the present time; by the internal differences within the *umma* that undermine its coherence and integrity; and by the erosion of religious commitment among adult Muslims, as a result of living in non-Muslim societies. Such threats bespeak a radical disruption in, or loss of, a way of being-in-the-world with others rather than the momentary 'moral breakdown' in an on-going order of which Zigon (2007) writes – a world felt to be lost, not through transient, reparable intersubjective failures, but through migration and large-scale political changes and the loss of an experience of the transcendent as a presence that is held in the rhythms of life in a Muslim majority society.

Most sermons implied, or specified, the need for human action in the world, but some presented the remedy as having a divine source. *In one such sermon, the safety and unity of the umma were seen as part of God's promise of the rewards of practice, among which was the provision of a protective barrier around Muslims against the threats posed by others. The sermon consisted of large sections in Arabic with only brief remarks made in English. The imam said that Ramadan was a month of blessings, a month given by Allah for this purpose. He spoke of the tally of blessings which would be received for reciting the Quran when standing, when sitting, or when performed at a specified time and then related how one of the first Muslims wanted to recite the Quran, not for one month, but for a thousand. As no one would live long enough to accomplish this, Allah told the Prophet that if you recited the Quran on the 'night of power', it would count the same as a thousand months of recitation. The imam finished by saying that the recitations of Ramadan created a barrier around Muslims that shielded them from the unbeliever and from jinn and shaitan.*[15]

The Guyanese and those who identified with them valued engagement with with non-Muslims in and of itself, and some preachers indicated that Muslims should accept the reality of living among others, invoking a narrative of the early Muslim community as having done so. However, in this sermon, it is living within a pluralist society *per se* that poses a threat to Muslims gaining paradise and against which the *umma* needed divine protection. The solution – an impermeable barrier – created not by human action but by the power of God through the efficacy of a certain number of recitations.

Another sermon started with a doubt about the capacity of the individual to be transformed inwardly by reciting the divine words and the need for Muslim practice to take place in an external context that also reflects God's revelation; the preacher first located the impediment to establishing the sovereignty of God within the individual, then identified the problem as lying in the absence of divine sovereignty in the external world. In this, he was critical of Muslim majority societies as much as non-Muslim societies. The imam spoke of how all constitutions in Muslim countries refer to sovereignty but then asked, rhetorically, how many Islamic constitutions reflect the values of Islam? He said, interjecting that he hoped this did not offend brothers from Algeria,[16] that articles in the Algerian constitution state that 'the people are the source of power' and 'we confer our power on our delegates'. He went on dismissively: 'It's all by the people, for the people and so on. These constitutions are all just cut and paste but this is a direction that is contrary to Muslim aqeeda (belief)'. He then said that in Bangladesh, 'the people' were also sovereign, and that this was 'directing the generations away from the deen of Allah'.[17] Although there was a reference in the Pakistan constitution to the sovereignty of Allah, in practice, the situation was worse there than in other countries. He reached a climax saying, 'We are engulfed by this reality'. The imam acknowledged that sometimes people said he was too political but that 'without a certain reality, we can't practice Islam. We recite [the Quran] but what does it mean if the reality we live in is engulfed by a social and political world order that is contrary to Islam? It is not enough to be an individual Muslim'. The preacher insisted that there was a collective need to establish the divine order in the world. It was not clear whether this was because, without such a context, religious practice was difficult to fulfil or because, more radically, it was 'not enough to be an individual Muslim' since the state of the Muslim umma was critical to the integrity of God's order. While the former would imply a human need for a shared way of being in the world and the practical and moral implications of its absence, when the preacher questioned the meaningfulness of reciting the Quran in a material context that was contrary to Islam, he implies a semiotic stance that prioritises the material and the public over the private and immaterial domain of meaning.

Among congregations such as the one in which I did my fieldwork, the very diversity of Islamic traditions and divergent forms of belief and practice among those living as Muslims within the UK may be experienced by some people as disturbing since it disrupts a previous sense of unity. In the sermon I describe below, the preacher tried to create in the congregation a collective sense of being Muslim which did not distinguish between them as to the level of piety or type of practice. His rhetoric sought to manage internal differences and the doubts this might engender about the integrity of Islam by creating a secure space that would enclose all Muslims, shutting out feelings of incomprehension and doubt which were now located in the non–Muslim world beyond.

The preacher alternated between ordinary speech and angry, passionate shouting. He was condemning Muslims who criticise other Muslims for following this or that practise and this or that sheik. In particular, he was castigating those who were critical of Muslim women who wore the hijab and niqab. *'It's not just a piece of cloth, it's bigger than that, it's a symbol. Like the minarets in Switzerland ... there are only four but people in Europe want to say, "We thought you would have changed your values by now and become like us"'. He added, mockingly, 'democracy, freedom, do what you like when you like ... but second- and third-generation Muslims are coming back to their deen [religious way of life], alhamdulillah [thanks be to God]'. He said the Arabic word hijab meant 'drape', as if to minimise it, but then went on to say that some scholars say it should cover the face. He said that personally, he didn't think that, but everyone should defend this view because it's an Islamic opinion. 'No sister wears it except because she believes it is part of the deen. So, we shouldn't attack it; they attack it because Islam is becoming more and more powerful'.*

I had attended this Friday prayer with a Mauritian woman from the Saturday class and her children and I drove her home. Standing outside her door she described the sermon to her brother-in-law, voicing just the mixed feelings and concerns with how the situation might look to non–Muslims in Switzerland and how they might feel that this preacher had represented as evincing a lack of solidarity with fellow Muslims. Though my presence may have heightened her awareness of multiple competing perceptions of the situation, it was an opinion consistent with views she expressed at other times. Jouili (2015: 2) recounts in the opening pages of her book the experience of a woman trying to pray in her workplace and her surprise at meeting with a friendly reception when her expectation and that of the other women in the group had been of a negative stigmatising response. This briefly opened a moment in which the idea of a different link with those from other faiths arose within the group. In the incident I described above, there is a further opening onto a curiosity as to what others might be feeling. Though many of the women in the Saturday class spoke of finding the practice of their religion easier since moving to the UK as young adults, there were some I met who felt it their religious duty to separate and protect themselves from the secular world they were now living in by reaching back into more traditional ways of being, creating a divine protective barrier as was described in the first example.

In their different ways, the sermons addressed an anxiety about loss or impending loss. The continuing integrity and well-being of the *umma* required, above all, that a Muslim form of life was preserved and handed on intact to the next generation. All migrants may be concerned for the safety of traditions carried from a lost homeland, though there is here, in addition, the fear for the future spiritual welfare of children. One sermon I heard brought this matter home in a particular way. It began with the imam thanking Allah for 'guiding us, protecting us and bringing us together again', conveying a strong sense of the congregation being brought back together safely after another week. He went on to talk about the dangers that militated against this sense of continuity and then said that he was going to talk about something that affects all of us – the raising of children.

'*They are in danger in this society. Imagine a one-year-old left in the middle of the jungle by its father. We would say this man is mad. We all know this. We are bombarded with the ideas of this society. In the streets, there are adverts of naked women; in school they are not safe. I heard about a French class where the boys were told to practice chatting up the girls. In the playground they say to each other, [here he adopted a sarcastic tone] "Do you listen to your father? Really?"'* He talked of Muslim children in danger from ideas that are not from '*our deen*' *(our Muslim tradition). 'These people say, "You're young ... don't worry ... be an individual ... it's your business... fun is the most important thing, don't listen to your parents or read the Quran ... live life as you want"'*. He went on to place the responsibility for '*saving ourselves and our families from the nar [the fire of hell]'* with Muslim parents but then acknowledged that '*there are some things we do that don't help. What is it we want? What is our goal for our children? To be practising Muslims who love their deen ... not just as a burden but an understanding of Islam so that even when we are gone, they will continue to practice ... and whose job is this? The parents ... yet sometimes we forget this. When we are choosing a school, we find a private school which costs a lot of money, and we think about the exam results, but we ignore the fact that there are few Muslims there and that it will be difficult for them to pray. We say, "Oh, they can pray later". I'm not saying they shouldn't be lawyers and doctors, but that won't help on Yawm al Qiyamah [the Last Day when all rise from their graves]. We have the wrong objective for them. Islam must come first and other things after'*.

He emphasised that the people who have the job of raising the young are the parents '*and the answer isn't just to send the child to the madrasa. It's not for the imam to build a child. What is he learning at home? We must spend time with our children. We live in a society where people have to earn money, and this can become a 24/7 preoccupation outside the home'*. He said that as adults we are affected by society and come to think that loving a child means a Nintendo Wii and a new bike ... '*but the young child raised in the deen (the faith) ... it's a gift'*. He spoke with increasing urgency of the need for adults as parents '*to push ourselves to practice the more because we live in this jungle. Otherwise, the ideas of this society will take root and we will lose them'*.

The external world, the non-Muslim world, is described as a jungle, but it is presented as a jungle that Muslims are drawn to, not only by the necessity to participate through work and school but by the desire of Muslims for what is available in that world. The dimension of time in relation to the ethical is present in the sustaining of a commitment over time, here in the passing on of a heritage from one generation to another. A process is being described by which adults lose their sense of what is important to them as Muslims and, as a result, they find that what had been a gift to them from their parents is no longer available to pass on to their children. The preacher presents this as a shared and rather public predicament brought about by the nature of British society; in the more intimate atmosphere of the classes, an account of such failures was more likely to be given in terms of the individual's loss of trust in God and to that turning instead to material objects that is implicit in this loss of trust.

The never-ending and unavoidable nature of this struggle was the subject of a minority of sermons that sought to give a more internal account of failure. One attributed the difficulty in remaining steadfast (*istiqrar*) to human nature, a nature that the Prophet described as constantly moving, like water boiling in a pot. The preacher said that the word for human (*insan*) was linked to the word meaning 'to forget'. 'We say we worship one God, but at the back of our minds we know we are in fact relying on other things ... Being steadfast means there is no one but Allah'. He ended the sermon by relating *istiqrar* to a quality carried by the community: 'We stand and pray in the same building side by side but the moment we leave the building we are disunited. Yet *istiqrar* means continuing to be united and steadfast'. This sermon used an idea of our common human nature, rather than the lure of an external amoral jungle, to understand both individual failure and the shared failure to realise and sustain the communal dimension of Islam, the *umma*. It gave an image to this instability of human being, the water boiling in a pot, through which the processes of failure could be recognised and owned and a language in which it could be thought about as an intrinsic aspect of the human.

Dispersing back into the mundane

After the prayers that follow the sermon, there would be announcements which extended, in a different form, the experience of being part of a community, though some of the congregation would have already started to leave. Those who had died in the last week and those who were sick were named, details were given, and prayers sought for them; coming events at the mosque were announced; and people reminded to give towards its upkeep. In this way, the congregation, past, present, and future was evoked but as a vulnerable, only partially united, human community rather than as an ideal object, the *umma*. The needs and uncertainties of the wider world were present not only in announcements of special collections in support of a religious school opening in a neighbouring borough or the vans of medical aid going from the mosque to Palestine but also in collections for the victims of natural disasters, whether Muslim or not. However, not everyone agreed, and, on a Friday, following the raising of money for victims of an earthquake a week earlier, the senior mosque imam announced that some in the congregation had objected to giving money for non-Muslims, making it clear that he himself did not agree with this view. There were also announcements about swine flu to counter the fact that some in the congregation thought this did not concern Muslims and about events to be run at the mosque by the fire service or encouragement to attend a mobile health-screening vehicle located outside.[18] The pull of the mundane was visible even as these announcements are being made – people jostle to pass into the non-ritual spaces in which social activities take place or to leave the building, while at the gates, they come into contact with those who are leafleting for religious lectures, language classes, *hizb ut-tahrir* and on occasion, the Socialist

Workers Party. Though small knots of people pause on the pavements outside to talk, some waiting to be collected in cars, most disappear down the surrounding residential and shopping streets.

The contrast between a religious reality instantiated in ritual and the complex worldliness of what lies beyond leads some to wish to ritualise larger areas of life than those which other Muslims see as limited to the forms of worship practiced by the Prophet. While movements of religious renewal are present within Muslim majority societies, Roy (2007) suggests that the enlargement of the scope of religious obligation, the ritualisation of everyday life, and the emergence of individualised forms of religiosity are also responses to the loss of a concrete community through migration and the encounter with an increasingly pluralist society. A different response to this situation, that one sees among the Guyanese, has been to bring the concerns of everyday into the mosque in the form of semi-ritualised social gatherings and, by beginning and ending such events with prayer, to extend the reach of religious experience. Beyond the prayer hall and the balcony, there are areas where some of the congregation gather, talk, and socialise in a way that also expresses, for them, though not for others, a moral world in a way that blurs the distinction between the ritual and the mundane.

Notes

1 Excluding individual mistakes in the proper form of the ritual.
2 A litany in which different objects of concern are brought before God.
3 Between an exclusive and inclusive religious stance (Lambek 2013: 2).
4 Bilal had been appointed by the Guyanese, who saw him as being in sympathy with their way of thinking and, having been born and brought up in the UK, as particularly suitable to act as the public face of the mosque at youth and community events. He only rarely preached at the mosque as he generally took Friday prayers at a local mental health unit, but his way of speaking and conducting himself gave expression to the religious sensibilities of the Guyanese.
5 This festival celebrates Ibrahim's willingness to sacrifice his son, Ishmael, and the substitution, through divine intervention, of a goat for the child.
6 As this was problematic for those in the UK, many people give to charities which then dispense financial donations to the poor in Muslim countries. However, at least one of my interlocutors expressed concern about how well this system operated in reality.
7 Though the Trustees exercise a degree of oversight, it is unclear how complete or consistent that could be.
8 Among those I came to recognise, there were preachers who were originally from Egypt, North Africa, Nigeria, Bangladesh, and Guyana.
9 Members of the congregation sometimes sought religious opinions from the preachers after prayers and Azzim, who I referred to in Chapter 1 and who also taught adult classes at the mosque that are described in Chapters 7 and 8, seemed to be taping some of his lectures.
10 Some words are said in Arabic if they have a religious meaning that is assumed to be familiar.
11 A similar limitation has been experienced by some Catholics with respect to the use of the vernacular after the Second Vatican Council (BBC World Service – Heart and Soul 25 October 2021).

12 The men's prayer hall could only be seen from the very front of the women's balcony. I rarely occupied a space there as it was more difficult to then remain seated while others prayed.
13 There is the possibility to stay on to complete the cycles of prayer that one has missed.
14 Yet, at the same time, there were little or no explicit references to theological differences and the contradictions and uncertainties this may have created for the congregation.
15 The *jinn* are a parallel creation, made out of fire rather than clay; like humankind, the jinn have free will. *Shaitan* (satan) is a *jinn* who refused to bow before Adam, rather than a fallen angel as in Christian thought.
16 There was no mention of sisters. Some preachers did seem to assume that they are talking only to the men they could see in front of them.
17 *Deen* refers to the religion of Islam and a way of life consistent with it.
18 From time to time, an NHS van could be seen parked inside the mosque grounds offering different services – blood-pressure testing, information on diabetes, and cancer screening.

References

Cenker, M. (2015) 'Ummah in the translocal imaginations of migrant Muslims in Slovakia', *Contemporary Islam* 29(2): 149–169.

Deeb, L. (2009) 'Emulating and/or embodying the ideal: The gendering of temporal frameworks and Islamic roles models in Shi'a Lebanon', *American Ethnologist* 36(2): 242–257.

Eickleman, D. F. (1992) 'Mass higher education and the religious imagination in contemporary Arab societes', *American Ethnologist* 19(4): 643–655.

Ghannam, F. (2011) 'Mobility, liminality and embodiment in urban Egypt', *American Ethnologist* 38(4): 790–800.

Hirschkind, C. (2006) *Ethical Soundscapes.* New York: Columbia University Press.

Jouili, J. (2015) *Pious Practice and Secular Constraints.* Stanford: Stanford University Press.

Lambek, M. (2013) 'What Is "Religion" for Anthropology? And What Has Anthropology Brought to "Religion"?' in Lambek, M. and Boddy, J. (eds) *A Companion to Anthropology of Religion.* Oxford: Wiley Blackwell.

Mahmood, S. (2005) *The Politics of Piety.* Princeton: Princeton University Press.

Rappaport, R. (1999) *Ritual and Religion in the Making of Humanity.* Cambridge: Cambridge University Press.

Rasanayagam, J. (2013) 'Beyond Islam: Tradition and the Intelligibility of Experience', in Marsden, M. and Retsikas, K. (eds) *Articulating Islam: Anthropological Approaches to Muslim Worlds.* London: Springer.

Roy, O. (2004) *Globalised Islam: The Search for a New Ummah.* London: Hurst and Co.

Roy, O. (2007) *Secularism Confronts Islam.* New York: Columbia University Press.

Schielke, S. (2010) 'Being Good in Ramadan: Ambivalence, Fragmentation, and the Moral Self in the Lives of Young Egyptians', in Osella, F. and Soares, B. (eds) *Islam, Politics and Anthropology.* Chichester: Wiley-Blackwell.

Shively, K. (2014) 'Entangled ethics: Piety and agency in Turkey', *Anthropological Theory* 14(4): 462–480.

Tarlo, E. (2005) 'Reconsidering stereotypes: Anthropological reflections on the jilbab controversy', *Anthropology Today* 21(6): 13–17.

Zigon, J. (2007) 'Moral breakdown and the ethical demand', *Anthropological Theory* 7(1): 131–150.

5

BEYOND FRIDAY PRAYER

The life of the community

This chapter looks beyond Friday prayers in the men's prayer hall and on the women's balcony towards the old hall, the kitchen, and the shop – spaces in which different kinds of religious, life cycle, and fundraising events took place interspersed with the unscripted encounters of everyday life. Here the pull towards unity in the sounds and movements of congregational prayer and the verbal exhortations to a united *umma* in the sermons were replaced by gender-mixed gatherings for the sharing of meals and informal religious rituals in which non-Muslim friends and spouses were often included as well as passing conversations in which news was exchanged or private thoughts voiced.[1] Though unscripted and often impromptu, this sociality had a coherence and patterning that reflected the underlying commitments and preoccupations of the Guyanese, preoccupations communicated through the embodied movement and musicality of the background as well as in speech. It was immersion in the flow of everyday life that created for those involved, both Guyanese and those who joined them, the shared ground that rendered lives intelligible to both self and others and created the experiential basis of moral reasoning (Rasanayagam 2013: 102).

The mosque was a focus for the social and family relationships of the Guyanese and expressed a commitment to their view of the world. Mauritians, who share a similar migration history, families of Pakistani and Bangladeshi descent, and individuals from a variety of other countries formed a group between whom there was a more or less shared view of what it meant to be Muslim and how they wanted to use the mosque. This group recreated something of the diversity of Guyana, as the Guyanese described it and as it appears in the records to have been. If their history placed the Guyanese on the outer reaches of the Muslim world, they spoke of it as having offered them, directly and indirectly, experiences from which they derived strength, energy, and direction. Through their communal life, the Guyanese actively generated experiences of belonging in

DOI: 10.4324/9781003080008-5

which being Guyanese and being Muslim were interwoven as a positive moral presence that sustained, and was sustained by, participation with others in the building of the mosque and in weathering the vicissitudes of life within it.

While the piety and religious renewal movement sought to bring daily life within the ritual prescriptions of Islam (Mahmood 2005), the Guyanese brought the relational concerns of ordinary life into the mosque and sometimes into religious rituals. Some of those I got to know did not fulfil the formal obligations of five daily prayers or perform *hajj*, but they did attend the mosque on Fridays, though not necessarily regularly; they joined with others during Ramadan and for festivals and, on occasion, came to the mosque for private prayer. This situation might be variously described as a failure of religious obligations, as the reality of religious practice within the lives of ordinary Muslims, or as the positive fulfilment of a different view of what it was to live a Muslim life. If participation in the core rituals of Islam brought all together, the events described in this chapter made differences visible and exposed those involved to challenge.

These hybrid events between religious practice and ordinary sociability took place in the old building – the *iftah* meal in the kitchen and the old hall during Ramadan, the use the Guyanese and Mauritians made of the shop as a space of their own, and an improvised prayer event that expressed the passage of time among the group who had built the mosque. The Ramadan meal was particularly a matter of living and doing, a way of being together in the material activity of the moment, the familiar feeling states this generated, and the moral values that were carried and communicated in the activities themselves for those who participated. But there were also indications of impending changes.

Breaking the fast together

The mosque has a long tradition of cooking and serving, on Saturday and Sunday evenings, the meal (*iftah*) that breaks the fast in Ramadan. It brings together a large section of the congregation for a ritual of food and prayer. It draws on the resources that the congregation has accumulated over time – the sense of an accumulating history as Ramadan comes around again and the possession of a familiar physical space in which food is offered, accepted, and eaten. It also involves the practical task of food preparation and distribution, and relationships of collaboration and sharing among a smaller group and, in a sense, celebrates the practical and social skills of those who organise it.

The moment at which fasting ends coincides with sunset and the timing of the fourth prayer of the day. After the *iftah* meal, the fifth and last of the five daily prayers takes place, followed by a prayer cycle specific to Ramadan, with Quranic recitations going on into the early hours of the morning.[2] Although it is set within a ritual framework, *iftah* is also an occasion that meets the practical need for food and drink after fasting within the dynamics of a social event. It brings together both a dispersed network of individuals who know each well and those from the wider congregation who choose to break their fast at the mosque rather than at home but do not necessarily participate in the more social aspects of the event. Because of the overlapping ties of family and friendship, some non-Muslim Guyanese and Mauritian friends may also be present at these meals, thus reinforcing its social aspect. In contrast to the exacting timetable and choreography of Muslim prayer that surrounds it, the meal itself is an un-ritualised, even chaotic event to which many come in family groups. Some people come for the meal and then stay on to chat in the hall while waiting to go through for the whole evening of religious ritual and recitation, while others, particularly those with young children, leave after the meal. Still others, such as the more religiously dressed women in *niqab*, do not attend the meal, arriving only for the later prayers, while a number of men attend *iftah* alone, without their families, wearing long white religious dress and lace caps, re-asserting the religious dimension amid the sociability.

Though communal eating forms an element of most religious and social events at the mosque, *iftah* attracts by far the largest and most diverse grouping since it is part of the mainstream rituals of Ramadan, which the congregation attends in large numbers. The provision of the meal has a long history. Before the move to the single room hall-mosque in the early 1980s, food was cooked at home and brought to whichever house was then serving as a prayer space. Now the gathering for *iftah* can attract up to five hundred men, women, and children, requiring more centrally organised catering and a large commitment of time, effort, and money. Sometimes individuals still brought small dishes to the kitchen to add to the mass catering; this seemed incongruous but might have been a hangover from earlier times. Calls for extra donations are made just before and during Ramadan to cover the various additional expenses during this period of intensified religious practice, such as the expense of hiring *hafiz*, men who can recite the Quran from memory and who come from outside the UK, especially for the occasion. It was clear from these announcements that many use the mosque without involving themselves in the practicalities of its maintenance or the organisation of events. This disparity between the outlay of effort made by those individuals who make the *iftah* meal possible and those who come to eat it is sometimes commented on, for example when men come to the hatch and ask for 'take home' parcels for their families. At the same time, those who gather in different combinations to prepare the meal are all Guyanese or Mauritian or have close ties with them; the activity contributes to establishing and maintaining their own conception of the mosque. Unlike congregational prayer, where, by turning up, anyone can take their place in the line of worshippers, confident of what to expect, it would not necessarily be so straightforward to move from being a member of the wider congregation to becoming more involved in the organisation of events such as *iftah*. Yet *iftah* is also an event that the congregation as a whole value and have come to expect. One year it was decided that a meal would be served on Saturday nights only, as the burden on those who produced it was too great, but there were so many complaints that the two weekend meals were reinstated the following year. The hall started to fill up with individuals and families about 45 minutes before the fast ended. Elderly women 'reserved' chairs around the walls for one another and sat together to chat. Young families 'camped' out with bags of possessions and additional supplies. As sunset and *maghrib* prayer approached, large pots of tea were brewed, and trays of fizzy drinks poured in readiness for the moment when the hours of abstinence would end.

The kitchen as a gender-mixed social space

Though the catering arrangements have changed from the days when the meal was prepared and cooked at home, the kitchen has remained a space occupied by the Guyanese and those individuals from other south Asian communities who most closely identify with them. The mosque has a large catering-style kitchen adjoining the old hall with low gas burners near the floor that can accommodate the huge cooking pots, which require two men to lift. Perhaps, for this reason, the actual cooking was always the province of the men, although the women sometimes joked that this gave them a rightful and well-earned break from their usual domestic role. When the food was being cooked on the premises, the event began a couple of hours before with the preparation and cooking of curried meat and vegetables, dahl, rice, and salad; tinned fruit and ice cream were served for pudding. The men attended to the vats of food in a spirit of cheerful camaraderie reminiscent of a barbeque, while the women stood around the large central work surface preparing bowls of salad for the meal and little paper napkin parcels, containing one or two dates and a small fried 'dumpling', which were distributed, together with a drink, at the point when fasting ceased.

While all the marginal spaces of the mosque were gender-mixed, the kitchen and the shop were the spaces most fully given over to the expression of the Guyanese conception of gender relations. During the preparation and serving of the meal, the kitchen was full of informal, sometimes slightly risqué banter with none of the formality of Muslim etiquette. Warm greetings and embraces were exchanged between people, both men and women, young and old, as they arrive to help or just 'look in'. Those adults who were not free to help, because they had children in tow, brought them in to greet relatives and be admired by them before going out into the hall. Older teenagers, and unencumbered young adults, gathered just outside the kitchen and chatted, waiting to perform their task of distributing the food. Thus, the kitchen was at the centre of a noisy, gender-mixed, multi-generational gathering – great-grandparents, grandparents, parents, young adults, teenagers, and children – and, though the ties between them of kin, marriage, and friendship varied, everyone knew everyone else. Members of older generations were addressed by younger people as 'auntie' or 'uncle', and young men and women who had known each other since childhood exchanged affectionate greetings and kisses. The Islamic forms of address, 'brother' and 'sister', and the formality between the genders associated with it, were absent. The older of the two mosque imams, coming over to collect his plate of food, might sit down to eat it with the young women involved in the serving of drinks. When I first went to these meals, a middle-aged Bangladeshi woman had charge of the drinks. During the first year, she was assisted in laying out and piling up tray upon tray of plastic cups filled with cola and lemonade by a teenage girl of Pakistani descent, whose mother regularly helped in the kitchen, and later by two very young Guyanese sisters. Young people who arrived as part of family groups and stayed to help did so as an adjunct to their own social relationships. Later, many would gather in and around the shop, joking with one another, while others spilled out to the area outside to chat. Parents seemed to accept that for the young adult members of their families, Ramadan at the mosque would need to be fitted into ordinary life and that, once the meal was over, some would leave to continue celebrations elsewhere.

A shared history ran through the face-to-face immediacy of the relationships in the kitchen. One elderly woman remarked to me as if caught by surprise at the thought, 'We came here together when we were young in the 1960s, and now we are old'. While this was a statement of fact, it also suggested that the gathering opened a space for reflection on what the years had amounted to and the value to be placed on them. The meals themselves were 'sponsored' by different individuals and families, whether through financial contribution, the involvement of family members in its preparation, or by arranging outside catering. In this way, the accumulation of relational ties was present within the activity itself – communal life as a practical and moral resource. Some Ramadan meals were a regular annual undertaking by certain families; others were provided by families where there had been a death during the preceding year, as part of their understanding of the religious rituals of Islam as well as a public remembrance of the dead person. Whereas for many, this interweaving of the religious and the social enriched the meaning of the occasion, for the Guyanese imam and teacher of the Saturday class, Azzim, this involved both the confounding of a religious ritual and a human event of remembrance and misrepresented the relations between the living and the dead in Islam. He taught that the living can do nothing to assist the dead. However, while the senior mosque imam attended *iftah* alone, in his official capacity, Azzim sometimes came to *iftah* and to funding raising events with his family as a member of the general congregation. So, despite his very different theological views that I will describe in chapter 7, one was left to conclude that Azzim continued to value the Guyanese community and to regard himself as part of it.

Praying in the midst of things

The mixture of the religious and the social in *iftah* was manifested in the use of the old hall first as an eating area and then as an overspill space for prayer while the kitchen remained a more distinctly Guyanese space. However, the concept of 'everyday religion' cuts across the idea of the religious and the social as separable domains, seeing ordinary living as carrying religious values (Orsi 2012). Being Muslim *and* being Guyanese were interwoven in unpredictable ways. Thus, among the Guyanese and others in the kitchen and in the shop, a particular idea of being Muslim was implicitly maintained – an idea in which gender mixing and joking, the wearing of ordinary high-street clothing, and a willingness to see themselves as living alongside non-Muslims were elements of moral significance that kept alive in the present the religious world that the older generation had been brought up in. Islam was sometimes invoked in the kitchen, but lightly, as when a man enquired teasingly of a woman struggling to open a large tin of fruit salad as to whether she had said *bismillah* (in the name of Allah) before attempting this task. However, while there are many short prayers and religious forms of greeting that can be said in the flow of daily life with the intention of bringing God into the midst of things, I rarely heard them used by the Guyanese. The remark over the tinned fruit was offered, accepted, and answered, in the same joking spirit, a little piece of creative theatre; yet those who joke in the kitchen also went into the hall to pray.

Although a relaxed attitude predominated in and around the kitchen during the preparation of the meal, there was a point at which the religious nature of the occasion suddenly reasserted itself. The distribution of the snack parcels took place just before the call to prayer sounded among those gathered in the hall and the area leading to the kitchen. Many seemed not to hear it at first, while others paused to adjust themselves in expectation of what was to come. People switched from a lively, disorganised engagement with those around them to an individual attention to prayer. A young Guyanese woman who had been sitting chatting with others near the kitchen now sat with her hands open in a supplicatory gesture, and, despite the distracting movements of the two-year-old on her lap, she seemed able to focus herself on this moment of prayer. On one occasion, the Bengali imam announced over the loudspeaker that the meal had been donated by a family who wanted to remain anonymous but that they had asked for prayers for themselves and for some sick members of the family. There was then a short recitation in Arabic before the imam continued by asking in English, in a familiar formula, that those present should 'open their hands and their hearts'. While this is an image of the body as containing an emotional space in which to receive divine blessings, other perspectives were also invoked. The imam asked God's blessings for success in this world and the next then referred to 'the delicacy that people are waiting to eat in Allah's time' and ended by asking blessings for 'all the people of the world'. This prayer suggested that the everyday world in which people hoped for success and the sensual pleasure of eating could and should be brought together with all humankind as in need of blessing. This inclusion of non-Muslims, by the Bangladeshi mosque imam, not only acknowledged the presence of some non-Muslim Guyanese within the gathering but also made explicit and public the positive moral value that religious diversity holds for Guyanese Muslims.

After the 'snack' had been eaten, lines were formed in the hall for prayer, though with none of the aesthetic qualities of the later prayer on the women's balcony where, in winter, the chandelier is the only form of lighting. Rather, there was a haphazard, un-stewarded move towards forming lines that were far from straight under the full glare of the lights in the hall. Children milled about and such was the informality at this point, spilling over from the social activity that preceded it, that sometimes people I knew well from the kitchen tried to pull me into the line to pray with them, a thing they never thought to do upstairs. Doubtless, this arose from the sense of good feeling and communality in the kitchen that I could share in while helping to prepare, serve and finally eat the meal. Unlike on the balcony, in the hall, I could remain standing on the margins of the prayer lines where there were other women who were not praying, presumably because they were menstruating or were non-Muslim family members or friends. This prayer was short, and few people stayed on to pray in private, as they did on the balcony. The hall was immediately needed as an eating area, with individuals and families seated on the floor along the lines of cloth laid to protect the carpets – the men with some of the boys in one area of the hall and the women with the younger children in the other – separated, but visible to one another, during the first Ramadan of my fieldwork, a situation that was to change the following year.

Large, round trays piled with paper plates of food would start to leave the kitchen, returning empty in an endless chain until the word came back that no more food was needed. Although both men and women were standing around together to receive the trays, the serving was undertaken separately by gender. A hectic level of activity took place and then came to a sudden halt as the meal ended. Plates and leftovers were gathered into black plastic bags by helpers, the cloths were folded up, and the carpet hoovered by a man who often made a joke about hoovering up the women. Children and toddlers ran about. The congregation dispersed, leaving little knots of people talking together. There was a hiatus after all the activity, particularly if, because of liturgical timing, there was a lengthy gap before people needed to go into the new section of the mosque for the next prayer.[3]

Whatever the success of the event at a practical level, there were tensions between the different meanings that the event itself held in play – the meal as an element in the rituals of Ramadan, its place within the life of the community, and the fact that it was an event which the Guyanese could shape to meet their own sense of how things should be in the face of those who took a different view. In the past, some Guyanese had resisted the transition from using private homes for collective prayer to the building of a mosque, open to all, precisely because they feared the loss of their way of doing things and the values this carried for them. Others had felt that it was nonetheless an important element in those values that they should open their mosque to different Muslim groups. If the *iftah* meal was an act in which the community consumed together what the community had provided, it was complicated by the reality of different views within the congregation about the way the meal should be conducted that marked out different conceptions of about how to be Muslim.

Apart from Friday prayer, the *iftah* meal attracted the largest gatherings in the mosque; yet unlike prayer it was, to a large extent, shaped by human concerns.

The timing and reason for the meal lie within a framework of Muslim worship, but much else about the occasion was shaped by the styles of gender and generational relationships among the Guyanese. The social atmosphere established in the kitchen flowed throughout the whole event. Relations between men and women were characterised by the sort of joshing that expressed both sexual vitality and the tensions that were created by gendered demarcations elsewhere in the mosque and the disputes that arose around them. There was sometimes a sort of game about those tension that all joined in. When those in the kitchen heard about a remark made by a non-Guyanese male member of the congregation which seemed to challenge the religious appropriateness of a woman's dress, another woman replied with an elaborate joke, 'Oh there is a *he* who is upset by what he sees ... if that *he* doesn't like it then that *he* doesn't have to look ... does he?' This is not to say that such a reply would have been given had the remark been made face to face, or that what was at stake with respect to gender within the mosque was not taken seriously, but that this was one way in which the tensions caused by the differences within the congregation and within Islam itself were managed. Through an ironic performance of 'being Guyanese', a familiar world was summoned up within which opinions about gender relations that were now contested could be voiced and their value reasserted.

The provision of a communal meal brought to life, in the present, the social ties and moral commitments that have endured over time within this post-migration community. The preparation and serving of the meal made visible and real the moral world of the Guyanese that they felt connected them to those who had gone before.[4] Yet the nature of this moral world was not uniform or fixed nor is its enduring presence as a shared resource inevitable. The young people who helped to serve in the kitchen but gathered later in the shop were in a different relationship to this inheritance than were their parents and grandparents.

The shop as a place to speak one's mind

The shop, like the kitchen, was in the old building near the entrance to the hall. It was open on weekday evenings when children's classes were held, Fridays during the period when the two congregational prayers took place, and during festivals and other events. The small space was crammed with religious literature – books, pamphlets, and CDs – devotional objects of various kinds, and articles of religious clothing, alongside sweets and soft drinks. A rota of Guyanese women helped in the shop when it was open. Men served there too but less frequently. Although it was cut off from the main prayer area, there was a closed-circuit monitor and sound system on the wall above the counter showing views of different parts of the mosque. On Fridays, one could hear the sermon through it, but no one in the shop paid any attention, although the women serving often prayed there rather than going to the trouble of closing the shop and going to the balcony.

The shop served the congregation as whole but in the absence of either the harmonies of ritualised prayer or the mediation of familiar practical and social activities, such as the *iftah* meal. It was a space for lively informal exchanges but where turbulent feelings, doubts, and anxieties emerged with respect to religious matters in a way that, uncontained by familiar patterns of activity, could seem stark and awkward. On one occasion, a female Trustee of the mosque came in and examined the sweets on display saying that someone had complained to her that they were not all *halal*. She was sure they were but felt the need to check. She described this as but one of a series of similar challenges. One year, the pictures in the calendar had been challenged as, inadvertently, they had shown an image of a cross formed by the glazing bars of a window. Finding a substitute picture was not so easy because, as she pointed out crossly, all sorts of things could be construed as a cross if you wanted to see it that way. The calendar was a recurrent point of discord. This year they had prepared a series of old views of the mosque because they wanted to mobilise financial support for a large new extension that would start as my fieldwork ended, but human figures would have to be removed from the photographs before they could be used as someone would object. There was also an on-going, unresolved dispute about 'contested festivals' such as the birthday of the Prophet and whether they should be listed in the calendar. She complained that they would put them in one year and the next year they would take them out: 'You can't please everyone'. She felt squeezed between a feeling that one should try to accommodate others and avoid unnecessary provocation while at the same time wanting to protect those elements that were felt as essential by the Guyanese, but this was not an easy path to follow.

A subtler problem attached to occasions when individuals needed to speak in their own words of religious things without the protection of ritual forms. Arriving at a time when I thought the preparations for an event would be starting, I found no sign of activity in the 'old hall' although I could see some men sitting or praying individually in the male prayer hall. In the shop, one of the Guyanese women was helping an African woman dressed in black to choose a Quran. The woman, whom I took to be a convert, or at any event not from an Arabic-speaking country, kept saying she wanted a green Quran. The woman helping duly searched and produced a green Quran with a translation by Yusuf Ali, which was rejected. The woman then said that it should start '*alif lam meem*'[5] and was told 'they all started like that'. Eventually, it seemed that the woman wanted a transliterated Quran (in which the Arabic is rendered phonetically in Latin script) and another search was undertaken among the stock kept upstairs in what is referred to as 'the library'.[6] This conversation had taken place in an atmosphere of some awkwardness. I was conscious that, though surrounded by religious objects that implied a shared world, one might still lack a shared language in which to discuss them. Sometimes there was an actual language barrier, but more usually, it was the absence of a shared mode of communicating about religious things that exposed differences or a lack of knowledge or created the fear of such exposure. This dilemma seemed to be part of the motivation for those who joined the classes. Seeking knowledge together as a group was also a search for a common language within which to safely voice and share religious experience without fear of rebuff or embarrassment.[7]

The shop is open to all, but for the Guyanese and the Mauritians, it functioned as a space for informal conversation among older men and women and, during social events at the mosque, it was also a retreat for the young who, by taking over the job of serving customers, took over the space as a gathering place for their friends. The bantering, theatrical style of speaking that filled the kitchen also flourished in the shop so that the conversation had the quality of a display of being 'at home', though often with an ironic twist. At one fundraising dinner, the meal was provided by a member of the congregation who owned a restaurant. When I asked the young Guyanese woman I was sitting with about the food, she looked down at her plate and said with a flourish, 'Looks Guyanese', then, bending closer, went on, 'Mmm, smells Guyanese'. She paused and then added dramatically, 'But wait! What's this? I think I see a carrot!'[8] – indicating that it was not, after all, *absolutely* Guyanese. Despite the confident mode of comportment displayed by the Guyanese, there was often an edge to their performance. It created a lingering sense that 'home' might not, after all, be something one was so securely and physically in occupation of since it was now an imagined place. The play on a suspicion that ingredients had been added to the food that were not Guyanese was a familiar way of managing, within the idiom of a joke, tensions around change, new situations, and particularly contact with other Muslim traditions.

Much of the conversation in the shop among the older generation revolved around news of fellow Guyanese and Mauritians – particularly about who was sick and who had visited them – not only in London but 'back home'. Migration has created a dispersed network of relationships between the Guyana that the older generation had grown up in, and current ties of marriage and friendship not only in the UK, but in the countries, such as the USA and Canada, to which other family members had emigrated. A conversation in the shop between a group of Guyanese about gardening in London and what could and could not be grown here was interrupted by a joyful ironic cry of, 'Oh look, foreigners!' as they spotted the arrival of friends from Canada who were calling in for Friday prayer and to make contact. There were also recurrent and poignant references to loss, and to the complex situations of belonging and not-belonging, created by migration. The jokes, like that about foreigners, seemed to be a riff on the years of their lives spent in the UK and what it all amounted to. Were they now British or were they still seen as foreigners by the majority population? Were they at home here or would they one day go back to Guyana, where some were sending money for the upkeep of what had been their childhood homes? Or was it, as Mr Rahman put it, that, though they would not return there when they said 'home' they still meant Guyana? Though often disguised as a joke, feelings of vulnerability were sometimes expressed more directly. One woman took advantage of a time when we were alone together in the shop to tell me that she and her husband had bought a plot in a local cemetery. If they died abroad, they wanted their bodies to be returned to the UK for burial. She said that having made her life here in London, where her children had been born, the idea of being buried in a strange place made her feel anxious such that this anxiety overwhelmed any concern about what other Muslims might think of such considerations. On an earlier occasion, during a long coach journey – a mosque day trip to the coast – she had told me the story of her arrival in London, her shock at the bleakness of the country and the single room her husband had found for them in which to start their married life. A number of the women saw me as a person to whom they could safely talk without fear that I would criticise them or gossip to others. In this way, from time to time, I came to hear passing references to family complications and the existence of marginal activities, such as the use of an amulet to ward off the magic that was said to have been deployed against the speaker by someone else. Though it would have been interesting, it was difficult to follow up on these hints without appearing to be focusing on practices about which people felt particularly anxious and defensive.

Aside from these more personal confidences, the shop was a location in which critical opinions, theological differences, and doubts occasionally surfaced. Though anyone could enter, it was sufficiently separate to feel one was in a different kind of space, and, realistically, one could check who was likely to hear and so pick one's moment to speak. At a time when the shop was displaying posters for *hajj* groups that various companies were organising, a conversation started about the cost of making the pilgrimage. The north African caretaker said he felt the trips were too expensive and poor value for the money spent. Several men described the poor accommodation and the difficulties they encountered; it was clear that they felt some Muslims were making a lot of money out of other Muslims. No one present seemed inclined to disagree. Though conversation is certainly more guarded when unknown customers are present, even among those who know each other well, there is always the possibility of discovering that, in making something explicit, you have opened yourself up to an unexpected response. When two women were on their own, sorting out stock just after Christmas, there was a discussion between them about Christmas dinner, which it seemed they both had cooked, but when one made a reference to decorating her house, the other said rather sharply that she didn't do that. Her companion did not seem put out by this, but it drew my attention to the differences that may underlie what appears to be a comfortable consensus. It may be that more recent experiences of globalised Islam have prompted the emergence of a new concern with correct practise and the need to point out when someone else has crossed a line between what is and is not religiously acceptable.

The most serious theological disagreement I heard voiced in the shop followed some jokes about heaven and hell among a small group of men standing around at the entrance, some were Guyanese and there were others whom I did not recognise. Someone told a joke about a man who wanted to go to hell so that he could light his cigarettes, and another added that he wanted to just get into heaven and no more so that he could remain at the entrance and smoke. Normally this would have been an entirely light-hearted conversation, but on this occasion, someone broke with convention. A man I did not recognise suddenly said, in a serious voice, 'We are not like the Christians who believe that when you die you go immediately to heaven or hell. Muslims believe in *barzakh*'. *Barzakh* is an intermediate period after death but this speaker implied that you were confined to this marginal state if you did not know the answers to the questions asked by the Angel of Death. From a corner of the shop, a Guyanese woman said quietly, 'We don't know if that's true', to which the man replied, tartly: 'We don't know if Allah exists'. Nobody seemed to want to take this further and the group disbanded. The general disinclination to make religious thinking explicit beyond a certain point preserved the appearance of an unchanging Guyanese consensus and protected people from the disruptive consequences of some individuals coming to adopt new positions or continuing to practice in ways that others now reinterpreted in the light of contact with other Muslim traditions. On this occasion, for reasons that were unclear to me, the woman challenged the speaker but in a way that was neither from within an Islamic scriptural framework nor a Guyanese position of tolerant common sense. She may have known the speaker, but such radical questioning of what we can ever know was unusual.

The Guyanese were well aware that they thought and acted in ways that were different from other Muslims and that some people regarded these differences negatively, in the light of the warning of the Prophet that there would be seventy-three ways of being Muslim, of which all but one was in error. I never heard this concern with error voiced by the Guyanese, but it made some who attended the Saturday classes anxious about their practice and prompted them to wonder how they could ever be sure where they stood. Others, however, felt quite certain. A young French woman, who I thought was a convert, stopped me after Friday prayers to say that she understood I was studying Islam and that it was most important that I studied only the one correct form of Islam; she then handed me a leaflet. Early in my fieldwork, I met an Islamically but stylishly dressed Ugandan woman at a study group near the mosque. I was surprised to learn that she had only just started to wear the *hijab* and that, until recently, she had been working in advertising and film. I had occasional contact with her during my fieldwork. After her marriage and an extended visit to Yemen, she became increasingly firm in her religious views and adopted the *niqab*. When I saw her for the last time, she told me, 'You have to remember, Judy, there is only one right way' and it was clear that she felt I was not on that path and, therefore, at risk of hell.

For the Guyanese, it is not only that, in the eyes of others, they are not following that one right way, but that they themselves did not see difference as contrary to Islam. This was indicative of something 'more positive and productive than a passive tolerance of difference' (Rasanayagam 2013: 104). Valuing pluralism was something rooted in their perception of Guyana that they felt had been a resource in managing their lives in London. Since building a mosque entailed opening the doors to all who chose to worship there, the mosque was itself an expression of their ethical position on this matter and their hope in the future, but it also made them vulnerable.[9]

Sustaining a community through time

The disagreements about the nature of ritual in Islam recurred in many different forms. To some people, it seems entirely natural that God should be invoked in times of need, not only privately in the repetition of a verse of the Quran deemed appropriate to the situation but also in public. Events such as the one I describe below would cross the line on which Azzim, the freelance religious teacher insisted, whereby ritual is limited to the forms of practice of the Prophet: everything else was deemed an 'innovation' that interfered with the form of worship revealed by God.[10] This was at the heart of the dispute between the Guyanese and two earlier, Saudi-educated, Guyanese imams. The two Bangladeshi imams at the mosque during my fieldwork were willing to accommodate the sensibilities of the Guyanese in these matters, participating and leading rituals for mixed gatherings in the hall, which included prayer that brought the concerns of everyday life into contact with the comfort of divine blessings.

> On one such occasion I arrived one Sunday afternoon for a meeting of the 'Sisters' Circle' and was surprised to see a very large gathering in the hall. Someone explained that it was a meeting to offer prayers for a Guyanese 'auntie' who was very sick. A lot of older men were sitting along one wall, with older women in a group at right angles to them. Though this constituted a degree of segregation, there were also a lot of younger women in bright clothes, short-sleeved dresses and without head covering and men sitting among them. I learned that they were non-Muslim members of the family of the sick woman. One of the mosque's Trustees, Harry,[11] sat down next to the imam who then started to speak, saying that the sister had asked for this gathering. When he had visited her, she had asked about the times when prayer is always accepted by Allah and he began to enumerate the different circumstances when this was so, one of them being prayers for the sick.
>
> Then an elderly woman arrived accompanied by two younger women, perhaps her daughter and granddaughter. They carried a stool and a rug and settled her between the imam and Harry, who held her hand quietly throughout the rest of the meeting. The imam acknowledged the woman, saying that we were going to pray for her recovery. Her daughter thanked everyone. I noticed Mr Rahman hovering in the background looking much older or rather looking his age, in a way he usually does not. The imam said, 'When a group sits together and remembers Allah, the angels will circle around and praise those people to the angels in the sky. If we open our

hearts and pray sincerely, Allah is remembering us as we remember him'. On several occasions during the meeting, the woman groaned as she sat with her head bowed holding Harry's hand. Then the imam asked if others wanted to speak and one older man began, 'Every good thing we do is an act of worship … like being here today to encourage our dear sister … it is *ibada* [worship]'. Another man with a good voice chanted some verses that I mistakenly took at the time to be from the Quran. Then Mr Rahman said a few words in his usual jocular style but with a note of sadness. He said he had played cricket with this sister in the old days to raise money for the mosque. 'You don't believe me, but how fast she could run.' He then couldn't resist saying something about the new calendars that were on sale. The imam was about to start the prayer, when Mr Rahman said that some who were present were not Muslim, but they should just pray in their own language because 'prayer doesn't have a language'. The imam said people should 'open their hands and open their hearts', the gesture for supplicatory prayer, and began, first briefly in Arabic, then in English, 'Allah accept what we are offering here today.' As his prayer finished, the call to the (regular) afternoon prayer sounded and the crowd moved into the mosque, reassembling afterwards for a communal meal provided by the sick woman's family.

Shuttleworth (2010)

This occasion had drawn in a very mixed group of people both Muslim Guyanese, Mauritians, and others. Some people who had married into Hindu and Christian families were accompanied by their relatives. There were also some British non-Muslim widows of Guyanese and Mauritian men. Some were friends – I was introduced to a Hindu Guyanese woman who was the friend and former work colleague of a Mauritian member of the congregation: 'We were nurses together'. This diversity was reflected in the women's dress, creating a complicated hybrid event but as the mosque secretary once commented to me, 'Not all Guyanese are Muslim and not all Muslim Guyanese are practising'. In its inclusive reach, the event was part of the social life of the community, but in its religious frame and intention – to seek God's blessings – it was an expression of trust in a transcendent reality. From the perspective of the Guyanese, it was a natural expression, within a Muslim tradition, of the moral concerns that attach to living one's life alongside others. The group had come together for mutual support as much as for the support of the woman who was its focus – an improvised event that calls on collective memories to create a feeling of solidarity in the face of time passing and the doubts about the future that this may engender. Those who may not have thought they were going to spend the rest of their lives in the UK find that they are. Here the need for mutual support found expression in a focus on Allah and the angels, the seeking of God's blessing by the imam, and the hope that was invoked by his assertion of the certainty and dependability of God's response. At the same time, it remained a very *ad hoc*, even a mundanely human occasion, in which those present were also invited to draw emotional

strength from the practical communal achievements of the last 50 years, manifested above all in the meeting itself. The social and religious were interwoven
in the event in a way that reflected the moral world of the gathering. The prayers
were improvised and in English in a manner that explicitly sought to encompass
the diverse group that was present. I realised later that the man who sang was
reviving a practice, *qasida*,[12] that had since been given up by the Guyanese under
pressure from other Muslim groups. Mr Rahman's sentiment – that prayer has no
language – comes out of his own religious feelings, as does the view expressed by
another man that all such gatherings are a form of worship.[13]

Everyday religion and ordinary lives as the ground of moral experience

Schielke and Debevec (2012: 3) suggest that not only ritual but the ordinary
practices of daily life naturally carry religious meanings through ways of doing
and feeling that reflect the imaginative patterns of a tradition. Orsi (2012: 156)
argues that religious meanings are felt as real by virtue of the material reality of
the everyday practices through which they are expressed and through the way
that the affective states they manifest are rooted in the reality of human relatedness to those who are present, absent, or dead. Thus, rather than contrasting the
events and encounters described in this chapter with moral qualities of religious
practice, 'sociality is itself a moral source' in its own right (Rasanayagam 2011:
14). Social life embodies the relationships and values of a shared moral world,
and its materiality may be said to add to the sense of the reality of that world for
those who participate.

From this perspective, the *iftah* meal is not only a material process that enacts
familiar external forms of sociality but a work of imagination that sustains an
idea of being a Guyanese Muslim, creating a moral significance that such events
did not have for others who brought different ways of seeing and feeling with
them to the mosque. Eisenlohr (2006) describes the way a relationship with the
ancestors is kept alive among Hindu Indo-Mauritians in a post migration present through the privileging of classical Hindi and the recreation of the sacred
geography of pilgrimage. In this vein, the way the Guyanese occupied the non-
ritual spaces of the mosque not only re-created the complexity of Indo-Guyanese
culture but sustained a creative dynamic imaginative relationship to it and to
their forebears who, like the 'ancestors' of Eisenlohr's informants, were both a
source of vitality and values – an acknowledged inheritance that was an object of
continuing responsibility and concern. Werbner calls attention to the generative
nature of imagination in the way a diaspora community carries the rituals practiced in a former abode into a new context such that rituals acquire the power 'to
reconcile past and present' (2018: 319). It is this capacity within the imaginative
life of an individual and a community to reconcile and deepen commitments
across time, space, and mortality that flows through ordinary sociality creating a
source of moral experience.

While the event for the sick woman was a more self-conscious celebration of shared memories and of commitments fulfilled, it was also the revitalisation of a shared religious and social imaginary through the accomplishment of a successful gathering, through its framing as a prayerful request for blessings and a collective recognition of vulnerability and loss, of time passing and of change that was coming. In the ordinary flow of things, individually or perhaps without the confidence invoked by the imam's view that such prayers are always answered, this reality was sometimes too difficult to face. I was aware that, during my fieldwork, a situation was developing in the kitchen in which the continued presence of some elderly women, who had been central to the establishment of the mosque, was making it difficult for younger women to ever be more than just helpers. For this change to happen, a new phase had to be imagined, and a space had to be made for it. By the time I left, there were indications that this was underway.

Notes

1 There were also outward facing events that included local agencies and political figures and members of the wider community.
2 The length of time available for the *iftah* meal itself and for socialising varies with the time of year – in summer, the lateness of sunset reduces the time interval between the two prayers to the point where there is barely time to serve and clear up. On such occasions, announcements were made to encourage the congregation to speed up their meal and one year it was decided that no pudding would be served on this account.
3 It was only returning on occasions after my fieldwork had ended that I realised how different the time available between the breaking of the fast and the next prayer was at different times of the year.
4 MacIntyre (1981) suggests that ethical value lies in the capacity to actively collaborate *with* others in the form of practice that has been inherited *from* others.
5 Three letters of the Arabic alphabet with which the Quran starts.
6 The room is named after the man who befriended Mr Rahman in the 1970s and who helped him to gain a religious education.
7 Liberatore (2013), writing of newly practising Muslim Somali women in London, describes one young woman beset by feelings of ambivalence becoming able to manage better once these experiences were named for her as a state known to others as *fluctuating iman* (faith).
8 When I came to write up my notes, I realised I was uncertain as to whether it was a carrot or some other vegetable that was named as the intruder!
9 The mosque is Sunni and as such, though there are a range of different views about the legitimacy of certain rituals and practices that are familiar to the Guyanese, it is open to all. During my fieldwork, there was a competition run by a UK Muslim television channel to find the 'model mosque'. What this 'model' entailed was never made clear, but it seemed likely that it was linked, though in a complicated way, to an idea of 'British Islam' that was prominent in the media at the time (and scorned by some of the visiting preachers). The Guyanese entered the mosque for the competition and though they didn't win they did well while at no time hiding the differences which they knew existed between themselves and other Muslim communities – the most obvious difference being that their entry was fronted by the female secretary of the mosque.
10 Some practices, including rituals that are held at a specific time after death or annually on a specific day, such as the birthday of the Prophet, or the extra fast on the tenth day of the month of *Muharram*, would for some fulfil the criteria for a religious innovation.

11 Some older Guyanese had both Muslim and European names. This was linked to the tradition of having 'calling names' that were used in school in Guyana although how they were selected could be quite individual. One elderly man explained that he had acquired his calling name during playground war games in which his job was to raise the American flag on Iwo Jima. However, the circumstances that gave rise to calling names have ceased to exist and most of the younger members of the community have Muslim names.

12 A form of Arabic and Urdu poetry.

13 Azzim would certainly disagree with the first of these statements. As to the latter, for him, it would depend on whether the speaker meant that worship resided in the ritual aspect of the event in which case it would be a forbidden innovation.

References

Eisenlohr, P. (2006) *Little India: Diaspora, Time and Ethnolinguistic Belonging in Hindu Mauritius*. London: University of California Press.

Liberatore, G. (2013) 'Doubt as a Double-Edged Sword: Unanswerable Questions and Practical Solutions among Newly Practicing Somali Muslims in London', in Pelkmans, M. (ed) *Ethnographies of Doubt*. London: Tauris and Company.

MacIntyre, A. (1981) *After Virtue*. London: Duckworth.

Mahmood, S. (2005) *The Politics of Piety*. Princeton: Princeton University Press.

Orsi, R. A. (2012) 'Afterward: Everyday Religion and the Contemporary World: The Unmodern or What Was Supposed to Have Disappeared but Did Not', in Osella, F. and Soares, B. (eds) *Islam, Politics and Anthropology*. Chichester: Wiley-Blackwell.

Rasanayagam, J. (2011) *Islam in Post-Soviet Uzbekistan: The morality of experience*. Cambridge: Cambridge University Press.

Rasanayagam, J. (2013) 'Beyond Islam: Tradition and the Intelligibility of Experience', in Marsden, M. and Retsikas, K. (eds) *Articulating Islam: Anthropological Approaches to Muslim Worlds*. London: Springer.

Schielke, S. and Debevec, L. (2012) 'Introduction', in Schielke, S. and Debevec, L. (eds) *Ordinary Lives and Grand Schemas: an Anthropology of Everyday Religion*. Oxford: Berghahn Books.

Shuttleworth, J. (2010) 'Faith and culture: Community life and the creation of a shared psychic reality', *Infant Observation* 13(1): 45–58.

Werbner, P. (2018) 'Ritual, Religion and Aesthetics in the Pakistani and South Asian Diaspora', in Chatterji, J. and Washbrook, D. (eds) *Routledge Handbook of the South Asian Diaspora*. London: Routledge.

6

REFLECTIVE CAPACITY AND THE CHALLENGES OF DIVERSITY

The gender, ethnic, and religiously mixed gatherings that took place at the mosque expressed the moral world of the Guyanese. This was shared with those who joined them on these occasions and perhaps by some who, nonetheless, chose only to attend the mosque for prayer; but it was not shared by all. Those who had joined the congregation through later migrations brought with them traditions and expectations founded in societies that were more ethnically and religiously homogeneous, while a few, who were visible among the women by their dress, had adopted new stricter forms of Muslim practice. Though religious diversity and the different ways in which individuals managed this reality were a constant presence, much of the time, the implications of these differences within the congregation were not the object of explicit comment. The Guyanese themselves rarely spoke about religion as something separate from their participation in Friday prayers, their attendance at other mosque events that began and ended with prayer, or the practical tasks involved in running the mosque with the day-to day-management of uncertainty and challenge this entailed. For them, this *de facto* accommodation of difference reflected both the diversity of Guyana and the pragmatic stance they associated with it. To some, such as those I met in the Saturday classes, this diversity offered a greater awareness of their own and other's point of view as something to be thought about. But this was not the only possible outcome. Some individuals within the congregation sought, from time to time, to challenge aspects of how the mosque was being run. While these challenges were no longer a major threat, they took place against the background of a time of more serious challenges that had never entirely disappeared.

This chapter looks at the responses of the Guyanese to these contestations, the way 'Guyana' and the values attached to it surfaced in this context, and the reflective capacities associated with it. Opportunities for a diverse 'cosmopolitan' experience have been linked to the growth of the capacity for self-reflection

DOI: 10.4324/9781003080008-6

(Nussbaum 1997). However, seeing one's own position in relation to other per-spectives is not a matter of the diversity of external experiences *per se* but what is made of them – the relationships that can be imagined as existing between those who are different and who hold different views (Laidlaw 2002; Parkin 2007; Marsden 2008). Kresse (2013) describes the experience of a Muslim com-munity on the Kenyan coast that he calls a 'double periphery' – a group on the margins of both the Muslim *umma* and the Kenyan state. Yet this position was experienced as 'creating mutual exposure to the way others live – Muslims [and] non-Muslims'. Through 'having the wider world in mind' they could develop 'open-minded and cosmopolitan attitudes and behaviour' (ibid: 96). This, as Kresse points out, is not something inherent in Islam but rather a capacity that 'grows out of the conditions of experience that shape people's lives individually and socially' (ibid: 97).

Here, encounters with difference are described from the perspective of the Guyanese and how they understood and managed them. A quite different account of the challenges of diversity and reflective capacity would have emerged had my focus been on other sections of the congregation. As Jouili points out, commitment to a religious tradition can have the potential to complicate the suggested link between 'cosmopolitan' experience and the capacity for self-reflection (Jouili 2015: 194). As she puts it, standing outside one's own discursive tradition and adopting the perspectives of others including that of a pluralist, secular, non-Muslim world was problematic for those with a 'strong attachment' to a strict interpretation of their religious obligations, though there would also be other Muslim perspectives that the women in her study would have found it difficult to think about.

The creation of a new post-migration home

Migration and resettlement in a new context create obvious and continu-ing external material challenges. Yet diaspora experience and the emergence of post-migration communities are, in important respects, generated through imaginative processes (Jayawardena 1980; Roy 2004; Werbner 2002; Eisenlohr 2006, 2013; 2015; Mohapatra 2006). As Eisenlohr puts it, 'I treat diaspora not as a simple consequence of migration from A to B, but as a form of identification in which some continued relationship or allegiance to a necessarily imagined, and sometimes even invented, homeland is made relevant for such processes of identi-fication … diasporas are not created by the mere fact of displacement' (Eisenlohr 2006: 8). While Jayawardena (1980), who undertook research in Guyana in the 1950s, argues that when a home is lost in external physical reality, as India was lost to the Guyanese, its values are transferred to the domain of imagination.[1] Jayawardena's argument draws a distinction between values carried within imag-ination and those carried in familiar material forms. While both are dimensions of everyday life, he presents the losses of migration as creating, like 'cosmopoli-tan' experience, the possibility of new forms of awareness and the emergence of new meanings. This potential for transformation and development within the imagination has been described by later anthropologists of diaspora – the paradox of a 'changing same' (Shukla 2001), of human beings 'who cannot but produce change even when they mean to produce stability' (Baumann 1999: 138) and the power that accrues within the imagination to '*reconcile* the past and the present' (Werbner 2018; *my italics*). While reconciliation can refer to the equating one thing with another, here Werbner implies a creative process by which emotional relationships, that might otherwise be felt as in conflict, are integrated within a shared imaginary.

Among the Guyanese, this imaginal dimension was expressed as a conscious identification with earlier generations who lived on in the moral life of their community.[2] They sometimes spoke of their history as contributing to their sense of how they have lived their lives in London and as underlying the difference they felt to exist between themselves and other Muslim groups at the mosque and within the UK. But this awareness is built, at least in part, on registers of experience beyond conscious verbal thought – an embodied connectedness with the past that generates the relational resources with which to manage new and uncertain circumstances in the present. Keane writes, 'we come to be who we are within, and by virtue of, relationships with others … their ways of inhabiting our imaginations and our emotions' (Keane 2010: 66). Yet this is not necessarily restricted to actual others once known in external reality but includes the qualities carried by those relationships that come into being within our imaginations through the internal elaboration of experience. This is imagination not as fancy and fantasy, nor as a copy of the external world, but as the human capacity to create meaning through what Marchand (2010) calls 'the indissoluble relation between minds, bodies and environment'. Through listening to sermons, young men in Cairo sought to develop this internal imaginative life as a distinctively Muslim ethical sensibility within themselves, but it is a capacity the potential for which already exists in the mind that can be fostered and developed or can be allowed to erode and deteriorate – a possibility that preoccupied some of the preachers at the mosque. When Mattingly refers to 'moral work' (2012: 167), it carries the implication of something serious that is potentially at risk within these imaginative processes – something that involves contending with a gradient of painful uncertainty and anxiety. These stakes and these risks become visible in the uncertainties and challenges of new situations, in the mosque as elsewhere in social life.

Though the adult Guyanese I got to know may have attended religious classes as children and learned to recite some passages of the Quran by heart, this was not the primary source of their sense of what they felt it was to be Muslim. For the older generation, it was the form of life in which they grew up in Guyana in which Islam and other faith traditions were elements within a pluralistic society and invested with socially integrative qualities akin to those the Mauritians refer to as 'authentic religion' Eisenlohr (2011). This is not to say that in external reality, Guyana was unproblematic or unchanging.[3] Jayawardena (1980) suggests the importance of imaginative processes by which the past shapes what follows through a comparison of the diverging transformational paths of two Indian populations from a similar geographical area who migrated in the nineteenth century to Fiji and Guyana, respectively. He argues that while Indo-Fijians maintained an actual link to India, the Hindi language, and private styles of Hindu and Muslim religiosity, this was not so for the Indo-Guyanese. For them, India became largely a place within the imagination, knowledge of both the spoken and written forms of the Hindi language disappeared, and a more public form of religiosity emerged among both Hindus and Muslims. Yet paradoxically, as Jayawardena puts it, for the Guyanese, 'India' and 'Indianness' became invested 'with more *useable meanings*. By this I mean that if a cultural entity exists mainly in the imagination, then it is the more susceptible to interpretations prompted by the need to shore up an ideal in times of anxiety and crisis, personal or public' (Jayawardena, 1980: 432, *my italics*). It is in this sense that a complex idea of 'Guyana', transformed through imagination into an object invested with shared values was carried forward through a second migration and into the later experience of being Guyanese in London as a resource to meet the challenges of a new situation.

The resources of imagination

If being Muslim for the Guyanese, or for those like the Mauritians and others who joined them, was something mainly to be lived out collectively, elements of this world were nonetheless sometimes acknowledged and elaborated on verbally. A sermon drew a moment of recognition from a Mauritian woman, Samira, whom I knew slightly, as we descended the stairs after Friday prayers. The imam had spoken about how our good and bad deeds are written down by the angels and how, on the Last Day, some of the merits from our good deeds would be given to those we had oppressed. He then talked of the behaviour of the Companions of the Prophet and how, when they visited new cities where they did not speak the language, they were nonetheless able to impress others through 'the beauty of their characters'. As we left, Samira said approvingly that the sermon had been 'short and clear', adding 'not like those who get into strange new things'. I took these 'new things' to be the more Salafi and politically oriented sermons that she did not feel able to assimilate into her way of practising her faith.

These 'new things' were among the currents of change that had to be absorbed or resisted. During the period of my fieldwork, I became aware that some Guyanese, who had been wearing ordinary 'modest high-street clothes', seemed to have started to adopt a version of South Asian Muslim dress or the generic style of Islamic dress on sale in the shop when attending the mosque, though they did not dress in this way outside.[4] Some of those who had previously worn colourful Muslim dress started to wear black to the mosque. If this current of change was experienced by some as due to external pressure and responded to with a degree of irony, the debates about what Islam demands raised doubts and concerns for others whose changed style of dress may have been the outcome of subtle personal accommodations to new ways of perceiving their religious obligations. I was used to seeing Jasmin wearing short tunic dresses over trousers and a colourful, casually tied scarf, with some, if not most, of her long hair showing, so I was surprised when she appeared in the kitchen one day in my second Ramadan dressed in black with a black scarf wound around her head. When I remarked on the change, she pulled a wry smile. However, the hijab kept slipping and she repeatedly tried to re-fix it with a clasp. Another Guyanese woman, who was wearing more colourful clothing and a casually tied scarf, offered some advice as to how to wind the material. Jasmin expressed her exasperation and eventually removed both the black scarf and the black under-cap, which was supposed to completely hide her hair. She re-gathered her long hair into a ponytail and started again to try and get it right. It was difficult to read what was going on in this adoption of a more Islamic style of head covering since Jasmin was, apparently, quite comfortable, within the mixed company of kitchen, to remove the whole lot and adjust her hair before retying it. On this occasion, her changed style of dress may be associated with the impact of the additional religious rituals of Ramadan; I saw her again later in more Western clothing, so it was not a permanent change. By contrast, the Bangladeshi woman who helped with the drinks remarked casually to me that someone, unspecified, had told her that the style in which she tied her hair up – in a kind of bandana which leaves her neck and sometimes her ears visible – was not Islamic. She shrugged, making it clear that she was not minded to change her way of dressing. This suggests not only the range of views present within the wider congregation but the willingness of some people to correct others. Since clothing is taken by some as a direct indication of piety and theological allegiance (Tarlo 2005) this critical remark about a style of head covering may have been motivated by a wish to help a fellow sister sustain her religious obligations, but there is a constant need to either stand one's ground or accommodate externally or at least give serious consideration to the perspective of others.

While the range of views and practice within the mosque allowed some space for me as a non-Muslim, there was always the possibility of some people noticing that I did not look Muslim and should not be there. Among the Guyanese, only one of the women I knew well ever seemed troubled by my clothing. She would sometimes comment, for no apparent reason, that I was 'looking more Muslim today'. On an occasion when she and I were opening the shop and hanging out the Islamic dresses, she wondered if I would buy one. I said I thought I would feel odd in it, meaning that I felt I would look as if I was pretending to be Muslim. Later she tucked my scarf down into the top of my shirt, which to my mind already had a high neck. This was done light-heartedly and though she herself did not wear a *hijab* outside of the mosque, her concern with my religious appearance was perhaps indicative of her sensitivity to how other Muslims might perceive her in the light of her friendly relations with me.

The challenges I witnessed were made and responded to in the moment rather than by recourse to authoritative religious opinion, but this is not to imply that such judgments were random or contingent reactions to events. There is a pattern and coherence in the examples below that implies a sustained sensibility to the moral qualities at stake. Such occasions might be framed as moments of 'moral breakdown' Zigon (2007), which require a conscious 'ethical' response as to where one stands, but they also bespeak the presence of an on-going moral sensibility that is of a piece with a way of being in the everyday world that has developed over a lifetime. It is this that Keane (2014) argues an ethnographic stance can reveal, rather than, as the ethical may appear through the lens of an experimental research design, a capacity only called into existence by the demands of a particular situation. Our variable, and not necessarily conscious, awareness of the mutually affecting presence of others underlies not only the capacity to infer the intentions of others but also the potential to experience, in a more direct sense, a feeling of responsibility for the 'state of things' within a social world. It is the capacity to inhabit, sustain and hand on such an imagined intersubjective domain as a shared moral endeavour that constitutes the ethical as a mode of being in the world. Though the contours of that domain may become sharper under situations of challenge, the ethical has been framed as intrinsically related to the capacity to live within the complexity, uncertainty, and ambiguity of human reality and the doubts and anxiety this stirs about one's commitments and failures in meeting obligations to others (Lambek 2000, 2010). Accepting the world as it is also creates a complex object of concern beyond ourselves (Faubion 2011: 72) that is vulnerable to the vicissitudes and limitations in our capacities and that of others whom we have nonetheless to depend on and trust in.[5]

Facing uncertainty and challenge

The contrast between the *iftah* meal and Friday prayer was apparent in the unscripted, improvised nature of the former but also in the anticipatory uncertainty that surrounded it – who would arrive and how it would go? – and the social judgements passed afterwards as to its success, especially where the meal had been provided by a particular family. While religious rituals may also go unattended, and many daily prayers during the week attracted only a handful of people, they are protected by their canonical status from the anxiety of failure in a way that social events are not. There is risk inherent in un-ritualised events founded in the immediate capacity of a group to respond to the needs and expectations that are in play – in this case, to manage a situation in such a way that it is recognised as an authentically 'Guyanese' *iftah*. Beyond this, again, are the risks inherent in an event open to a diverse group with different expectations. Though the sermons often spoke of the absence of a religiously appropriate social context and the consequences of a failure to maintain religious practice, they rarely referred to the differences of view within the congregation itself as to what those practices, and that social context, should be. Only in one sermon did I hear an imam make a clear reference to the contestation between traditions when he spoke in passing of an additional fast, outside of Ramadan, that would soon be undertaken by some groups. He indicated that not everyone recognised or agreed with this practice and left it at that. However, differences that were obscured at Friday prayers or were managed by people self-selecting with respect to which events at the mosque they attended came to the fore in a direct and visible encounter within the mixed gathering that *iftah* attracted. Such contact resulted not only in overt challenges but also in the presence of other religious possibilities and a sense of responsibility for one's own choices and commitments.

The production of the *iftah* meal made visible to others the place of gender mixing within a Guyanese way of being Muslim laying them open to criticism and as with modes of dress there was an impression of a change underway. During the first Ramadan of my fieldwork, there was no curtain dividing the hall into male and female areas during the meal and when prayer was called, the men went into the main prayer area of the new mosque, leaving the hall space for the women to pray in. This lack of segregation for eating in the hall had been remarked on by a young Ugandan woman whom I had met at another Muslim gathering and it was clear from her tone that, because of this, she would not be coming again for *iftah* at this mosque. When I saw her and her sister some months later at Friday prayer, their clothing had changed from carefully colour-toned Islamic dress to black *niqabs*. While individuals can grant themselves latitude to think about religious issues in their own way and may voice them as and to whom they choose, as happened sometimes in the shop, those involved in running the mosque were faced with public challenges that were presented as grounded in the only correct interpretation of Islam.

One evening during *iftah*, Leila, one of the Trustees, beckoned me into the entrance area by the shop, which was not exactly private but out of the main hall. She talked quietly, checking occasionally that no one else was likely to hear. She asked if I had noticed the argument that she had just had. She told me that she had to deal with the demand by an Algerian man from the congregation for complete segregation during the meal – that the curtain drawn during *maghrib* prayer should remain drawn. Leila was shaking and clearly very upset. She said that he had threatened that if this didn't happen, he would lead a walk-out, with others, from the mosque. She had apparently insisted that the curtains remain drawn back for the meal, explaining to me that if they gave in over this it would be another demand next time. Looking up, I could see that Mr Rahman, the president of the mosque and another male Trustee were, in fact drawing back the curtains. The Algerian caretaker of the mosque, who is warmly supportive of the Guyanese, came and asked Leila if she was alright. She said she was but continued talking to me about her outrage when, on top of what had happened, the man had then come and offered her a date from the snack that breaks the fast. When she refused his 'gift', he had challenged her accusingly, saying that one should not show anger during Ramadan. Clearly upset, she went on to explain to me that if he, and those who thought like he did, had their way, she would not be in the mosque at all: none of the women would be. They would all be at home. At that point, two young women passed by on the way to the shop. They were both very beautiful and colourfully dressed in the most casual degree of Muslim attire. Their thin sparkly scarves were sliding off the back of their heads, showing their long dark hair hanging loose. There was nothing unusual about this among the younger Guyanese. However, Leila broke off talking to me to tell them both to pull their scarves up and I heard her speak to them again later in the shop, even more urgently, saying that they really must be more careful as they would cause trouble. Without pause or comment, they both made some half-hearted gesture towards pulling their scarves back into place and carried on talking to their friends. Though Leila seemed clear about the need to defend the presence of women at the mosque, she was undecided about how and where to draw the line. I noticed that when the time came for the second prayer (after *iftah*), and the curtain was being drawn across again for that purpose, Leila was carefully tucking down the edges of the curtain where it would mask the praying males from the women who might be leaving through the shop exit as if to make clear that she understood and accepted the need for the curtain at this point (i.e. during prayer).

Though couched in religious terms, some of these challenges were deemed by others, such as the Guyanese religious teacher Azzim, to be cultural formations that had overlaid and obscured the message of the Quran. Yet all these disputes raised questions about the grounds for a particular interpretation and who had the power and authority to pronounce on it. While the Trustees felt they had a right to run the mosque according to their conception of Islam, they did not necessarily feel inclined to conduct a public theological argument, nor would they have claimed their legitimacy in that way. Rather, they saw a Muslim life as embedded within broader social and practical concerns and the acceptance of culture and history. In his capacity as president of the mosque, Mr Rahman's public pronouncements often demonstrated a style of thinking that was shaped by his practical engagement with the material project of building the mosque and by his absorption of the contemporary secular thinking necessary to protect it. This was certainly provocative to some people and Mr Rahman had had to defend himself both in the past and during the time of my fieldwork against the claims of others to greater religious orthodoxy. For example, there was a long-running dispute in which Mr Rahman and the other Trustees were challenged and threatened over their insistence on shutting the doors when the mosque was full on Fridays. Though I could not see what was happening among the men on the ground floor, there were times when the women's balcony was so full that people had great difficulty in finding a space to pray while late arrivals continued to push in, resisting any restraint from the women who were trying to steward the balcony. At its worst, during Ramadan, the doorways and the stairs became blocked, and doubtless, the same situation was reproduced in the corridors and exits downstairs, so it was not just a matter of the Trustees conforming to empty bureaucratic requirements but a genuine 'duty of care' with its ethical implications of work and responsibility. However, the closing of the mosque doors on health and safety grounds created an on-going confrontation since, in the view of some of the men in the congregation, their right to pray took priority over all other considerations. On at least one occasion, some men barged Mr Rahman, he was knocked to the ground and the police were called. In subsequent weeks, Mr Rahman spoke at the end of prayers about the situation, complaining vigorously that these people were not proper Muslims.

This issue was a reminder of the strong feelings that attached to some of the different views within the congregation, the religious significance accorded to the distinction between the material and the immaterial, and how differently the same event could appear under entirely different descriptions. To talk of health and safety was to admit the legitimacy of material secular considerations external to the religious domain, bringing into sharp focus that, for some, the mosque was not an ordinary physical structure subject to material limitations of capacity and risk. However, in saying that those who were challenging him were not proper Muslims, Mr Rahman also gave the dispute a religious frame. He did not spell out his conception of what it was to be a 'proper Muslim' in these circumstances, though the implications were that it included living in the world as it is and acknowledging the need for the practical arrangements that this necessitated. As the account was reported at Friday prayers, the two perspectives were, and remained, incommensurable. As with the dispute about gender segregation during the eating of the *iftah* meal, practical efforts were made to accommodate the various parties, and one side of the women's balcony was sometimes screened off as an extra area for use by the men. The underlying dispute was, however, unresolvable because what was at stake was a way of thinking among the Guyanese that was radically at odds with others within the congregation.

Drawing on the past; thinking in the present

One of the characteristics that distinguished the Guyanese, and the wider group that identified with them, was an idea of being a Muslim as something you did alongside others in the world. One person who seemed comfortable speaking about this attitude was Ali, an active member of the congregation who was often called on to open meetings with a short prayer, which he did with great seriousness and a presence that was at odds with his usual sociable, jocular manner. When I asked him about these prayers, he said, 'Well, we start and end the day with prayer and so, too, every event', evoking the intimacy and simplicity of what is shared and religiously transformed in this way.

In addition to bringing the everyday within a religious framework through this prayerful framing, Ali did not seem to regard practical thinking as at odds with religious virtue and his readiness to respond to unforeseen contingencies conveyed a sense of rootedness in a space for thinking that was both coherent and open. On an occasion when I was standing with him in the shop, an announcement came over the sound system that a *janazah* (funeral) would be taking place after congregational prayer and that people parking in the road beside the mosque must keep the gates clear as the hearse would need to park. Ali then said the man who was being buried had been at the mosque for prayer only last Friday but had been taken ill on Saturday. He thought the man had had a heart attack and died that same night. He seemed to want to emphasise the suddenness and completeness of the change from life to death. I took the opportunity to ask about the delay in the burial, as I had understood that in Islam, the dead needed to be buried immediately. Ali said that that was in the old days when there was no refrigeration; also, people are living all over the world now: 'It takes time to get here, maybe twenty-four hours from the US and Canada, but maybe two or three days from Guyana'. He said that actually, a young man had recently challenged Mr Rahman about this delay in burials, saying that it was contrary to Islam. In reply, Mr Rahman had asked the young man what he would do if his mother was on holiday in Mauritius and his father died here – what would he do? Would he wait for his mother? The young man conceded that he would wait. 'So, there you are. That's your answer'. Ali repeated, 'It's the sixth pillar, the hidden pillar of Islam: common sense', and laughed. I thought he offered this joke to avoid seeming to have set up this position provocatively, in contradiction to the views of others – as if to say it was only everyday common sense he was talking about, not theology. Yet he did not see this capacity for practical thinking as being contrary to Islam. What Ali styled as 'common sense' was not just practical improvisation or doing what was convenient but an orientation to the human concerns and values of a Muslim life that was consistent with his responses on other occasions. Moreover, this way of thinking requires to be lived out through a way of comporting oneself if such an idea is to be carried off convincingly in the face of challenge from other ways of being Muslim.

During a conversation in the mosque office, Ali told me that he had been challenged by some Algerians within the congregation about attending a Christian funeral. 'As you know we have a lot of friends … not only Muslim … and not only friends but family members.[6] In *their* belief [those with whom he was in dispute] if a non-Muslim passed away you can go to the home and pay your respects, but you can't go to the burial ground or to the church … it's haram, forbidden. But I have been to several churches and cremations and so on, and I cannot see for the love of God what I would be doing wrong …. This is a dear friend who has passed away …. Probably they [the Algerian challengers] don't have non-Muslim friends or family so maybe it's straightforward for them but for us it's different …. Apart from that, I grew up with people of different faiths, in fact for me with neighbours of different faiths … it's helped me tremendously in my life'.

Ali was arguing that his appreciation of the perspective of others was not just an aid in managing external encounters but an on-going internal resource that helped him to live a meaningful life. For this, as he made clear, he was drawing on an experience of Guyana such that the moral resources of the present were rooted in a relationship to a past and to forebears from whom they had been handed on. Yet this heritage can be hard to hold to in the face of new theological positions. I was asked on one occasion why I was doing my research at this mosque rather than in others where, the Guyanese woman talking to me implied, Islam would be seen as more correctly practiced. I explained that I was interested in how she and others actually lived as Muslims rather than with what some other people might consider the correct way of doing so. This was met with the remark that, when she was growing up in Guyana, she had thought there was only one kind of Islam, that which had been handed on by her parents, but now she understood that this was not so. She realised now that there were different groups like *shi'a* and others whose names she was not sure of. She bemoaned the fact that there were groups who thought you should be killing people – 'this isn't Islam' – but did not mention theological differences closer to home, those within the mosque. Her response to my expression of interest in her way of being Muslim seemed to be the thought that it was no longer possible to be Muslim as one's parents had been, living without an awareness of other views.

An older woman, Amina, was aware of other views, the questions they posed and the gap that was opening between Guyanese traditions and new ways of being Muslim. Some of the resulting changes were presented as forced on them and as matters of real regret, while others were seen as offering something of value that could be integrated with the practice they had inherited. Amina said that in the early days in London they had organised social events for local elderly that involved tea and singing old (English) songs, but this had been dropped due to pressure from other Muslims, which she felt had been wrong. (I learned later from someone else that the singing of religious songs, *qasida*, that had been widespread in Guyana, had also been given up in the UK.) However, talking about a recent death, she explained that when they first arrived in the UK, the Guyanese had held long gatherings as they used to in Guyana. She referred to such gatherings as 'like a wake', in which individuals would recite whatever verses they knew from the Quran. Now they understood that this was seen by other Muslims as 'a cultural thing' and this had resulted in generally shorter events led by an imam who recited something appropriate to the occasion. Though she did not contest this reference to their former practice as 'a cultural thing', and seemed to feel the present arrangement was better, this did not appear to transform past practice into idolatry. Amina conveyed a contentment with the Islam she grew up in and that had sustained both her long and active involvement with the mosque and a capacity to think for herself about religious matters.

Though Guyana was no longer the external social context of her life, it was very present within Amina's conversation as current news, in recollections of how it had once been and as a presence constantly re-imagined into life within the present. That the world she grew up in and her parents' way of being Muslim was something that provided an enduring point of orientation and meaning adds an internal dimension to the idea of a sustaining external social context of the ethical in the present (Keane 2014). Whether and how accurate a portrayal of the past it might be is less important from this perspective than the way Guyana, as a multi-faith society, gave the Guyanese, at least of her generation, a common ethical orientation, an idea of a collective good. Though there were some references to the political unrest between Indo- and Afro-Guyanese in the years just before and after independence, what had survived in the accounts I heard from those who grew up before the People's Progressive Party split along ethnic lines, was the experience of inter-faith contact. Amina described the fact that Hindu, Muslim, and Christian Guyanese children went to school together, and from there, they went to church and sang hymns. She said they did not have to go, but she had wanted to. There was a catechist who taught religion and Hindi, so, she said laughing, she had done that too. The children celebrated Eid, Diwali, and Christmas. Even though her father considered himself a religious Muslim, she had a Christmas stocking, little presents, and a tree: 'not a proper tree, just a plant brought in from the garden and decorated'. She acknowledged that some people were now very hostile to this practice, but it was quite usual in Guyana for Muslims and Hindus to celebrate Christmas. When they moved to the UK, she was content that her children went to a church school and continued these practices since she regarded them as a way of learning about others. One of her sons is married to a Guyanese Christian and I heard references to his attending midnight mass with his family at Christmas. The implication of this 'mixing', as she called it, was pointed up in relation to one of her grandsons who had married into a Hindu family from India rather than a Hindu-Guyanese family. She explained that in India, they do not celebrate other people's religious festivals, and her grandson's wife seemed to know nothing about 'these things' concerning the religion of others.

Amina had grown up deep in the countryside in Guyana – 'it was really a fantastic place … lots of outdoor life'. She described running around with her cousins, fishing in the channels and walking along the seawall in the moonlight. 'Really very good games … our children can never get those games we had …. Even when I went back [as an adult] I would want to get my fishing rod!' She talked of how creative girls had been in Guyana, always cooking and making things. She was quite clear, however, about the lack of educational opportunities and the greater limitations placed on a girl then. She felt she had done well in school and would have liked to continue her education beyond the age of thirteen but was instead sent to learn to sew professionally – a skill which eventually helped to support the family when they moved to London. Over various conversations, the Guyana of her imagination, the freedom she had enjoyed there and the disappointments and losses she had experienced were a continuing live presence in her mind and part of her engagement in the challenges of the present.

Though in public Amina generally kept her opinions to herself, she had her own views and when she chose to voice them, she was critical of those she saw as holding stridently orthodox opinions who felt they should be telling others what to do. She referred to them as 'fanatics', but these turned out not to be the distant fanatics of the media. She spoke of a relative now dead, who had been like this, and who would tell her, 'You can't walk bare-headed or in front of a man, a woman shouldn't allow her voice to be heard, you can't sing ….' He had left the mosque for another group. Over time, he had mellowed a bit, but Amina said sadly that, 'I couldn't go and give him a hug, as that was against religion as far as he was concerned'. She also described encounters with a Muslim man in a weekly health group she attended that seemed to echo this situation. He repeatedly told her to cover her hair and to dress differently. In the end, she decided to tell him, 'No, I can't do what you want. I'll do what I want. When I go to the mosque, I cover but otherwise not'. Then he began to say that she should not be going to the mosque to which Amina said she replied, 'You lot have women under your control, so they don't know anything about the mosque, but our people are not like that. We know how to mix with men without fancying them and things like that'. She said that he was annoyed, but she had just walked off and did not speak to him the following week. While she might feel she had dealt with the challenge this man posed to her view of things, her relationship with her long dead relative continued to sadden her, a reminder of the price paid for commitments and failures and the complicated and subtle nature of responsibility within the domain of the ethical. It is not, as Lambek writes, that a person is or isn't responsible for all the consequences of their utterances and actions whether or not they could have been foreseen but that, quoting Stephen Mulhall, a person 'is responsible for determining her relation to them' and living with those consequences (Lambek 2010: 53). It is the on-going nature of the relationship to past experience that sustains ethical capacity in the present.

Amina felt able to take issue with aspects of Islamic teaching. For example, she expressed strong disagreement with the view that menstruating women are unable to pray because they are unclean, insisting instead that the reason for the injunction against praying at this time should be understood as being for the comfort of the woman who was menstruating. This was of a piece with her view of God as not wanting us to suffer. Someone had asked her about a pregnant woman who had found that something was seriously the matter with her unborn child and had been offered a termination. Amina said they should phone the imam about that, but she thought that 'God is very understanding and didn't mean us to make more unhappiness for ourselves … we must do what we think is best'. While leaving space open for seeking the opinion of an imam, she apparently felt confident that 'doing what we think is best' was appropriate in the circumstances. For many Guyanese, the experience of living as a Muslim was a matter of trusting in one's own judgments. One could say that this confidence in exercising judgement is related to having internalised and identified with relationships, including that to God, that give the space to think and to act though without the certainty that one could not be wrong. One could argue that the capacity to form and trust such judgements is based on the acceptance that a point of view, and the ideas formed from that perspective, are just that – ideas, not facts, and cannot guarantee the outcome. This distancing allows that one's own thoughts may be seen and judged differently by others and opens a dimension of human existence in which human beings, though constrained by both biology and culture, are nonetheless potentially free to think, to make judgments as well as to take (or evade) responsibility for them and to forgive and be forgiven Keane (2014). While ethical capacity may emerge through the 'affordances' of particular social encounters, it is developed over a lifetime of relatedness to others within the social-moral background of everyday life.

As well as these practical concerns, Amina also had abstract questions about theological issues. During a recent visit to Mecca, outside the main *hajj* season,[7] she had had difficulty performing the requisite number of circuits of the *kabah* on foot and had paid someone to push her round in a wheelchair. Other members of her group could return frequently to repeat this ritual of seven circuits, but she could not. Instead, she started to query why one was supposed to go around seven times: why *seven*? Amina felt no one could answer to her satisfaction. She had asked the guide what happens if you cannot walk and cannot afford to be pushed. He answered that you would be forgiven, but Amina complained that that was not what she wanted to know. Indeed, it only complicated matters further as far as she was concerned. Another guide had indicated that 'it was alright as long as you tried', but she remained dissatisfied with these answers though she could not say exactly why. In a sense, this question may have stood in for a host of other unvoiced concerns. Certainly, she had an expectation of being able to question and understand within the framework of her own thought and experience rather than through taking on a new theological system and new forms of reasoning. Amina was critical about some aspects of what she had experienced in Mecca that seemed inconsistent with the religious nature of the occasion, such as the crowds of people pushing – 'They don't care a lot about anyone else – only themselves'. When I pressed her, she said, 'I have seen it now and I'm glad about that, but it didn't change anything for me. I don't think it changes anything'.

Loss and the re-imagining of a community

Guyana was often referred to as 'home' and many of those I got to know may have once thought that they would go back eventually; it was clear now that for most this was not going to happen. Though new ties had been made, what had been gained through migration to the UK was accompanied by an awareness of what had been given up. Amira had made trips back to Guyana in the past, but she did not plan to return again as the people she would have wanted to see were no longer alive. By contrast, she continued to visit her relatives who had settled in Canada and the USA with their growing families. A time is approaching when the nature of the tie to Guyana among the Guyanese in London will cease to be based on first-hand experience of a place one grew up in and the link will become increasingly attenuated, a place to visit or just to hear about from others.

This pervasive sense of loss among the older generation was given a particular form in relation Mr Rahman. He had lost his mother when he was very young and once mentioned, rather poignantly, that he had no photograph of her and no memory of what she looked like. At the celebration of his eightieth birthday, among a display of pictures of the family, the community, cricket matches, and the mosque down the years was one in which Mr Rahman's father was shown standing, as if in a wedding picture, next to a woman whose face had been blurred. The picture was the creation of one of his sons; it was labelled 'Mr Rahman's parents'. At this event, various dignitaries from the borough, local churches, and voluntary organisations, and someone from the People's Progressive Party (PPP) of Guyana in the UK spoke about the achievements of Mr Rahman's life, but when Ali, the Guyanese Trustee I mentioned earlier in this chapter, got up to address the gathering on behalf of the mosque, he started by talking of how Mr Rahman had lost his mother at a young age. I later learnt that Ali had also lost his mother in early childhood. One can see this as simply a matter of private significance, but it has a more public resonance through its encapsulation of the experience of loss in which migrants all share to some degree. It also gives a particular meaning to Mr Rahman's drive to build a new religious home for the Guyanese Muslim community, a mosque in London, and his capacity to galvanise others to this end. While loss creates a gap in the external social context supporting an individual's ethical capacities, it may also stimulate the capacity to imagine into being a new context and a new focus of ethical thought though first the loss must be recognised and accepted. Lambek (2010: 59) makes a link between the loss of a world, albeit through failure to maintain the integrity of individual or collective practice, and the need to mourn that loss as the ground of ethical capacity. The sense of loss following migration may include just that experience of having damaged or put at risk one's religious inheritance as evidenced in the loss of faith of one's children that was described in one of the sermons.[8]

The rupture and loss of migration is something shared by many, if not most, within the congregation, but a new post-migration life is neither simply imposed by circumstance nor waiting to be taken up. In an important sense, it must be imagined into being. This draws on an elusive quality of human imagination – hope – as much as on the practical capacity to build a community as a material reality. In his reflection on an interview conducted in the nineteenth century with the last chief of the Crow people about the destruction of their world, the philosopher Jonathan Lear (2006) writes of what he calls 'radical hope'. For the most part, we live within an already existing, though slowly changing, form of life in which mourning losses is a constant accompaniment. By focusing on the catastrophic loss suffered by the Crow, Lear calls attention to the human capacity to imagine into being something which had not previously existed, yet it is a capacity required to some degree in the face of all loss. Crapanzano (2004: 99) suggests that hope for an as yet unknown future state depends for its fulfilment on some locus of agency other than the self. The Crow chief located the origin of his vision in a dream and his experience of the presence of an ancestral spirit. Earlier generations of Guyanese had 'kept the lamp burning' and handed on that hope to those who came after them as a presence within the imagination of those who went on to build a mosque in London. In a paper drawing on literary and clinical sources, Waddell suggests that hope lies in being able to face difficult realities without losing the capacity to love life (Waddell 2019). The decision to build a mosque entailed facing difficult realities, but in doing so, it created a communal project as a new source of hope and meaning.

In Mr Rahman's account of the Muslim Guyanese project to build, by stages, their own mosque, it was described as taking place in the context of a rupture within the community in London in the early 1980s. One of the differences between the groups concerned whether they needed to have a new home – a mosque. 'We always wanted a building. I don't know why they didn't want one, but I said no, we need something to identify with – a room or a house or whatever it is'. The group that Mr Rahman led lost all their existing material resources in the split. 'We had to start from scratch … so that's what we did, and everyone pitched in'. When he was asked to lead the rump of the society, he said he had agreed because he felt he had 'a vision to get somewhere, to establish ourselves'. He told the Guyanese that he was going to move ahead on this path and those who wanted to come could join him; those who did not were free to leave. In telling me this Mr Rahman emphasised his own single-mindedness, saying, 'If anybody slip, my hand will be stretched backwards so grab it [he demonstrated several times the action of reaching behind him], because I am not going to turn back to pick up nobody. If they don't want to come along, they don't have to take my hand, you see'. Sometimes the building of the mosque was presented as beginning as a collective idea in the UIA; at other times, it was more clearly felt to be his own vision in which others joined him. 'I know I may not finish it before I get to the door (of paradise) but God will know that I tried my damnedest'. Yet the project required the community to commit to it and it would only have been possible, and would only have made sense, to the extent that they did come together around it. The physical struggle to fund and build the mosque as a material structure for the Muslim Guyanese in London required both an act of ethical imagination, 'an expanded sense of what can be' (Rumsey 2010: 118), and the on-going moral work to sustain this as an enduring focus for the community over time (Mattingly 2012). Mr Rahman's image of the Guyanese Islam of his childhood, its limitations, and inadequacies, as well as its survival in difficult circumstances, was a source of moral value as well as an object of continuing responsibility – the responsibility to go beyond simply 'keeping the lamp burning' by undertaking formal religious training in London and by building the mosque.

New circumstances; new challenges

What the Guyanese felt they had inherited was a form of religious sensibility and a style of moral reasoning within everyday life that maintained a porous boundary between Muslim and non-Muslim. If, among themselves, the Guyanese could seem confident in their own way of doing things, this was now increasingly challenged both theologically by movements that sought to purify religious thinking and by Muslims from other, more homogenous, cultural traditions who have settled in North London. However, there was another kind of interface within the large and diverse Muslim population in London – that with groups who also found themselves as marginalised minorities within the larger Muslim community in London. The mosque offered its facilities to the local Turkish community for funerals: sometimes, they brought their own imam, and sometimes the mosque imam took the ceremony. On those occasions, men and women arrived together in ordinary Western dress. When a two-year-old Kurdish child died at home, the mother had wanted someone to come and recite the Quran over the body, but she had been told by an imam at the East London Mosque that such prayers were unnecessary.[9] The woman became very upset, saying that she herself would recite the prayers if no one would come from a mosque to do so. When Mr Rahman heard about the situation, he visited the home, and said the prayers. This indicates the emergence of another sort of Muslim formation that is based neither in a scriptural view of orthodoxy nor in the continuity of pre-migration traditions but a new response to the diversity of actual Muslim communities in London in new circumstances with new unmet needs.

Those from other ethnic groups who joined the Guyanese may also have been seeking a way of being Muslim that accommodated their experience of living in London with its accumulating complexity and contradictions. Zahara, a Bangladeshi woman, often referred to her feeling of commitment to the community at the Guyanese mosque with which she has been involved in its various forms over 30 years. She described persuading her husband to buy the house in which she raised her family because of the plans for a mosque nearby. This sense of commitment and continuity runs alongside her accounts of difficulties with other Bangladeshis living locally. When I first got to know Zahara, she told me about the verbal attacks and threats she had been subjected to by neighbours in shops and in the street over the fact that her eldest son was fighting with the British army in Iraq. This was particularly upsetting as there were incidents in the press at that time concerning threats made by some Muslims to execute Muslim soldiers, but if she felt any doubts about her son's position, she never said anything. When he was home on leave, they would go together to the mosque. Zahara had been an active member of the congregation for many years and, in times of difficulty, had turned both to the mosque as 'her community' and as a place for prayer. There have been a number of occasions when she had asked for prayers to be said for herself and her family at the mosque, and times when I found her there, praying quietly by herself. This is a life of ethical engagement and, as Keane suggests, without 'differing and even clashing voices', and hence the need to manage conflict, 'there would be no occasion for ethical consciousness' (Keane 2010: 77–78).

The imaginative resources that sustained the Guyanese and those within the more diverse group around them surfaced in response to challenges and in moments of reflection. On one occasion, Mr Rahman put his understanding of the situation of the Guyanese in this way. 'Arabs think of themselves as more holy because they have the language of the Quran. Pakistanis think the same way because they speak Urdu … but Urdu isn't the language of the Quran [it is however written in a script similar to Arabic]'. He implied that the Guyanese, with their use of English, were thought of as inferior by other Muslims. He countered this situation by saying, 'We're open, and I see that our background helps us a lot – because we can see things differently from some other people who have not opened up their vision to the place where they (now) live …. Although we're here, we don't say we're at home … when we say home, we mean Guyana … but living in this society we have to be part of the society here'.

In talking about the differences and hierarchy between Muslim communities, Mr Rahman described the way languages had become invested with significance through the perception of a privileged link to Islam. The Indians who migrated to Guyana lost their connection with both spoken and written Hindi (a language related to Urdu but written in a different script) and took on the language of the colonial power and of the Afro-Guyanese. Yet here, Mr Rahman seems to see this loss of a language as linked to the freedom to approach the situation in London in a way which he describes as 'open' because, unlike Urdu- and Arabic-speaking Muslims, he sees the Guyanese as unencumbered by this kind of imagined hierarchical relationship to Islam. The argument then seems to reverse. The paradoxical statement about Guyana indicates that, for Mr Rahman, it was by retaining Guyana as a 'home' in the imagination that the Guyanese were enabled to live within the new context they found in London. This can be understood in relation to Jayawardena's (1980) analysis – that in becoming a place that many, like Mr Rahman, will never see again, Guyana became a resource within the imagination that could be used in new circumstances, just as the idea of being 'Indian' became a focus for a new collective meaning for indentured Indo-Guyanese workers of different faiths by becoming detached from material connections to India as an external place. Beyond this, the nature of Guyana as a place of social diversity and 'mutual exposure to the way that others live' (Kresse 2013) is felt to have created a style of thinking and feeling that enabled the Guyanese to settle and flourish in London. A conversation with a young British-born Guyanese woman, two generations on from Mr Rahman, implies that the idea of what it is to be a Guyanese Muslim is still relevant as a point of ethical orientation, albeit within a changing landscape.

Milly, a Guyanese woman in her thirties whose husband was a Mauritian Christian, described the complexity of making her way as a Muslim in London among others whose Muslim practice is different, as well as among non-Muslims. She referred to her family origins as South American, which is geographically accurate but one of only two occasions on which I heard it put like that. It was clear that she did not pray five times a day, except in Ramadan, when she said she made a special effort. She explained this in terms of her hectic life in which she had to combine childcare and work, but then added seriously that 'I'm not saying I don't want to give time to my Creator'. She contrasted her problems as a working mother with the situation in Pakistani families where she felt women tended not to work outside the home and where it was, therefore, easier to be more orthodox about prayer. She went on to talk about a new Pakistani girl at her work. 'In her family you don't go out and mix, that's her environment. She lives with her parents-in-law and they are very strict so it's difficult for her at work where there are non-Muslims'. Milly asked if I had seen a recent TV programme about Muslim faith schools and observed that it must have been very disturbing for non-Muslims to see it. She thought it must have set up all sorts of images of Muslims as hostile to non-Muslims 'so that when they see women in a hijab, they must feel that's what they are all like, hostile'. Of her non-Muslim work colleagues, she said that 'they don't see me as I am in the mosque [in a hijab]. I look just like any other woman, but they know I am a Muslim'. She described a difficult encounter with the new Pakistani colleague who had asked about Milly's husband. When she had said that he was not Muslim, the colleague had replied, 'I didn't think so'. Milly said acidly, 'Well! I wanted to ask her what she meant by that, but I didn't'.

The initial starting point, the placing of Guyana in South America, conveyed a location in the middle of another hemisphere rather than on the outer periphery of the Muslim world. In the light of what follows, this suggests an internal imaginative landscape that offers the space to see other points of view. Milly's train of thought and her perspective moved back and forth between her own religious commitments and how she managed them, her awareness of the different practices of other Muslims, and the perceptions of non-Muslims. Though it was the encounter with the Pakistani colleague and the conversation with me that might be said to have created the 'affordances' (Keane 2014) that brought these concerns into focus, they were live issues in her everyday life – how she thought of herself as a Muslim, how she saw other Muslims and how she imagined non-Muslims to perceive her. This train of thought remained in motion as the conversation ended; there was no resolution, only more uncertainty and ambiguity to be managed. Guyana and being Muslim-Guyanese seemed, at some level, be a sustaining presence in her thinking and her confidence, as it has been for earlier generations, but Milly was also making her way into new uncharted territory that engendered a sense of vulnerability. Concerns with what it means to live within a tradition is to be aware that its endurance depends on a willingness to acknowledge problems and to defend it before others who may perceive matters differently. An individual's sense of their inevitably limited capacity to embody its values in their own life are anxieties at the heart of moral experience. The concerns expressed at the mosque, in activity as much as in speech, were just these – the safety of their way of being Muslim, the need to open the mosque to others and the acceptance that not all Muslim Guyanese are practising or that they are practicing only to the extent that they felt it to be possible within the world in which they found themselves.

Notes

1 Jayawardena (1980) argues that the loss of a realistic, physical link to India for the Indo-Guyanese led to the emergence of a different relationship to being Indian and a different pattern of religiosity, among both Hindus and Muslims, from that which pertained among a similar population that settled in Fiji. He makes the claim that the importance of imagination in the meaning of India was in an inverse relationship to the material reality of that link – 'if a cultural entity exists mainly in the imagination,

it is the more susceptible to interpretations prompted by the need to shore up an ideal in times of anxiety and crisis, personal or public' (Jayawardena 1980: 432).

2 These identifications were present both as ideas that could be invoked and reflected on and as bodily identifications that could not.

3 The political and social upheavals that began prior to independence called into question the continuation in external reality of the earlier consensus and accommodation between ethnic and religious groups.

4 Fadil (2011) writes of the decisions of individual women not to veil as an expression of their wish to think independently. It is less clear that this was the motivation here. On the contrary, there seemed to be a pull towards conforming to a more conservative style within the mosque. Tarlo (2018) describes Muslims living in Bangladesh and Pakistan as increasingly regarding their hijab wearing relatives in Britain as old-fashioned and traditional.

5 Klein (1959) suggested that the emotional and cognitive developments that occur in the second half of the first year of life – among which are the achievements of what Trevarthen was later to call 'secondary intersubjectivity' (Trevarthen 1979, 1998) – brought new anxieties stirred by the dawning awareness of the separateness of others, of dependence on them and the vulnerability of the capacity for love and trust in the face of the anxieties that were stirred by these perceptions (Rustin and Rustin 2017). In this model, it is out of this constellation that moral sensibilities and ethical capacities develop.

6 He is here tacitly acknowledging the level of intermarriage between faith groups.

7 This was her first pilgrimage that had been organised by a younger Guyanese woman with whom she was friendly.

8 Absence, loss, and mourning have had a key place in psychoanalytic thought from Freud (1917) and Klein (1940) through to those writing today, for example, Paul (2018). The capacity to recognise and mourn what has been lost or damaged throughout life is seen as enriching the imagination and the creativity of the mind.

9 Infants and pre-pubertal children who die are thought to be in a pure state and so go to paradise immediately. No prayers are therefore required. However, the status of prayers and recitations for the dead, more generally, is a matter that some, like Azzim, would dispute since he held that there was nothing one could do for someone once they had died.

References

Baumann, G. (1999) *The Multicultural Riddle*. London: Routledge.

Crapanzano, V. (2004) *Imaginative Horizons*. Chicago: Chicago University Press.

Eisenlohr, P. (2006) *Little India: Diaspora, Time and Ethnolinguistic Belonging in Hindu Mauritius*. London: University of California Press.

Eisenlohr, P. (2011) 'Religious media, devotional Islam and the morality of ethnic pluralism', *World Development* 39(2): 261–269.

Eisenlohr, P. (2013) 'Mediality and materiality in religious performance: Religion as heritage in Mauritius', *Material Religion* 9(3): 328–348.

Eisenlohr, P. (2015) 'Mediating junctures of time: Ancestral shronotypes chronotypes in ritual and media practices', *Anthropological Quarterly* 88(2): 281–304.

Fadil, N. (2011) 'Not-/unveiling as an ethical practice', *Feminist Review* 98: 83–109.

Faubion, J. D. (2011) *An Anthropology of Ethics*. Cambridge: Cambridge University Press.

Freud, S. 1917. 'Mourning and Melancholia', in Strachey, J. (ed) *The Standard Edition of the Complete Psychological Works of Sigmond Freud*, 14: 237–258. London: Hogarth Press.

Jayawardena, C. (1980) 'Culture and ethnicity in Guyana and Fiji', *Man* (NS) 15(3): 430–450.

Jouili, J. (2015) *Pious Practice and Secular Constraints*. Stanford: Stanford University Press.

Keane, W. (2010) 'Minds, Surfaces and Reasons in the Anthropology of Ethics', in Lambek, M. (ed) *Ordinary Ethics*. New York: Fordham University Press.

Keane, W. (2014) 'Affordances and reflexivity in ethical life: An ethnographic stance', *Anthropological Theory* 14(1): 3–26.

Klein, M. (1940) 'Mourning and its relation to manic depressive states', *International Journal of Psychoanalysis* 21: 125–153.

Klein, M. (1959) 'Our adult world and its roots in infancy', *Human Relations* 12: 201–303. Republished in *The Writings of Melanie Klein*, Volume 3. London: Hogarth Press.

Kresse, K. (2013) 'On the Skills to Navigate the World, and Religion, for Coastal Muslims in Kenya', in Marsden, M. and Retsikas, K. (eds) *Articulating Islam: Anthropological Approaches to Muslim Worlds*. London: Springer.

Laidlaw, J. (2002) 'For an anthropology of ethics and freedom', *Journal of the Royal Anthropological Institute* 8: 311–332.

Lambek, M. (2000) 'The anthropology of religion and the quarrel between poetry and philosophy', *Current Anthropology* 41: 3.

Lambek, M. (ed) (2010) *Ordinary Ethics*. New York: Fordham University Press.

Lear, J. (2006) *Radical Hope: Ethics in the Face of Cultural Devastation*. London: Harvard University Press.

Marchand, T. (2010) 'Making knowledge: Explorations of the indissoluble relation between minds bodies and environment', *Journal of the Royal Anthropological Institute* 16: 1–21.

Marsden, M. (2008) 'Women, politics and Islamism in Northern Pakistan', *Modern Asian Studies* 42(2/3): 405–429.

Mattingly, C. (2012) 'Two virtue ethics and the anthropology of morality', *Anthropology Theory* 12(12): 161–184.

Mohapatra, P. (2006) '"Following custom?" Representations of community among Indian labour in the West Indies, 1880–1920', *International Review of Social History* 51: 173–202.

Nussbaum, M. (1997) *Cultivating Humanity: A Classical Defence of Reform in Liberal Education*. Cambridge, MA: Harvard University Press.

Parkin, D. (2007) 'The Accidental in Religious Instruction', in Berliner, D. and Sarro, R. (eds) *Learning Religion*. Oxford: Berghahn Books.

Paul, K. (2018) 'Mourning and the Development of Internal Objects', in Garvey, P. and Long, K. (eds) *The Klein Tradition*. London: Routledge.

Roy, O. (2004) *Globalised Islam: The Search for a New Ummah*. London: Hurst and Co.

Rumsey, A. (2010) 'Ethics, Language and Human Sociality', in Lambek, M. (ed) *Ordinary Ethics*. New York: Fordham University Press.

Rustin, M. E. and Rustin, M. J. (2017) *Reading Klein*. New York: Routledge.

Shukla, S. (2001) 'Locations for South Asian diasporas', *Annual Review of Anthropology* 30: 551–572.

Tarlo, E. (2005) 'Reconsidering stereotypes: Anthropological reflections on the jilbab controversy', *Anthropology Today* 21(6): 13–17.

Tarlo, E. (2018) 'Dress and the South Asian Diaspora', in Chatterji, J. and Washbrook, D. (eds) *Routledge Handbook of the South Asian Diaspora*. London: Routledge.

Trevarthen, C. (1979) 'Communication and Co-operation in Early Infancy: The Origins of Primary Inter-subjectivity', in Bullowa, M. (ed) *Before Speech*. Cambridge: Cambridge University Press.

Trevarthen, C. (1998) 'The Concept and Foundations of Infant Intersubjectivity', in Braten, S. (ed) *Intersubjective Communication and Emotion in Early Ontogeny.* Cambridge: Cambridge University Press.

Waddell, M. (2019) '"All the light we cannot see": Psychoanalytic and poetic reflections on the nature of hope', *International Journal of Psychoanalysis* 100(6): 1405–1421.

Werbner, P. (2002) *Imagined Diasporas amon. g Manchester Muslims.* Santa Fe: School of American Research Press.

Werbner, P. (2018) 'Ritual, Religion and Aesthetics in the Pakistani and South Asian Diaspora', in Chatterji, J. and Washbrook, D. (eds) *Routledge Handbook of the South Asian Diaspora.* London: Routledge.

Zigon, J. (2007) 'Moral Breakdown and the Ethical Demand.' *Anthropological Theory* 7(1): 131–150.

7

AN INDEPENDENT RELIGIOUS TEACHER

The impact of modernity and rationality and the spread of mass education within Muslim societies has been linked to the widening of access to scriptural knowledge among ordinary Muslims (Eickelman 1978, 1992, 2000). This development has also meant that it could no longer be taken for granted that an appropriate religious sensibility would naturally emerge, as it once had, simply through living within the embodied traditions of a Muslim society. Movements of religious revival and the conscious cultivation of individualised forms of religiosity both within Muslim majority societies and among diaspora Muslim populations arose in response to this situation. Roy (2004: 168) describes a 'crisis of transmission' within European Islam where the absence of a Muslim environment has driven a need for both textual knowledge and the immediacy of felt religious experience, needs that were met by independent teachers and the internet sites, creating a market in ideas outside the authority of Islamic institutional structures.

Azzim, a freelance imam who preached from time to time at the mosque, was such a teacher. His Guyanese background was described in Chapter 2. He was committed to an intellectual engagement with the text of God's revelation in the Quran rather than as it had come to be lived within his own or other cultural traditions, and, in consequence, he was also committed to a project of religious teaching, da'wa, among fellow Muslims in London Though in restricting the source of religious knowledge to the written text of the Quran and the Sunnah his stance in some respects reflected the rise of contemporary Salafi thinking within European Islam (Mandaville 2007; Roy 2007; de Koning 2013), Azzim's views also differed markedly from it. Rather than identifying with larger Islamic movements, he saw himself as an independent teacher and stressed the need for ordinary Muslims to develop their own capacity to understand the Quran so that they could think for themselves in religious matters rather than being overly reliant on others. His theology challenged both the place of cultural traditions

DOI: 10.4324/9781003080008-7

in Islam and the idea of an emotional relationship to God that had shaped the Muslim lives of many at the mosque. The gap that this opened between the clarity of the divine revelation with its appeal to rational thought and the emotionality and uncertainty of human experience was reflected in his view of the absolute nature of the distinction between the Creator and the created. However, he also maintained the distinction between worship, in which everything permissible has been specified in the Quran and the Sunnah, and the everyday living of a Muslim life, in which only those things specifically forbidden are excluded.

Though located in the mosque, the weekly Saturday classes and the monthly lectures on Sundays that he established took place independently of any organisational framework.[1] Within the lectures and classes, Azzim's view of the need for Muslims to engage with the text of God's revelation came into contact with the often confused and confusing concerns of those who attended these events, concerns gleaned from the traditions of their family, various internet sources, and the accommodations they had made to life in a non-Muslim majority society. Azzim's religious perspective placed Islam beyond the vagaries of the human, yet his commitment to being a freelance teacher, like his engagement with the society around him and his early life in Guyana, placed him firmly within the mundane. His commitment to teaching was primarily focused on what was theologically correct, but there were occasions when an ordinary intuitive understanding of the circumstances in which people found themselves came to the fore and a moral space opened in which new thoughts emerged. Like the freelance imam in Wesselhoeft's study, Azzim had a certain freedom to think and to surprise (Wesselhoeft 2010).[2] Adopting an attitude to secular European society as offering a perspective from which to reflect on the living of a Muslim life, Azzim could, on occasion, use his independent status to challenge the expectations of some questioners. In this, he had more in common with Mr Rahman, the president of the mosque, and other Guyanese in the congregation, than his theological position might indicate. Though the language Azzim used to layout his religious position was very different from that used by Mr Rahman, his attitude to gender relations was similar. He was also a local religious figure in the sense that, though his ideas had obvious links to global theological issues within Islam, his thinking engaged both with his immediate surroundings and his own Guyanese history.

Creating a space for teaching and learning

The account Azzim gave of how he came to hold the religious views he did echoes the wider transformation in the relationship to the Quran that, for many ordinary Muslims, had once been based solely in memorisation.[3] Despite the low level of general education in rural Guyana, Azzim managed to teach himself Arabic so that he could have direct access to the meaning of the divine revelation. Eventually, a preacher who was visiting Guyana selected him for sponsorship to study Islam in Saudi Arabia. Though one can trace aspects of his theological thinking to the religious ideas with which he would have had contact in Saudi

Arabia, there was something (never spelt out) that he disliked about this experience and he left after a year. He reacted sharply during one of the monthly Sunday meetings at which he gave lectures when some women from East Africa talked about a view that, as a Muslim, you were obliged to live in a Muslim country and that perhaps they should go and live in Saudi Arabia. He insisted that they were much freer in the UK; he meant freer to practice their religion. For Azzim, this idea of being free to practice did not mean, as the women perhaps meant, being able to live as a Muslim within a social context of a guaranteed Islamic form, but rather one in which one was free to think about Islam for oneself. While this view was consonant with the opinions voiced by some of the women in the Saturday class, it contrasted with those expressed by some who preached on Friday sermon and by some studies of Muslim communities in Europe.[4]

The idea of freedom was significant in Azzim's thinking in another sense. When he left Saudi Arabia, he came to the UK and trained to work in the public sector, which gave him the freedom to be an independent teacher of Islam. Although he lived some distance away, Azzim had an association with the mosque based on his Guyanese origin. He participated with his family in a range of religious, social, and fundraising events such as cricket matches. This allowed him to develop a space at the mosque for his role as a visiting preacher and a freelance teacher, a very different position from the two official Bangladeshi imams who have paid posts. Azzim's independent, freelance status, made possible by his job, was an important element in the way he conducted his life. It allowed him to be part of the rota of Friday preachers while retaining a critical distance from the religious views he disagreed with as well as the diversity of practices within the congregation.[5] It also gave him the freedom to devote time to informal and voluntary religious activities in various other places, including teaching Muslim students at a university near his work. He claimed no fee for the classes at the mosque, though the women organised a collection from time to time as a way of thanking him, and it seemed that his other activities also arose from his sense of the religious obligation to engage in *da'wa*.

The complexity of Azzim's position was apparent in the way he comported himself. Though he sometimes wore a white religious robe, he generally arrived for the classes dressed in ordinary casual attire with only a small white lace cap to indicate that he was Muslim. At the same time, there was a composure and a sense of purpose about him. His appearance contrasted with the obviously Islamic dress, beards, and styles of self-presentation of some other freelance preachers. Although I usually sat at the back of the women's balcony for Friday prayers, on one occasion, when I knew Azzim was preaching, I managed to position myself near the front railings. I was struck by the vulnerability of the position of an imam, standing alone in front of the men (whom I could not see), and by Azzim's quiet, unemphatic mode of delivery. Azzim's demeanour might be attributable to aspects of his personality, but it can also be linked to his stance towards Islam, his suspicion of those who seek to make themselves into intermediaries between ordinary Muslims and God, and the meaning to him of his chosen role as an independent preacher fulfilling the duty to undertake *da'wa*. In this, he saw his role and responsibility as being to set out plainly the nature of Islamic theology, not to persuade or to arouse others emotionally.

Having actively used the opportunities for study that had come his way, Azzim became committed to bringing his fellow Muslims back to an understanding of the core text of their religion and to the realisation that much of what they took to be Islam was the result of a proliferation of cultural traditions. His stance was characterised not only by its focus on the Quran but also by his confidence in his own ability to read and understand the text for himself. In keeping with this, Azzim saw his task as encouraging others to think for themselves about Islam.[6]

I first met Azzim at a Ramadan meal near the beginning of my fieldwork when he was only just thinking about setting up a class at the mosque. At this meeting, the fact that my research echoed his experience of continuing adult study gave us something in common. He seemed happy for me to join a class he was hoping to start if the venture got off the ground. During our conversation, he elaborated on this by referring to his experience, through his current job, of the value of 'a multi-disciplinary team'. Yet there is, of course, a huge gap between the sharing of different professional perspectives within a workplace and the idea of different perspectives on religion. So, though it was an opportunity for me to learn about Islam and, importantly, to observe others in the process of teaching and learning, I was aware that it also created some ambiguity about whether I would, in time, become a Muslim. However, if my presence as a non-Muslim in his class over two years was a source of ambiguity, and Azzim sometimes made comments about 'people who learn but don't change', he also commended my consistency and commitment to the class. And this recognition was mutual.

As with the task of building a mosque and sustaining a congregation, the dimension of time was relevant to the establishment of the weekly classes and the lectures he started to give to a group that met once a month. I frequently heard people exchanging information about different classes and groups across north London, and I sampled a few. As Huq (2008) indicates, practice-oriented classes and study circles are a global phenomenon, but I got the impression that many such groups started and then faded out. It became apparent that establishing and sustaining the necessary individual and collective commitment was not straightforward. For Azzim, being a teacher was a considerable outlay of time and effort. In fact, it was a family commitment, as he would sometimes drive over with his three young children, leaving them to mill about with the children of those attending the class; at other times, his wife came as well and looked after them or would oversee their Islamic studies elsewhere in the mosque. Azzim's efforts to maintain the weekly class and the monthly group continued through many setbacks. During the early months, there were some occasions when he and I would be waiting alone; on other days, the class that formed would be a completely different set of people from the week before. Eventually, a stable committed group became established.

A major point of contention for the religious study groups I encountered was whether they could involve both men and women. Azzim's venture in this mosque came into being because of an earlier failure on this front. He had been teaching a group of women in a small mosque in a neighbouring borough, a few of whom were Mauritians who sometimes attended the Guyanese mosque. Then the group came to the decision that they should become a 'women only' group so he could no longer be their teacher. I think Azzim might have preferred to teach a genuinely gender-mixed class but although he made various attempts to include men in the monthly lectures and succeeded to some extent, it was only ever women who joined the weekly Saturday class. This group of women seemed to have no problem with a male teacher.[7]

At first, Azzim's class at the mosque consisted of a rather disparate collection of young, single women, mostly Turkish, dressed in ordinary Western clothes and a headscarf. Their motivation was hard to pin down and their attendance was very erratic. Some seemed simply to have time on their hands, having finished college or university and not yet found a job. Certainly, there was none of the strongly expressed desire to know about their faith that I heard from the group that emerged later, and their existing knowledge of Islam seemed very slight.[8] However, despite repeated setbacks, after about a year, a group had formed with eight to ten members of whom a core of about six would attend regularly. They differed substantially from the earlier groups, being older, with children or jobs or both, and having come to the UK from different countries as adults. Unlike those who attended more general ritual and social events, they quite explicitly joined the class because of a wish to develop themselves as Muslims through study. It seemed that there was a much better match between what they were looking for and what Azzim had in mind, and, over time, they became a committed working group where difficult ideas and feelings could be discussed. But first, the foundations for this teaching and learning had to be created from scratch, covering not only the obligations and practice of Islam but also the task of learning to read, understand and recite the Quran, beginning with the Arabic alphabet, but not the memorisation of the text.

In his lectures and classes, Azzim questioned what his listeners had taken for granted. While some were unable to consider this question, others, particularly the women who attended the Saturday class became increasingly aware of their own practice. This set into motion a complex, mutually affecting engagement between Azzim and a class of Muslim adults who felt torn between the wish to be better Muslims, the living of their lives within British society, and the traditions of religious thinking they had grown up in and remained to some extent attached to. Yet despite Azzim's consistent adherence to a strict textual form of Islam and the clear distinction he made between Islamic theology based on God's revelation and culture and tradition as human creations (Boyle 2006), his teaching offered both the focus of a text and support for a process of learning. Drawing on the difficulties he felt he had encountered in developing his religious understanding in Guyana and his active participation in a wider, non-Muslim society in London, his classes created a space for others to learn about Islam – a space over which he did not have, and did not seem to seek, any real control. He saw his responsibility as being to teach; it was then the responsibility of the individuals in the class to decide whether and how to use what they had learned.

Getting 'the basics' right

In contrast to the piecemeal human struggle out of which the class, as a working group, gradually emerged and the complicated encounter with his ideas that took place there, Azzim insisted on the simplicity, logic, and coherence of Islam. A pivotal issue in his thinking was the ontological separation of the Creator from his creation that restricts contact between the human and the divine to the study of the revelation of God's will in the Quran. The contradiction between this and the unpredictability and ambiguity of human life surfaced frequently in the classes and had to be managed while remaining ultimately irresolvable for the class, who were mostly unable to fully adopt Azzim's viewpoint. He firmly maintained that Islam's basic concepts – the unitary nature, or oneness of God (*towheed*), and God as external to his creation – were straightforwardly accessible to reason rather than dependent on passional modes of apprehension, which he regarded as leading to self-indulgence and wish fulfilment. For Azzim, it was the widespread lack of clarity with respect to these two concepts about the nature of God, and their implications, that gave rise to confusion and error in both the thinking and practice of many Muslims. Though he might sometimes correct something someone had said, it was more usual for him to prompt questions concerning the implications of a practice: 'What concept underlies this (practice)?' and 'What are you really saying?' Though he did not always succeed, Azzim sought to encourage others to think about Islam by building up a logical argument about the nature of God and looking at Muslim ideas and practices in the light of it.

Azzim insisted on the logical necessity that you cannot both create something and be located within what you have created. From this, he maintained it followed that 'Allah is not in the world in any way whatsoever', and that Allah could not be envisaged imaginatively since he is not like any humanly perceived object. For Azzim, knowledge of the conceptual structure and grammatical articulations of the Quran, rather than feeling or imagining a relationship with God on the model of human emotional intimacy, formed the only sound basis for a religious life. He saw these central tenets – the oneness and radical otherness of God – as engulfed by religious currents among Muslims that flowed continuously in the opposite direction, pulling the divine back into the domain of the material and the human. His concern to re-establish an idea of God as outside Creation echoes the 'work of purification' that sought to free Protestant Christianity from the materiality of ritual and dependence on religious mediators between the individual soul and God (Keane 2007: 23–25). For Azzim, to treat the Quran as if its material form, a book within the human world, was itself to be equated with the divine revelation was, at best, confusion and at worst, idolatry. However, in the classes, the power of the immanent and the material kept reasserting itself. From the point of view of Azzim's reforming project, the experiences that emerged in the classes were a concrete manifestation of the impediments to 'the work of purification'. He found it necessary to counter repeatedly, and in different ways, what he saw as misconceptions. However, Azzim was inhabiting the same human world as those in the class and a different perspective would occasionally emerge in the challenge of the moment that was neither that of a transcendent divine revelation nor that of an embodied taken for granted tradition but a view that integrated, momentarily, the rational and the bodily and emotional in a thoughtful human response. While this was consistent with the distinction between what is specified in Islam with respect to worship and religious obligations and what has been left unspecified with respect to everyday life, they were often none the less moments of moral creativity.

Azzim's theological stance and these moments of unexpected integration can be seen in the context of the long history of secular scientific preoccupation with the nature of the relationship between the rational and the embodied within human experience, both the connectedness of these modalities and the inherent tension between them. Marsden describes the way Chitrali villagers in Pakistan expressed anxiety about the potential destructiveness of a failure to maintain the proper balance between the rational and the affective that was needed for a mindful Muslim life (Marsden 2005: 262). Something of this unstable but unavoidable paradox was apparent in Azzim's class, but never itself became an object of thought though it was implicit in the individual stance of some in the classes.[9]

The Saturday afternoon class brought questions indicative of the women's preoccupation with detailed issues of practice and the dilemmas of the everyday, often in a spirit of anxiety. These concerns were about the validity of variations in the movements of prayer, enquiries about whether one could attend weddings where one of the parties was not Muslim, and whether men and women could exchange Islamic greetings. Azzim repeatedly responded in terms of the need to get the 'foundations' right, without which, he implied, their many highly specific questions would not lead to the development of a capacity to think for themselves about the underlying issues. To many questions, such as one about a sleeping position that was said to be religiously favoured, he replied that 'it was a pity that very weak *hadith*[10] were drilled into us [when we were young] while substantial things were ignored'.

Azzim regularly challenged what he felt to be the widespread confusion about the radical separation between Allah and humankind and the assumptions of immanence implicit in certain widespread understandings among the women, such as 'God is everywhere'. Thus, an often-quoted reference in the Quran to 'Allah being closer [to you] than your jugular vein' (50: 16) was generally understood by the class and by other groups I attended to mean that God was everywhere. Azzim would challenge this as based on an assumption of a literal physical presence, whereas, he maintained, Allah is 'present in creation [only] through his abstract qualities', as expressed in the ninety-nine names of Allah. From Azzim's standpoint, the correct understanding of the 'closer than your jugular vein' quotation was, therefore, that Allah is omniscient, and his *knowledge* is everywhere. Similarly, as he put it, 'Allah is not *in* creation; he *is* creation'. Azzim felt this distinction was essential to avoid slipping into a view of God as physically present and from there to a confusion between the nature of God and the nature of humankind. Azzim's stance is captured by Lambek (2000: 318) when writing about ethics – 'while I have privileged Aristotle over Plato it may well be that Plato's model is closer to the way some religions themselves operate, setting off a transcendent or ideal unchanging order from the mundane flux of everyday life'.

Studying of the Quran as the only link to God

There were discussions among the women about their experience of belief (*iman*), but Azzim countered this with the view that such feelings were subject to inevitable vicissitudes, and for this reason, it was only knowledge of the divine revelation that could provide a secure basis for a Muslim life. This focus was sharpened through his descriptions of his encounters with Christians who, he said, described elements of their theology, such as the Trinity, as being 'a mystery' or referred to their 'feeling' of being saved as the basis for their expectation of paradise. Azzim felt this was completely unsatisfactory. He held that the foundational premises of Islam could be understood rationally as a scientific reality without resort to faith with its association to the holistic grasping of 'a mystery' beyond rational thought and its associated ontological confusions. He stressed that Islam is rooted in what are and will ultimately be shown to be scientifically provable realities. As an example, Azzim pointed out a reference in the Quran to the 'two easts' as something puzzling until one thinks of the fact that the sun rises and sets at different points throughout the year – the reference to 'two' being explained as indicating the two most extreme points of difference during the year.

Like the unity of God, the divine revelation was a coherent whole and the Quran contained no contradictions. However, Azzim did not specify whether the basis for this claim was empirical or whether it logically followed from a prior acceptance of its divine origin. Unlike the Shi'a Muslims in Deeb's study, who distinguish between that which is premised on faith, the existence of God, and that which is open to rational enquiry – the nature of a God-given order (2006: 27), Azzim made no such distinction. Thus, he did not say that if one has accepted that the Quran is God's revelation, then it must follow that it is without internal contradiction and any apparent contradictions must be due to human misreading but rather *since* the Quran is without contradiction, it must be of divine origin as no humanly produced text could attain such perfect coherence. Azzim discussed passages of apparent contradiction and gave explanations which sometimes drew on the precise grammar of the language. One such example concerned God's command to all the angels to bow down to Adam 'except Iblis [Satan]' (2: 34 and 18: 50). He explained that this can be misunderstood to mean that, as in Christian theology, Satan is a fallen angel. However, in another *ayah* in the Quran, Iblis is said to be a *jinn*.[11] This could therefore be taken to constitute a contradiction, but Azzim carefully explained that while the phrase *'except* Iblis' would, in English, imply that Iblis was an angel, this he said is not the case in the Arabic construction (*ilaa*). Though the women found the grammatical basis of such an explanation difficult to follow, the point that there was no contradiction in the Quran, and could be none, was easy to grasp, yet they did not abandon completely taking their emotional responses as a compass to steer by.

Resisting the pull of the human

Though Azzim's conception of God as intrinsically and absolutely separate from the created world was the primary source of the theological imperative to purify religious understanding and practice of human materiality, he also maintained that the widespread lack of such a separation brought mundane difficulties in its wake. For him, it was the culturally elaborated errors and additions that made Islam into a religion that its ordinary members could not understand, so that they required others, with claims to special knowledge, to tell them what to do. Imams, sheiks, and 'saints' set themselves up as intermediaries between the believer and God based on their own claim to piety and the use of other books and devotional literature written in other languages in place of simple and direct access to God's revelation, the Quran. This, in turn, led to the transformation of optional practices into burdensome additional obligations and created, in place of a universal community of Muslims, enclaves of social, cultural, and racial exclusivity which he maintained was a violation of Islam as a revelation for all. The women in the class readily supplied examples of these phenomena both locally and in their home countries.

Azzim explained to the class that the on-going growth of cultural traditions since the Prophet breached both the principles with respect to worship, the form of which is limited to what has been clearly specified, and the freedom of daily life, except for particular prohibitions. This had led to two related forms of transgression: the proliferation of forms of religious ritual and devotional practices that are not part of the practice of the Prophet and the development of additional prohibitions that are not founded on an explicit textual prohibition, such as the view that music is forbidden. As a result, over time, the forms of Islam in different cultural traditions, shaped by local circumstances and the exercise of human will, have made it difficult for Muslims to distinguish the 'basic tenets' of their religion and left them prey to social norms at odds with Islam.[12]

Azzim insisted that no claim to a special relationship to God, to being a 'friend of God' (*wali*), could be legitimately made because, like piety, the relationship of *wali* only existed between God and the individual. In his suspicion of an emotionally driven form of religiosity, he told of Muslims who had suddenly taken on excessive additional religious practice rather than slowly building up their commitment; then, finding it impossible to sustain extreme levels of practice, they had then given up Islam altogether. For Azzim, this failure to sustain a religious life had to do with taking the desire to *feel* pious as a religious aim in itself. He was also critical of Muslims whom he characterised as loud in stating their views but ignorant of the most basic aspects of their religion: 'They don't know the *faraid* of *wudu* [the obligatory forms of ritual ablution] but they want to establish a caliphate'. It was, by implication, only proper knowledge of 'the basics' that could moderate the pull of human emotional needs and impulses, whether expressed as individualised piety or political action.

Azzim did not regard his theology as an expression of personal feelings, as they were for many others I encountered. For him, the revelation of Islam must be grasped intellectually through constant study rather than absorbed without reflection from an environment of lived religious practices or as ideas cut loose from the textual framework of a revelation and handed down informally within families and communities or over the internet. He talked as if his own understanding arose solely and directly from reading the Quran. Though he was, no doubt, influenced by his year of study in Saudi Arabia; he almost never referred to it. This accentuated the sense of the Quran as an object which could be grasped intellectually by an individual given sufficient effort to understand the language of the revelation. It was a link to the divine that was free from both human feelings and culture.

Since the world, all human beings and the *jinn* were created by God and all are therefore Muslim, all other religious traditions are departures from an original natural sense of God. Unlike many other Guyanese, for whom Christianity is a kindred tradition, Azzim saw Christian thinking and Sufi-influenced forms of Islam as alike built on the erroneous conceptions of God as being *within* creation – *within* us – and ideas of a union with God or even the possibility of our becoming *like* God. Yet, as he pointed out, these sorts of ideas were widespread among Muslims too. Troubling thoughts were stirred up in the class as to how such errors might have arisen and this discomfort was expressed in different ways. One of the women said, 'This was how our parents brought us up to think when we were children'. An older woman in the group was prone, at such moments, to say, 'We got these ideas from the Hindus [in the sub-continent before partition]'. By contrast, a young Mauritian woman with children anxiously contemplated her own part in the dissemination of error when she admitted, 'I have always told my children that God is everywhere'. Though he conveyed a robust sense of being able to live as a Muslim within a non-Muslim society, Azzim thought that these errors came originally from contact with non-Muslims rather than having their source in human nature. Since he saw humankind as originally both innocent and Muslim, the currents of misconception that flowed through Muslim communities, as they did through the class, could not be understood as having their source in the nature of humankind.

Seeing the hidden presence of idolatry in its various mundane manifestations was a recurring theme in Azzim's classes and sermons. Since there are no other sources of divine power and no favoured intermediaries to intercede for humankind, one should rely only on God in case of need. He explained that this did not mean you should not take practical steps to help yourself, for example, by seeking medical treatment in the case of illness. It was the use of material objects, as if their efficacy stemmed from 'religious' power located in them, that was idolatrous (*shirk*) since this was based on human beings trying to take control of power that belongs only to God. At one end of the spectrum, this error might be the sale and use of little religious objects, such as the tiny Qurans on sale in the mosque shop and frequently to be seen hanging over the dashboard of cars parked near the mosque. Azzim felt that it was essential to be clear whether this was merely intended to be decorative, in which case it was permitted but point-less since they were too small to read as some decorative inscriptions on wall hangings might be read, or whether the object was supposed to have power, in and of itself, in which case it was idolatry. Azzim was systematic in trying to clar-ify the real reasons for even such apparently small matters as these little Qurans, as he felt that it was through these areas of unexamined ambiguity that serious religious confusion, superstition, and idolatry was spread among Muslims. A question raised in class about the ritual in which a Quran is held over the head of a bride was met with the response from Azzim that 'it needs to be inside her head not over it!' Otherwise, he said, 'you could just fill your house with Qurans without reading them'. Equally idolatrous, in Azzim's view, was the tendency to use Quranic verses to generate new ritual forms (*bid'a*), or their inscription on objects designed to bring about events in the world, as 'medicines', 'love potions' or to ward off *jinn*. This was something he knew about from experience and, although the way he had told the story, in Chapter 2 about trying to find a job in Guyana was from the perspective of error, no doubt, at the time, his need for a tangible intervention had been great, and it was only afterwards that he came to the view that he must put his trust only in Allah.

The presence of *jinn* as an invisible, parallel creation was a very active, real, and frightening idea for many of the women in the group. Although Azzim accepted both the existence of *jinn* as part of creation and the legitimate forms of prayerful supplication to God for protection as practiced by the Prophet, he was critical of the widely held view among Muslims that the *jinn* are a powerful force in human lives. Beyond their legitimate place within Islam's view of creation, Azzim felt many Muslims accorded the *jinn* a space that implied an infringement of the integrity of human agency. Rather than being passively at their mercy, he insisted that the *jinn* only had access to human affairs if human beings themselves allowed them entry. He argued that if we were not clear about this, we might use the *jinn* to evade responsibility for our own wishes and actions – 'the *jinn* made me do it' – as well as giving rise to the need for special, humanly improvised, ritual measures against them. In a similar vein, he maintained that these confusions, innovations, and idolatrous practices were the result of an inability to trust in God alone that was widespread among Muslims, despite the frequent invocation of the name of Allah in Arabic greetings and interjections that were interspersed by some in conversation, though not often among those in the class. There was an implication that such interjections might give a misleading impression of piety and trust in Allah. He often spoke about the willingness of Muslims to be taken in by appearances rather than substance. He maintained that a good Muslim name, the right kind of beard and pious dress was enough to convince many people that you were a good Muslim. In his view, this reliance on appearances betokened a lack of trust in Allah and led instead to a willingness to rely on religious leaders of various sorts who used these external trappings of piety to gather dependent followers, to set up shrines and dispense idolatrous material objects for money. He also felt there was a serious confusion in the minds of some people between God and Mohammed. In an appalled tone, he quoted those who said that if you removed the veil covering the face of God you would see the face of Mohammed. The widespread desire to 'see', going back, as Azzim pointed out, to Moses' desire to see God was, he implied, based on a misconception about the nature of God and the limitation of human senses before the power of God. He argued that such misconceptions also led to dreams being given a misplaced status by many Muslims. He spoke of a *hadith* in which the Prophet said to the *sahaba* [his companions] that if he appeared to them in a dream, they should trust that it was him; this had since become generalised to include everyone's dreams. After telling this story, Azzim paused to see if people understood why this extension of the *hadith* was an error. He then explained that while the *sahaba* knew what Mohammed looked like, we do not, so we have no way of knowing that it is not *shaitan* [Satan] who appears in the dream. An active awareness of both our human impulses and the threat posed by *shaitan* was needed if human agency and judgement were not to be subverted.

One Friday in a sermon, Azzim spoke about a widespread tendency to speak of the 'miracle of the Quran' as if, as he put it, in doing so, people were conferring a special status on themselves as Muslims by association. He linked this phenomenon with the tendency for great excitement to be caused by the appearance of the name of Mohammed in the internal structure of a tomato or an aubergine, as if this was also a miracle. He insisted that the Quran was there to be studied and if there was a miracle, then the miracle was in the language of the revelation, not in the book itself [as a material object]. During one of the classes, he talked of how people put great store by treating the book of the Quran with respect, putting it in a high place, not on the floor, but that this was mistaken. The book itself was not what should be respected. The original revelation was not a book. It was, he said, like thinking your respect for your mother was shown by putting her picture on a high shelf rather than in the way you treated her. For Azzim, this confusion underlay the supposed prohibition against a menstruating woman touching the Quran. He insisted that the reference to the purity of the Quran concerned only the original book of the revelation and referred to the permanent state of purity of the angels who surround it. However, despite the otherwise rather challenging attitudes of some of the women in the class, this opinion about menstruation did not seem to settle the matter for them. Though Azzim would say firmly that there was no reason for a menstruating woman not to touch a copy of the Quran and, indeed, that he thought menstruation was a difficult time when a woman might be particularly in need of the Quran, the question would often resurface as if the class shared a residual doubt on the matter.

Despite teaching the need to free oneself from the human cultural forms that masqueraded as Islam, Azzim would often acknowledge a natural tendency to do as our parents did. However, on the Last Day, each person would be responsible for themselves and their own practice. It would be no good saying that others had guided you. He sometimes referred to his admiration for reverts (converts) who had to undergo a particularly severe form of rupture from their family backgrounds. He felt that they were not usually welcomed by other Muslims as they should be and must feel very isolated. Such discussions evoked many painful questions in the class about the spiritual safety of family members. Azzim tended, if pressed, to say that, of course, one did not know how things stood between an individual and Allah while at the same time maintaining firmly that some element of practice and belief, described by a member of the group in relation to a family member, was not part of Islam. He was also of the view that you only needed to deny one of the core tenets of Islam to cease to be a Muslim. He said that you could practice in all respects, but if you maintained, for example, that we would not be judged on the Last Day, that denial negated everything else. Thus, Azzim moved between a pragmatic attitude and a firm line on what was required – or rather what he felt was required of himself since he made it clear that in teaching them, he had done his duty and it was for the women to decide and act for themselves. During one such discussion, he asked a young woman why she was staring at him, and she replied, 'Because you scare me'. It seemed to have been the uncompromising aspect of Azzim's religious thinking with its spare approach to theology that he sought to separate off from a context of family commitments and human feelings that had frightened her. Yet if one aspect of his thinking aimed to purify and abstract religious concepts from their embedding in the complexities and vicissitudes of life, another aspect was his willingness to think about human failures, provided fundamental religious concepts were not at stake.

'A thinking mind'

Azzim sought to present his theology as logical, definite, and unchanging, dis-embedded from a human context; Allah was to be known through study of his revelation and by means of rational thought and worshipped through a form of practice rooted in this knowledge. Yet study itself is a human activity and there is an inevitable tension between the nature of God as an object of perfect coherence and logic and the idea of study as a never completed process founded in the inherent uncertainty and incompleteness of human forms of knowing. The classes themselves enacted this gap between divine perfection and the imperfect struggle to learn in the women's continuing attempts to bring the reality of their lives to bear on the process. Yet just as de Koning (2013) describes the struggles of ordinary Muslims in the Netherlands as bringing to life the otherwise rigid and unfulfillable demands of Dutch Salafi organisations, so the classes created a space for live human contact, allowing the concerns and challenges of the women to sometimes evoke a new and different response from Azzim.

When sufficient members of the class had gathered, and Azzim judged it time to begin, he recited, in a low voice, a brief prayer in Arabic. The class ended in a similar way.[13] The implication of this framing was made explicit when someone in the class asked about an often-repeated idea that those who died while on *hajj* went straight to paradise. Without either endorsing or rejecting this view,[14] Azzim responded by elaborating on the idea that paradise was the reward for the giving of our time to the worship of Allah, in which he included attendance at classes and the struggle to learn. Here his response opened up what had been a rather rigid question that had invited a binary answer. Instead of a 'straight to paradise' reply, what the class heard was an answer that took in the idea of a religious struggle that needed to be sustained over time. An important but unacknowledged dimension of Azzim's religious thinking emerged in such moments when he did not accept the restrictions of a question and responded from the larger perspective of a religiously committed life.

If the effortful nature of learning was all too clear to the women, Azzim often referred to the pleasure of using one's mind. His own struggle to learn and the pleasure he got, and continued to get, from 'learning something new every day' were part of his conviction that what you needed to live as a Muslim in the present was 'a questioning attitude' and a 'thinking mind'. This created an image of a continuous flow of living, questioning, and thinking reminiscent of the work of William James cited by Crapanzano (2004: 18) – a thinking mind embedded within the unfolding, unfinished, open-endedness of human experience in contrast both to the conceptual structures of abstract thought and the complete and perfect nature of the divine revelation. Such 'a thinking mind' was to be developed through a continuing process of study rather than the acquisition of knowledge in childhood or after a period of attendance at adult classes. Through this lens, knowledge was something that had to be meaningfully lived and developed through on-going experience. In a discussion about the scene in the grave, in which an angel is said to ask the recently deceased person who they had worshipped and which prophet they had followed in life, Azzim took issue with the usual account of this scene as it seemed to assume that the angel was seeking simply 'a correct answer' rather than an understanding of what had, in fact, guided the dead person during their lifetime. He said, otherwise, 'perhaps we should just put a piece of paper with the answers on it in with the body!'

Seeing Azzim speak in different settings, in the classes, at Friday prayers, and in lectures, it was apparent that at any onetime certain issues that preoccupied him were being worked on and would then be presented in different places. He identified with the task of teaching and seemed to know that he had some talent for it, while his own commitment to learning was central to his impact on the Saturday class. The link between Azzim's presence as a teacher and the process of learning that it sustained within the class can be understood as the taking in of live qualities that become, through identification, the resources needed to encounter new situations and the emotional capacity to learn from experience.[15] The sustained contact offered by a class, in contrast to the one-off contact of a lecture, provided the opportunities for these processes to become established.

Azzim never referred to imagination as a reliable or valuable element in a religious life, rather the contrary. Yet his many references to the development of 'a thinking mind' evoked a quite different image of learning to think for oneself from that expressed in the certainty of logical relations within a conceptual system as the only possible form of contact with the abstract qualities of a divinity outside creation. The idea of 'a thinking mind' suggested images of an organic process of absorbing and reflecting on new experiences akin to the processes of respiration, digestion – or of circulation as in Pelkmans' (2017: 103) description of the 'pulsations' of affective commitment to collective ideas and a group endeavour. Azzim's use of language and whether it conveyed an abstract or an embodied form of knowing shifted according to whether his referent was the divine revelation of the Quran or a Muslim life engaged in various ways with the world that fell outside what was specified in Islam. With respect to the former, he generally presented an implacable stance, yet there were times in the class when the impact of an emotional situation brought an unchanging transcendent order and the painful vicissitudes of daily life into contact within a 'thinking mind'.

Azzim said that he had a friend in Guyana, whom he referred to as a 'very good imam'. From other things he said, I assumed he meant that this man was not motivated by pride or greed as he clearly felt some imams were. However, he went on to say that 'his education level is zero and yet he is teaching [other] Muslims ... of course the quality of information [he is passing on] is poor'. He did not complete this account as he was interrupted, but it carried the implication that though this man's religious knowledge was poor, his motivation was not self-serving, and this gave a certain moral value to his presence as an imam. The woman who interrupted about the poor level of education said it was just like that in Mauritius: 'If you fail in your academic studies, they send you to study the Quran'. Azzim replied, 'it's because they think it's easier but actually it's more technically demanding'. He added that 'unfortunately most of our scholars have no knowledge of other academic fields and that's a big problem. You need knowledge of both [kinds]'. Another member of the group asked, 'How many people want their children to be an Islamic scholar? They want them to be doctors'. To this Azzim replied that 'any knowledge that benefits *is* Islamic'. In this exchange, Azzim created a space for ordinary human qualities, the uneducated man who is nonetheless, in some respects, 'a good imam'. Though he challenges the assumption among Muslims that religious study is easy and not something to be highly valued such that parents prefer their children to become doctors, he does so by evoking a larger context – an Islamic approach to *all* knowledge linked to the idea that *all* creation is naturally Muslim. All knowledge is, therefore, good, and all correct knowledge is Islamic. This way of reasoning – the valuing of 'secular' scientific knowledge by encompassing it *within* the scope of Islam – was different from that with respect to the possibility of an imam who knew little being nonetheless 'a good imam' by including his human qualities in the consideration. However, both moves gave a sense of his mind at work and contrast with the drawing of sharp distinctions described earlier, where the space for thought was reduced by Azzim's insistence on one correct interpretation of practice to the point where the young woman said, 'you scare me'. Here the concerns of the group found a wider, more encompassing mental space in which ordinary reflective capacity had a place.

If Azzim generally adopted the language of evidence and logical reasoning, at other times, he spoke as if the divine nature of the Quran could be perceived through its aesthetic qualities. He would refer to the beauty of the language, the elegance of the grammar, and the musicality of its recitation by those who knew how. He was critical of the speed with which some imams led the prayers and spoke of the time required between each movement for the mind to focus and the bodily process of prayer to have its proper impact. Through an idea of the complexity of a whole human life, he responded in a rather striking way to a member of the class who was worried about the situation of a couple in her extended family who were living together but were not married. He said that though this was *zina* [the sin of unlawful intercourse] it was not the whole of their lives, implying that it was possible that there were areas of their lives in which they were living in accordance with Islam. This might be seen as at odds with his assertion that any negation of the basic tenets of Islam rendered one a non-Muslim, but there was no indication that the couple was denying the validity of Islam, only failing to fulfil its demands. Here Azzim was talking of human living in a way that evoked the idea of the time and space of 'a whole life' and the possibility that the perspective of God's judgments could not be anticipated by human beings.

Notes

1 In their variable and informal organisation, the adult classes at the mosque more closely resembled a large number of madrassas attended after school and at weekends by Muslim children, who are otherwise educated within the mainstream educational system.

2 Wesselhoeft (2010) describes the teaching of a freelance imam in Paris and the independent quality of his thinking about the predicaments of Muslims who sought his opinion.

3 From a text accessible to ordinary people only through memorisation (Eickelman 1978) at the beginning of the last century, through mass education, migration, and globalisation, the Quran became a source of religious knowledge available to a wider population Eickelman (1992, 2000).

4 Jouili (2015) links the difficulties encountered by her informants to the political cultures in France and Germany that created inhospitable environments for Muslims seeking to develop their religious practice. Whereas the Netherlands, the UK, or Sweden, where more 'multi-cultural' policies have been pursued in the past, have been more open to Muslim difference she suggests this situation may be changing.

5 This seemed mainly to do with officiating at rituals for the sick or the dead that he deemed to have no basis in the Quran and the sunnah and being involved in marriages based on family pressure or on the merely nominal conversion of one party.

6 Islamic scholarship has sought to reconcile the implicit freedom of human rationality with submission to God's revelation, seeing both acquired and revealed knowledge as divine in origin (Halstead 2004; Sayyid 2006).

7 It is hard to know what inhibited the development of a mixed group. When some men eventually joined the Sunday lectures, probably mainly the husbands of women who already attended, they were markedly less open to the ideas Azzim introduced than the women.

8 However, one of the members of this group who dropped out early on greeted me some time later in the mosque, dressed entirely in black, her face completely covered, and wearing black gloves.

9 Connolly (2006) looks to Spinoza to explore the relationship between the 'higher and lower' registers of experience. The neuroscientist McGilchrist (2010) describes the inherently problematic relationship between the abstracting function of the left hemisphere of the brain and the right hemisphere's openness to the direct impact of unprocessed bodily experience as giving rise to a predicament in which the right-hemisphere capacities needed to live an embodied life in the world are continuously and inevitably undermined by the claims to clarity and certainty that come with abstract, left hemisphere rationality. Within psychoanalytic thinking, the capacities of embodied *and* symbolic modes of functioning have been thought of as two fundamental human states that shift from one to the other throughout life under the impact of raw external and internal events and the potential, but uncertain, capacity of the mind to contain these impingements and transform them through thought into experience (Britton 2001).

10 Collected accounts of the practice and pronouncements of the Prophet that differ in their reliability.

11 The *jinn* are a separate part of creation that has free will like humankind and so were capable of behaving contrary to God's will.

12 Azzim referred particularly to patriarchal power that had eroded the rights given to women by the Prophet.

13 This was in addition to the collective afternoon prayer that would fall at some (variable) point during the class.

14 He was sometimes very tactful and careful not to provoke dispute, but it was unclear whether this was a matter of mood or part of a larger understanding within which the point at issue was deemed insufficiently important for an overt disagreement.

15 The psychoanalyst Wilfred Bion (1962) used the phrase 'learning from experience' to indicate the capacity to learn from the *impact* of experience and the changes this made in the 'learner', the time it took and the anxiety it stirred up, as opposed to learning *about* something which did not include these internal processes.

References

Bion, W. (1962) *Learning from Experience*. London: Heinemann.

Boyle, H. (2006) 'Memorization and learning in Islamic schools', *Comparative Education Review* 50(3): 478–495.

Britton, R. (2001) 'Beyond the Depressive Position: Ps (n+1)', in Bronstein, C. (ed) *Kleinian Theory: A Contemporary Perspective*. London: Whurr.

Connolly, W. (2006) 'Europe: A Minor Tradition', in Scott, D. and Hirschkind, C. (eds) *Powers of the Secular Modern*. Stanford: Stanford University Press.

Crapanzano, V. (2004) *Imaginative Horizons*. Chicago: Chicago University Press.

Deeb, L. (2006) *An Enchanted Modern: Gender and Public Piety in Shi'a Lebanon*. Princeton: Princeton University Press.

de Koning, M. (2013) 'The moral maze: Dutch Salafis and the construction of a moral community of the faithful', *Contemporary Islam* 7: 71–84.

Eickelman, D. F. (1978) 'The art of memory: Islamic Education and its social reproduction', *Comparative Studies in Society and History* 20(4): 485–516.

Eickelman, D. F. (1992) 'Mass higher education and the religious imagination in contemporary Arab societies', *American Ethnologist* 19(4): 643–655.

Eickelman, D. F. (2000) 'Islam and the languages of modernity', *Daedelus* 129(1): 119–135.

Halstead, M. (2004) 'An Islamic concept of education', *Comparative Education* 40(4): 517–529.

Huq, M. (2008) 'Reading the Qur'an in Bangladesh' Modern Asian Studies: the politics of belief among Islamist women', *Modern Asian Studies* 48(2/3): 457–488.

Jouili, J. (2015) *Pious Practice and Secular Constraints*. Stanford: Stanford University Press.

Keane, W. (2007) *Christian Moderns: Freedom and Fetish in the Mission Encounter*. Berkeley: University of California Press.

Lambek, M. (2000) 'The anthropology of religion and the quarrel between poetry and philosophy', *Current Anthropology* 41: 3.

Mandaville, P. (2007) 'Globalization and the politics of religious knowledge; pluralising authority in the Muslim world', *Theory, Culture and Society* 24(2): 101–115.

Marsden, M. (2005) *Living Islam: Muslim Religious Experience in Pakistan's North-West Frontier*. Cambridge: Cambridge University Press.

McGilchrist, I. (2010) *The Master and His Emissary: The Divided Brain and the Making of the Western World*. New Haven: Yale University Press.

Pelkmans, M.E. (2017) *Fragile Convictions*. New York: Cornell University Press.

Roy, O. (2004) *Globalised Islam: The Search for a New Ummah*. London: Hurst and Co.

Roy, O. (2007) *Secularism Confronts Islam*. New York: Columbia University Press.

Sayyid, S. (2006) 'Islam and knowledge', *Theory, Culture and Society* 23(2–3): 177–179.

Wesselhoeft, K. (2010) 'Making Muslim minds: Question and answers as a genre of moral reasoning in an urban French mosque', *Journal of the American Academy of Religion* 78(3): 790–823.

8

ENCOUNTERING NEW FORMS OF RELIGIOUS THINKING

PART 1 – DIFFERENT GROUPS; DIFFERENT EXPECTATIONS

For many of the Guyanese, and those associated closely with them, being a Muslim was experienced as the unproblematic outcome of having grown up in a Muslim community such that the nature of what it is to be an adult is to be a Muslim adult (Berliner and Sarro 2007: 5). Yet the more self-conscious theological currents that are increasingly present within Islam were also present in the mosque. This chapter describes the groups that Azzim taught at the mosque; the difficulties for many in taking in his theological ideas; and the complicated feelings of confusion, loss, and anxiety that were stirred up in those who tried. More traditional religious assumptions within the congregation as to what could, and should, be known by ordinary Muslims were apparent in the 'Sisters' Circle' and a lecture that followed it at which Azzim spoke – giving a sense of the background from which the Saturday class emerged. It has been suggested that the emergence of new forms of religiosity needs to be seen as taking place over time and in the context of competing life demands and the experience of ambivalence and failure (Schielke 2009). Different ways of engaging with a complex society (Fadil 2013; Shively 2014) and individual modes of accommodating to life in Europe may include not only adaptations of Muslim practice but also non-practice and the adoption of other forms of spirituality (Fadil 2011; Jeldtoft 2011). Yet if the classes brought to the fore feelings of ambivalence and doubt and conflicting commitments, they also brought a measure of religious development.

A Sisters' Circle, led by women for women, met once a month on Sundays and was largely devoted to the encouragement of pious feelings as something natural and within the compass of all. During my fieldwork, Azzim began to give a lecture in the second half of their meeting, and later some men joined in for some of these lectures. However, the audience for both the first and second half of these

DOI: 10.4324/9781003080008-8

meetings was variable, giving them the character of a series of individual events rather than constituting an on-going context of study that the weekly Saturday class came eventually to provide. Azzim presented his theological position in the lectures just as he did in the class, but the idea that an individual might take responsibility for their own religious knowledge was difficult for the lecture audience to engage with. Though the obvious barrier was a text in a language that no one except Azzim could read, it was also, Azzim insisted, connected to a particular attitude widespread among Muslims – an attitude of passivity and dependence on the mediation of religious specialists that he sometimes referred to as 'sheep following sheep'.[1] By contrast, Azzim saw real religious knowledge as requiring active engagement and regular study. Perhaps because he had mastered Arabic on his own, he glossed over the impediments to achieving this. The requirement of active study that Azzim envisaged was only met within the weekly Saturday class, where there was an effort to learn Arabic as the precondition for accessing the Quran. There was also in the class a more substantial engagement with Azzim's ideas and more of a struggle with the implications of his theology that reduced the gap that Woodhead ([2013] 2016) suggests must inevitably exist between an everyday form of lived religion and scriptural authority. Though experiences of 'ambivalence, incoherence and failure', that Osella and Soares (2010: 11) suggest should have a place in studies of ordinary religious lives, were present within all these groups, it was only in the Saturday class that these feelings could be consciously acknowledged and reflected on. The account of the Saturday class builds on work with Muslim women who feel able to voice 'controversial and often decidedly individual opinions' (Marsden 2008: 426), the range of attitudes towards practice and non-practice expressed by individual Muslim women in Europe (Fadil 2011, 2013; Jeldtoft 2011) and the complicated responses of Dutch Muslims, both men and women, to Salafi ideas (de Koning 2013) that arise from the fact that those who are Muslim also live with other commitments and among non-Muslims.[2]

The process of learning that I both observed and participated in was a complicated and multi-layered transformation generated through the embodied processes of apprenticeship learning (Marchand 2010), the internalisation of relationships (Lambek 2007), and the subtlety of what it means to experience a sense of understanding (Berliner and Sarro 2007). Cognitive, emotional, and imaginative qualities are transformed and integrated into the experience as new capacities such that living and knowing are the same thing (cf Toren 1993).[3] From this perspective, learning is inherently and profoundly emotional and relational, whether in the struggle to cling to the idea of a religious specialist as I will describe in the lectures or in the hopes and expectations that the women brought to the classes. Within the class, this process of learning involved the attempt to assimilate Azzim's view of Islam with its new religious ontology of transcendence and the idea of thinking for themselves. By contrast, those involved in the more limited didactic experience of a lecture seemed to find themselves faced with something it was too difficult to engage with.[4]

The Sisters' Circle

The monthly Sunday afternoon meetings of the Sisters' Circle were led by two Mauritian women and attracted an ethnically mixed group of individuals mainly of Mauritian, Guyanese, Somali, and Ugandan origin. They were drawn from grandparental and parental generations, the latter sometimes accompanied by their children. At its maximum, there could be 20 women present, but attendance was variable, as was the religious knowledge and engagement of those who turned up. A phone list was kept of those who had attended in the past, and sometimes women would ring around to try and encourage people to come. The purpose of the group seemed to be both religious and social, an opportunity for women to get together and to make use of the mosque as a space that was open to them. As one Somali woman explained to me, women did not attend the mosque in Somalia so being welcome in this mosque was one of the benefits of her new life in London, which she was keen to use. This contrasted with both the lack of facilities for women in many UK mosques and the widespread feelings of being unwelcome (Shannahan 2014).

One of the women who led this group often gave a talk on a religious theme that expressed a view of piety as a state of feeling that could be fostered by emotionally toned images of relatedness to God as immanent in the human world.

On one occasion, she spoke evocatively about a part of the night, in the early hours of the morning, when prayer is especially rewarded: "God comes down to meet us so as to help those who pray in the night".[5] She spoke of God as wanting to listen to our prayers and wanting to offer help. She went on to elaborate on the different states of need people might be experiencing and then exclaimed that "here is God coming towards us, but who is taking advantage of this opportunity?" Another woman joined in to stress the marvel of this situation: "a chance which is wasted if we are not there praying at this special hour". Another contributor expressed this expectation of reciprocity between God and the believer: "If we go one pace towards God, he will go ten paces towards us." These images of relatedness to God were described here in terms of their intrinsic value rather than linked to an account of the rewards for particular kinds and amounts of practice and the calculation of merit to be gained on the Last Day, as was often the case in the sermons. Moreover, this scene of the night prayer was rooted in the conception of a potential fit between human beings and God. As one of the leaders put it, "heaven is made for us." Such an idea removes the sense of struggle, and the anxiety about failure, that was often present in the way some women spoke in the Saturday class. In the Sister's Circle, references to failure were generally muted and mundane: "We should not just leave the Quran on the shelf getting dusty and only bring it down when someone dies. A page a day, it doesn't have to be a lot ... reading a lot without concentration isn't any good, better something short. When we approach Allah, he also approaches us. If we haven't prayed for a long time, we should ask for forgiveness – he wants to be asked … once we are dead it's too late"

Shuttleworth (2010)

There was no sense of the absolute gap between the individual and God that was so central in Azzim's teaching or the conditionality evoked by the insistence of some Friday preachers that God only accepts prayers performed correctly in conformity with his will. Here God is felt to engage with the human world of relationships.

Religious knowledge as the province of a specialist

Sometime after I joined the monthly Sisters' Circle, Azzim started to attend the second half of the meetings. While the character of the first half of the meeting remained that of a self-help group, in the second half of the afternoon, Azzim gave a short talk, after which he encouraged questions. Sometime later, men were invited to attend this part of the afternoon; initially, it seemed to be largely the husbands of women who attended the Sisters' Circle. Though the theme of the talk sometimes overlapped with a recent sermon he had given or with an idea that he had talked about in the weekly classes, this lecture often circled around the same points month after month with little in the way of development apparent among those present. Ironically, while Azzim's ostensible aim was to encourage ordinary Muslims to understand their religion for themselves, he became the focus for the firmly rooted idea that religious knowledge was something possessed by a specialist. This also had the effect of bringing to the attention of the women in the first half of the afternoon, the nature, and limitations of the knowledge available among themselves and they began to reserve an increasing number of issues for Azzim to deal with.

After his lecture, Azzim would invite questions and the voicing of disagreements. He encouraged those present to see themselves as engaged in study and as thinking for themselves rather than passively relying on others. This was an idea that had some substance among those in the weekly Saturday classes but was a problematic expectation on the basis of monthly lectures with erratic attendance. His aspirations also seemed at odds with what those who attended the lectures felt they were coming for or felt they were capable of. The questions that were asked indicated that while some of those present had taken in what Azzim had said, most were more interested in airing familiar, pre-existing ideas. The 'questions' asked were often really statements that cut across or even contradicted the theme of the lecture but were voiced without any apparent awareness of this. The questioners, often disproportionately male, did not seem to have any expectation of learning something new or clarifying a matter that would make a difference to what they already thought. Similar 'questions' were voiced in much the same way by different people over time, as if, reassuringly, entrenching known and needed positions.

At one of these gender-mixed lectures, Azzim announced that he would speak about the importance of religious understanding. Beginning formally with 'Brothers and Sisters in Islam', Azzim spoke about the importance of sound reasoning in religion and the fact that many people thought that you were not supposed to use your intellect in Islam. He quoted from the Quran to show that this was mistaken, that Allah had created human beings with certain organs and faculties, and they should be used – to observe the signs of creation and to understand the revelation. He said that people who accepted that the intellect is necessary in science nonetheless felt that you did not need to use your intellect in religion. Yet when Allah created the universe, he made human beings intelligent, and he revealed the Quran for mankind to study and understand. Azzim summed up this link between reason and the divine plan for human living as: 'reasoning is the sharia internally and the sharia is reasoning externally'.

However, he argued that this link between human reason and God's revelation had been undermined by the fear of not understanding the Quran. A feeling of doubt that was fed by those who claimed knowledge and looked pious. While acknowledging that misreading was a serious matter, 'this fear has led us to put the Quran aside and take up other books, written by other people that claim to be saying what Islam is'. He was particularly critical of the development of devotional literature. He said that he had heard a lecture in another mosque recently in which not a single *ayah* (verse) of the Quran had been quoted, but instead, other things had been added, such as what Azzim referred to as a fairy story about the *sahaba* (the companions of the Prophet) returning home from a journey to find their sins and the process for atonement written on their doors. He said that the speaker was trying to show how pious the *sahaba* were, but there was no basis for this in the Quran or in a *hadith sahih*.[6] The speaker had also said that every inch of the earth was covered with angels, at which point Azzim said he had asked himself, 'What about the hadith that the angels do not enter a house where there are statues?' He insisted that 'most of what this man said was invalid, but he had a long beard and a nice *thobe*[7] so we think that everything that comes out of his mouth is Islamic'. The idea that Muslims were easily taken in by appearances was a familiar theme in the Saturday classes that Azzim linked to the failure to rely on what was in the Quran and Sunnah and to a tradition among Muslims that implied you should *not* use your intellect or your common-sense to think for yourself. 'Instead, we follow traditions and customs, we follow our parents, and we think we are following Islam. We end up following things for which we have no proof or evidence but on the Last Day you will be responsible for yourself, and you will be asked how you used your intellect'.

On this occasion, when the time came for questions, it was clear from the comments that it had been difficult for some people to take in the implications of what had been said; for example, 'Not everyone understands the Quran so we must understand first from the *ulema* (scholars) and then go to the Quran'. Another comment from a man in the group consisted of a quotation in Arabic followed by the insistence that we need the *ulema*. Azzim replied that 'the brother has quoted an *ayah* which indicates that if you don't understand something you should ask those who do, and this is quite correct, but what this means is you should seek knowledge. If you haven't understood something, you should ask for guidance, but if you ask ten scholars, we all know you may get ten different answers, so it doesn't say you should just follow'. Holding his small, battered 'working' Quran that he took everywhere, Azzim said he was 'basing himself on the Quran rather than the hadith because the Quran is a book in which we have no doubt. Once you start on hadith …'. He trailed off ironically implying, without actually saying so, that there was no end to the disputes and misunderstandings if you go down that path. The discussion moved on and the women joined in with, by contrast, various very specific questions as to what was permitted. Despite the topic of the lecture, the group was expecting Azzim to have specialist knowledge and to give them clear opinions. While this was true of both men and women, it was striking that the men were preoccupied with reinstating the position of the *ulema* and that they did so by means of statements that might be said to enact their identification with male religious authority. The group as a whole seemed unable to respond to Azzim's attempt to invest it with the capacity to think. As will become apparent in the main part of this chapter, this was in contrast to the women in the weekly Saturday class who saw themselves more straightforwardly as coming to learn something, but they were also more able to be challenging with respect to areas of life with which they felt well acquainted.

If Azzim found the lectures frustrating he never said so, presumably hoping that at least a few individuals might be prompted to think and that all would derive some religious benefit from the act of attending. Thus, what from one perspective might appear to be the enactment of a fiction – that learning and development were taking place – might be seen from another perspective as the gradual establishment, through experiencing the regularity and solidity of Azzim's commitment to learning, of the pre-conditions for something new to be assimilated in the face of long established habits of thought and practice. Azzim sought to keep the lectures going, perhaps from an understanding of where the pious but religiously uninformed were coming from, a sympathy grounded in his experiences in Guyana, and perhaps from having a longer-term aim and because for him teaching was the fulfilment of a religious duty which was separable from the immediate outcome of the event. Whatever Azzim's aim, these Sunday afternoon events gave a public forum to some of the traditional points of view within the congregation. Certainly, no one seemed to be seeking a radically renewed form of Islam. However, as my fieldwork was coming to an end, some members of the Saturday class started to attend these lectures bringing with them their more developed understanding and I thought the character of the event was beginning to change.

Assimilating knowledge through commitment to a class

Though the Saturday class faced the same difficulty in accessing religious knowledge in that they were non-Arabic speaking Muslims, there were clearer feelings of having insufficient knowledge, a more focused desire to engage with the problem, and an awareness of being in the midst of a multiplicity of ideas about Islam. At the same time, there was also the pull of the Islam they had grown up with that was present as forms of practice and ways of thinking that did not easily give way in the face of Azzim's teaching. Unlike occasional attendance at lectures or the Sisters' Circle, the class provided a context not only for the acquisition of competence in Arabic and in recitation but for a sustained contact with Azzim's way of thinking, with each other and with the experience of learning itself. Though this may be seen as a project of religious self-development such as Mahmood (2005) describes, there are a number of contrasts to be drawn. The Saturday class was a diverse group engaged in complex ways with post-migration experiences and with the non-Muslim culture of the society in which they were now living. Unlike the hundred or more women who attended the religious lectures in Cairo, the class constituted a small, sustained group who came to know each other. In characterising the learning of those attending the Cairo piety groups as self-development, Mahmood draws on an individualised, one-person model of the mind and its capacities, albeit within the normative structures of a tradition. This may be a reflection of the thinking of her informants, but the processes within the class that I observed can be better understood in terms of webs of relationships – both within the group and in the sedimentation of past relationships that the women brought with them to the classes as identifications which both sustained *and* complicated their learning.

In the classes Azzim presented his theology (as described in chapter 7), the women struggled with it and Azzim then responded to their struggle. The situation was not just that of an individual woman disciplining herself in the face of the demands of a new view of Islam but of a group with a background of prior relational commitments who needed to find, or rather to imaginatively create, a new ethical space within which to integrate what they were learning with their existing lives. This sometimes happened and sometimes failed to occur. Azzim's religious project was based on asking the women to give up the religious world of their childhood and early adulthood and to stand outside their own emotional responses in the present so as to grasp the nature of God's revelation from a new disembodied, cognitive perspective.[8] This created painful uncertainties for the women as they oscillated between the sharply conflicting demands of Islam as an intellectual object and the emotional experience of being Muslim and living a Muslim life alongside others. The process of integrating a new thought that is at first external to one's own subjectivity is inevitably associated with some degree of anxiety and loss – for example, the pain of realising the limitations of one's own perspective or of seeing one's habitual religious practice in the light of a new way of thinking.[9]

It took Azzim about a year, and the weathering of repeated setbacks, before a regular group of women began to gather that was able, over time, to engage with his teaching. This is not merely to say that it took a long time but that it was a process that required commitment and it was this moral dimension, as much as knowledge per se, that was transmitted in the class. This group of women was older than those in the earlier failed classes mentioned in Chapter 7, ranging in age from mid-20s to late 50s. They brought with them not only their children, who played around at the end of the room but past religious experiences that impacted on their learning. The educational level of the group varied. Two young women had degrees but were not, for the most part, in employment. Several had trained for, and continued to work in, the fields of health and education and one worked in the finance department of a private sector company, but most had spent a large part of their adult lives bringing up families. Certainly, the group did not see themselves as the sort of graduate class that Huq (2008) describes, and they did not have the analytical skills that she describes to bring to bear on discussions. However, while not everyone attended every class, over time, a sense of commitment emerged, both to individual study and to a shared endeavour.[10] Azzim used to refer to some of the women as 'scholars' and the group shared humorously in this idea, but they also identified with his approach to learning, his seriousness, and his commitment. Parkin writes of this aspect of learning as a process of 'exposure to like-thinkers' and of the 'absorption of percepts and convictions such that ... they become unquestioningly a constituent part of the person' (Parkin 2007: 52). In some ways, Azzim was not a 'like thinker' as far as the women were concerned. Yet, as a Muslim who had taught himself Arabic in Guyana, had been a Guyanese student in Saudi Arabia, a Muslim working in a public service organisation and a freelance teacher, he knew about being an outsider having to slowly make his own way, and this was something the women, from their different positions as migrants, could identify with. Moreover, his approach to the place of women in Islam gave them equality in learning and worship and a space that allowed, or at least did not inhibit, a good deal of argument. Though the women were not knowledgeable about their religion at the start, and they accepted that they needed to learn from Azzim, they used the space to bring their own thoughts and actively engaged with him rather than passively submitting to his authority as the teacher.

The women brought within them their involvement with the wider society through work and family responsibilities, and their response to Azzim's teaching was complicated by the accommodations they had made, often without realising it, to the world around them. They were seeking to become better Muslims, but, for the most part, this was within the lives they already had rather than in the expectation of a radical break with the past. This latter radical path was sought by only a very few of those I met during my fieldwork and despite his uncompromising theological stance Azzim's attitude towards such a choice was one of concerned scepticism because, in his opinion, it often turned out to be unsustainable, so that the person gave up their practice all together. The stance of the women in the Saturday class can be contrasted with that of Liboratore's (2013) informants. While some of the young Somali women in her study veered uneasily between periods of devout practice and a wish to return to the world of shopping and clubbing, among the women I am describing a less extreme set of contradictions was brought into more sustained contact, at least as I encountered it within the classes. If these were individuals who had on-going engagements with worlds that were not framed in terms of Islam – the worlds of work, school, and contact with public services – they were not simply leisure pursuits. They had a desire to re-approach, as adult learners, the religion of their childhoods, now with the addition of something akin to what Berliner and Sarro (2007) describe as the transformative experience of understanding.

The Saturday class was an ethnically mixed group. Three were Mauritian women who had been involved in the earlier group at a neighbouring mosque that opted to become open to women only, one was Guyanese, while the rest were originally from North Africa, Pakistan, Bangladesh, Eastern Europe, Somalia, Eritrea, and Sri Lanka. On the whole, the women wore Islamic dress, though it was mostly colourful and sometimes more like an adaptation of the short tunic dress worn over trousers that was generally in fashion at that time. Only a young North African woman, her friend who came across London to the classes, and an older Bangladeshi woman dressed entirely in black. Apart from the two young North Africans, everyone had grown up outside the UK. Although they had all been brought up as Muslims within their own countries of origin, there were frequent references to how notional the Muslim character of their society of origin now seemed.[11] As adults in the UK, they now felt there was something they needed to learn about their religion. Migration removed them from a familiar setting and created a different relationship to their religion and the need to take greater personal responsibility in a society in which they were now members of a religious and ethnic minority. Roy (2004) suggests these upheavals create a need for a more defined personal religious identity, but it also involves managing the past in the light of this new knowledge. For example, during a discussion about making time to pray at work in the UK, one of the Mauritian women said that although they were given time off for prayer in Mauritius, 'many people, and I'm sorry to say, many women used the time to shop'. She even felt that it was more manageable to pray here than in Mauritius, implying that non-Muslims left you free to pray here and your actions did not carry the same burden of an implicit social pressure on others to do so.[12]

Though the women wanted to learn about what was deemed a correct form of practice, Azzim's view of what it involved was sometimes difficult to reconcile with the other demands of their lives. That the classes continued was in no small part due to Azzim's commitment, the coherence of his own religious project as it had developed over time and its consistency both with the way he spoke about his earlier life and with the way he behaved in the classes. The women could identify with Azzim's seriousness and commitment and with each other in their common experience of migration and the uncertainty about the nature of the religious legacy that their home societies had bequeathed them. This suggests a different kind of coherence from that sought by the women in Mahmood's study – not a coherence sought through identification with the coherence of God's revelation but a humanly generated coherence, acquired slowly through the integration of study and life experience.[13] In this process, the social support of the class was an important element, and in addition, some members of the class knew each other outside as friends: as de Koning (2013) suggests, these attachments are important elements in both embarking on and sustaining projects of religious engagement.

PART 2 – THE STRUGGLES OF RELIGIOUS DEVELOPMENT

Initially, the classes were rather informal but as the membership became more regular, elements of a curriculum emerged consisting of learning the Arabic language (from scratch), the rules governing recitation through reading aloud short *suras* rather than through memorisation, theological principles, and the rules of practice with respect to ablution, prayer, fasting, charity, and *hajj*.[14] Rather than describe these individual elements in detail I will explore the kinds of difficulties the women encountered. At the start, no one spoke Arabic or understood its grammatical structure – even the young North African woman had only picked up a little of the dialect spoken by her parents. As he had had to teach himself, Azzim seemed rather deaf to the pleas of the women who found it very difficult to understand the grammar or to keep up with the homework, given all their domestic responsibilities. The women could be quite combative, and a bantering atmosphere developed around ironically 'gendered' disputes as to who had the greater domestic responsibilities, to be replaced at critical moments by a sudden shared seriousness – how will I be judged on the Last Day and where will I spend eternity? By the time my fieldwork ended, there had been a marked improvement in the group's knowledge of Arabic and recitation, and, somewhat reluctantly, Azzim let them know that they were now the most advanced of any group he had taught. They had reached a point where they had sufficient understanding of Arabic for Azzim to attempt to expand on some points of interpretation through an explanation of the grammatical structure of a sentence in the Quran. Yet the process of learning was more than the acquisition of competence in Arabic or recitation. What was being learned also involved taking in an idea of Islam that was at odds with both the identifications the women had grown up with and with many of the ways in which they had so far managed their adult lives in London. Yet, despite the difficulties, there was evidence of development in their religious lives.

At the start, they all expressed feelings of ignorance about their religion and there were many dismaying moments when the women were faced with the realisation of how little they knew. Equally painful was the discovery that something they thought they knew, was not, in Azzim's opinion, part of Islam at all. This also created concern for the spiritual well-being of parents and grandparents, not only in life but also in death, as these family members were now understood to be beyond the help of traditional rituals for the dead. The acquisition of a new perspective was experienced as a complicated process with gains and losses that created anxiety. Learning was, therefore, slow, uneven, and painful. Aspects of this process can be compared to mourning in that it involved the giving up of old ways of being and thinking with their 'sense of coherence and belonging' (Berliner and Sarro 2007: 5) that had been taken for granted and relied on (Zigon 2007).[15]

As a culturally diverse gathering, the class itself embodied Azzim's argument that Islam stood outside any one culture. Moreover, he felt that given all the changing meanings of a living language, native speakers of modern Arabic were not necessarily better placed to interpret the Quran than someone, like himself, who had learnt Classical Arabic without previous knowledge of the spoken language. As a non-Arab Muslim, he pointed out the failure of many Muslims to embrace the universality of Islam and the racism implicit in its internal hierarchy. Many discussions in the classes revolved around examples of this as well as the recognition of such processes closer to home. Talking about the need to marry within their own societies, a Pakistani member of the class spoke of the pressure within her community to choose a partner from within their own district of Pakistan, to which Azzim added dryly, 'preferably from within your own village'. On an occasion when someone repeated the Prophet's warning that there would be seventy-three forms of Islam, but only one would be correct, Azzim added, 'and each group think they are the ones who are correct'. He saw in this the tendency of Muslims to form cliques and cults, to which people are drawn, rather than following Allah through the Quran. He insisted that there would be no separate spaces in paradise, 'no special place for the Guyanese. We are all in the same ship, all making the same journey'.

However, within his idea of the unity of Islam, a space for different perspectives and for the complexity of the interaction between them was created by his references to different scholarly traditions. When Azzim first introduced the idea that there were different schools of interpretation and asked members of the class which *mathhab* they had grown up in, it was clear that the women had never thought about this. They had all been brought up within a single, but different, *mathhab* linked to their different cultural origins, not realising it was not itself simply Islam: 'I didn't realise I was Hanbali. I just thought I was Muslim'. Azzim was critical of religious teachers who held that it was better to teach only one school of interpretation as otherwise people would become confused since he felt it deprived people of vital knowledge. Certainly, the idea that different schools drew on different hadiths to guide their thinking, or might interpret the same hadith differently, was something new to the class. They were not able to make much use of this knowledge during my time with them. If it created a space for legitimate diversity, it also generated uncertainty and the women still wanted to know what they should do and were reluctant to take responsibility for weighing the different interpretations for themselves, defaulting under the pressure to a position that was similar to that taken by those in the lectures. If, as Azzim insisted, the Quran could, and should, be thought about by ordinary Muslims living ordinary lives in the UK today, this required something different from the seeking of opinions or the following of your own thinking without an understanding of the text as seemed to be happening among some of Liboratore's (2013) informants. Yet it may be that it is precisely through individuals managing to live as best they can in the light of divine revelation within the challenges of a non-Muslim society that the ideals of a religious tradition are upheld as a living endeavour (de Koning 2013).

Many said of their past lives in Muslim majority societies, 'we were not taught to think about Muslim ideas', so the classes involved the women in a new relationship to knowledge, an idea which for some was linked to their experience of having children in the UK school system. They remarked on how different education was in the UK from back home: 'My children are taught to discover things'. However, the women had different capacities to take in the ideas that Azzim was teaching, and though he created an atmosphere in which they could be quite challenging in some areas, it was striking that there was never any direct questioning of Azzim's theological position. Even his insistence that the idea that God is everywhere was not Islamic went unchallenged, although this came closest to negating a deeply held and widespread assumption that never seemed to entirely disappear from the women's preoccupations and evoked quiet responses to the effect that 'I have always told my children that God is everywhere'.

Coping with myriad religious 'opinions'

Though the group made steady progress in Arabic and recitation, where the acquisition of competence was hard but not contentious, the women found themselves in the midst of all sorts of competing ideas about religious practice that complicated what Azzim was teaching. The women's experience of this was very different from the 'authoritative pluralisation' and 'latitude' to think about Islam suggested by Mandaville (2007) and Bowen (2012: 9). If the women in this class did not accept everything Azzim said without question, neither did they feel free to steer their own way through the divergent religious opinions they heard about. Most of the women, at some point, felt other Muslims had told them something about Islam which they urgently needed to bring to Azzim for his judgement. He addressed some issues and passed over others with little comment. One woman asked whether you should touch your arms to the ground when you pray. She said she did not but had heard other views. Azzim acknowledged that there were different opinions about this which had to do with the idea that men and women should pray differently. However, he explained that the Prophet had made no such distinction, saying only 'pray as you have seen me pray'. Many questions revolved around the use of the Quran – as a decorative item in a car, a gift when people moved to a new house or something you held over the head of a bride. At first, the group found Azzim's insistence that these practices implied treating the Quran as having magical powers difficult to take in. He asked why they would think of holding the Quran over the bride's head. When they said that the bridal Quran was for *baraka* (blessing) he answered, '*baraka* comes from reading, understanding, and practising the Quran – otherwise, you could just have thousands of Qurans in the house!'

At one time or another, most of the women used the class to express their confusion at the plethora of views on the Muslim TV channels, the internet and passed by word of mouth, opinions that, as Azzim would point out, were often from 'the limitless sphere of gossip'. These ideas would generally be reported as having come through 'a friend'. This sometimes gave cover for the discussion of embarrassing breaches of core obligations, but it also allowed some of the women to report phenomena that had a quality of 'New Age' spirituality – a 'saint' who was said to be able to fly or a claim that you could tell the future with star signs and tarot cards. While this is a common feature of current popular religiosity across different faiths (Roy 2004: 165), Jeldtoft (2011) suggests an eclectic range of practices have sprung up among Muslims in Europe. Insisting that the Quran was the source of 'her friend's ideas', one woman added, 'But of course, everyone has their own reading of it (the Quran)'. Azzim responded sharply, 'It's not a jigsaw puzzle … the Quran saves you from all of this [confusion] … it teaches you how to think'. Then, perhaps trying to avoid becoming himself such an alternative source of knowledge, he added that 'your evidence should be the Quran and the Sunnah, not me'. He complained that 'Nowadays people are quoting the TV … this sheik said this or that … there's an ayah that will answer the question of 9/11 and 7/7 … but the only way you can answer these things is by evidence … not by word of mouth'. Later, he took the opportunity of a discussion about family disputes that bubbled up in the middle of a class to repeat the point about evidence. Someone talked about a relative who had been saying things about another branch of the family. It seemed that the relative had heard something bad and now there was nothing anyone could say to him that made any difference. Azzim cut across her account to ask, 'Where does the problem lie? It lies in his concept of information – someone tells him something and he takes it for a fact'. He explained that this was what was happening in gossip but also in the way religious information was passed on, and he referred to an ayah in the Quran about people receiving information and spreading it without asking if it was right or wrong.

The class was often drawn into these discussions as if there was something irresistible about this rather wild way of speaking that took them away from the more pedestrian task in hand. However, one such conversation that took place in Azzim's absence was brought to a sudden halt by one young woman saying very seriously that she thought the problem was that Azzim said things that people did not want to know because 'once you know them there is no going back'. In saying this, she seemed to be voicing something from the experience of encountering her own ambivalent response to what she was learning in the classes and the underlying, non-negotiable implications of accepting Azzim's theology. This remark suggests that in the midst of a rather confused and excited discussion, this woman regained the mental space necessary to distinguish her own thoughts from those voiced in the group and, with it, the capacity to reflect on what was being said. Her intervention was striking in cutting across the prevailing atmosphere of confusion in the class.[16] The moment had something in common with the vignette Keane (2014) quotes, in which a Polish woman speaks in such a way as to create an ethical perception of a Jewish child in an external situation where that capacity had been lost among those present.[17] Where this capacity for what Keane calls an ethical intervention comes from is less clear since, as Lambek (2007) points out, it is not necessarily itself a conscious goal. This suggests it is rooted in unconscious embodied feelings of relatedness to others that become accessible to thought in a moment of need.

Accepting new obligations; facing new anxieties

On matters concerning home and family, the pull of tradition and habit often reasserted itself. Questions would arise about whether a family was right to want the body of a dead relative to be returned to Pakistan or whether one could accompany elderly parents planning to visit a shrine in India. The woman sitting beside me explained quietly that the shrine was the burial place of 'what they call a *pir*'.[18] The questioner said that she was under pressure from her father: 'They're saying you get everything you ask for there'. It was unclear whether the speaker herself felt drawn to this claim, which would certainly have been at odds with what Azzim was teaching, or whether she was uncertain if she had to refuse her parents' request. First, Azzim acknowledged it was 'an Asian thing' and that people in Guyana would go for three months to Pakistan and visit shrines instead of going to Mecca. He then passed on to saying something general about Sufis. The woman on the other side of me said quietly, 'I used to be into Sufism'. When Azzim finally returned to the question about the shrine, he said that the woman should ask her parents if this person is greater than the prophets because Islam doesn't allow this even for the prophets. The Quran says, 'Call on me and I will answer your prayer'. All this was very difficult for the group. One woman said, 'I can't tell my mother she's not praying in the right way'; and the original questioner also said she could not say this to her father about his planned trip. Two forms of Muslim life, that might manage to co-exist on a day-to-day basis where nothing is too clearly spelt out, were suddenly revealed to be incommensurable. In response to this painful atmosphere, Azzim softened his stance, first describing how, when he was young, he had thought he should tell older Guyanese Muslims of their mistakes but that he had learnt from experience that this was hopeless; he finished by saying that 'we know it's part of their heart because they believe it's part of Islam' – a moving image I never otherwise heard him use. As in the example in the previous chapter about an unmarried couple living together, it was Azzim's acknowledgement of the human cost of these situations and sympathy for the participants that produced a way of integrating rather than condemning these contradictions. But the tensions in the class had been considerable and he continued in a lighter vein. He mentioned some of the practices that went on around him when he was growing up in Guyana that included voodoo, to which the group replied, laughing as if with sudden relief, 'Ah well, we don't do that!'. At this point, I realised that the children, who had been playing as usual on the far side of the hall, had crept under our table, and were sitting listening as if they sensed that the conversation was about matters close to home – the state of safety and well-being of the grandparental generation and doubtless the earlier generations who were now ancestors.

Precisely because such matters were so close to home, they caused anxiety as to the source of these errors. For a while, at the start of my fieldwork, I attended another class which was run outside the mosque by a Bangladeshi 'freelance' imam. Here religious practices of dubious provenance were often humorously denoted as 'a sub-continent thing' – a designation that implicitly included Muslims themselves in the problem. However, in Azzim's class, customs that appeared within Muslim traditions that the group felt were strange and arbitrary were often attributed explicitly by a few of the women to the influence of Hinduism. They also brought recurrent references to the practices of a sheikh in a nearby mosque and 'the strange things people believe in Turkey' that they had encountered on holiday. In this way, some aspects of Muslim practice that seemed unusual or suspect could be, to varying degrees, disowned, but this was not so possible with ideas and forms of thinking they themselves felt more identified with. Anxiety about the *jinn* presented special difficulties. Everyone had encounters with practices used to ward off *jinn* that were not those of the prophet. Though Azzim was sympathetic towards accounts where he felt the idea of possession was the expression of psychological difficulties, he was critical where other people got drawn in, exacerbating the situation. A story was related about a woman in Mauritius who, as a result of contacting the *jinn*, was able to tell the future or make people do things. It was insisted that this woman was a Muslim and that this power had been in her family for generations, an echo of the blending of Muslim and traditional practices in Mayotte (Lambek 2002, 2007). Azzim's reply was 'Now I *am* worried'. In this vein, people would ask whether it was alright to seek ritual help from Hindus and some would insist that rituals performed by non-Muslims had been successful. Azzim said that he did not doubt the successful outcomes they were claiming but asked them to consider what must lie behind it – the power of *shaitan* (satan who is a jinn). He insisted that neither the *jinn* nor *shaitan* had power over you unless you turned to them and made a friend of them. This thought made a great impact on one of the women in the class who said that 'she had never thought that if you make a relationship with God, you cannot be overcome by *jinn*'. Azzim himself never spoke in terms of a 'relationship to God', only of trusting in Allah, but the woman's shock at this new perception seemed to be based on experiencing Azzim's response as returning responsibility and agency to her.

The whole domain of the *jinn* was extremely frightening to the women, and they found it difficult to speak of. One woman said that she told her young daughter to say her prayers so that she would not have bad dreams about the *jinn*. Azzim replied abruptly, 'But this isn't true – *shaitan* is not a scary animal. Children must learn to grow up to handle these thoughts in a legitimate way'. Rather than turning to forms of thinking and rituals that he saw as being themselves based on the power of *shaitan,* Azzim's reply emphasised the need for a serious engagement with these thoughts as impulses inside human beings that had to be managed by being known and owned. Though he did not put it this way, it might follow that taking such conscious responsibility is, for him, one of the functions of 'a thinking mind'. Coming to experience this domain as a matter of trusting in God, understanding something of one's own state, and taking responsibility for one's impulses, rather than claiming them to be caused by *jinn*, was central to Azzim's effort to detach Islam from culture and tradition so that the believer's mind was available for the understanding of God's revelation.

Berliner and Sarro (2007) write of religious transmission as taking place within a moral community, but for the class, there was a rupture from an earlier community that had first to be lived through. Perhaps on a par with conversion, this meant having to detach from the assurances offered by one set of familiar traditional practices and relationships before one had yet managed to establish oneself firmly in a new moral community and new identifications. One might question whether such a new, consciously acquired community can ever fully attain the status of a taken-for-granted moral world to be inhabited without further effort or the risk of returning to old ways of being. This perhaps accounts for the constant resurfacing of earlier religious ideas, voiced in whispers to me to which attachment could never be totally given up.

Meeting the obligations of practice

If more unusual views could be discounted or blamed on the religions of others, there remained a range of more mainstream interpretations to be navigated, and this created unease and uncertainty as to how one could know whether one's practice was correct or sufficient. This was a form of doubt from which some people sought refuge in additional practices. Yet such doubts are difficult to resolve in this way, and Azzim talked of those who felt the need to resort to ever stricter forms of practice so that what had been optional was interpreted by them as obligatory (*fard*), such as the wearing of the *nikab*.[19] In a discussion about the decoration of graves, Azzim had indicated that it should be limited to identifying information. Yet it was clear that the class knew of many elaborately decorated Muslim graves and one woman became troubled and preoccupied with the possibility that others might add such forbidden decorations to her grave after her death and against her wishes. She did not seem to be able to take in Azzim saying that she was not responsible for what others might do though he repeated it several times. Despite Azzim's attempts to make clear what Islam required and the freedom he felt to be pragmatic beyond that, this did not always reach the women's private anxieties.

For some in the group, contact with non-Muslims became a focus for this sort of anxious concern, prompting questions about visiting non-Muslims when they were sick or accepting a drink or food from a non-Muslim. Those who voiced these concerns were generally those who were least actively engaged with non-Muslims, while those with more day-to-day experience in this regard had already found ways of managing these situations. As Das (2013: 77) puts it in relation to the accommodations between Muslims and Hindus in India that happened not 'at a deep theological level or through deliberative reasoning – it was as if a certain mode of speaking and feeling ... [was] created by proximity and friendship'. However, there were times when any sense of 'proximity and friendship' was absent from the class and replaced by a series of concerns which, for the most part, Azzim did not share. He would insist that where the food or drink was itself permitted, it did not matter from whom you received it – 'It isn't the person [who gives it to you] that makes it *halal* (permitted); so as long as it hasn't been prayed over in a name other than Allah, it's fine'. But, for some of the women, this still did not seem to settle their concerns. Picking up on what he indicated were misplaced scruples, Azzim said with deliberate provocativeness that he thought some Muslims felt that even touching a pig or saying the word was forbidden and judging by the response in the group some did indeed feel this. If these scruples were about matters that Azzim felt lay outside religious obligations or were the traditional practices of family members for whom they were not responsible, there was nonetheless a gap between their religious practice and Azzim's interpretations of their religious obligations. As the young woman I quoted earlier had suggested, there was something they did not want to fully know about Azzim's teaching.

This, in turn, raised a further uncertainty about how one could know that one was practising correctly and with the proper intention. Someone asked, 'How do you know that you are on the right path ... does Allah send you a sign?' Azzim asked the group and they responded enthusiastically: 'For me, it's a peaceful feeling inside myself'. Someone else suggested 'a feeling of internal happiness', others that 'When you wake up, you do feel different' or 'If I'm doing something wrong, I feel that'. One of the Mauritians said. 'I learnt to be a better Muslim here than in Mauritius, even though there you are surrounded by Muslims'. As far as the women were concerned, their new attention to religious practice had an impact on their bodily-affective state and it was this that informed their responses to Azzim's question. However, after letting this conversation run on for a while, Azzim said firmly, 'The answer is that your knowledge must be pro-foundly established ... *that* should be your guide, not how you feel about it. Some people are waiting for a nice dream or a voice but that might be from *shaitan*'. He spoke of meeting a Christian on a plane who had told him, 'I'm a happy man because I know the truth. I feel it', Azzim said scornfully, 'That's no different from spiritualism ... they are basically just believing in their own desires'. Given the way the women had responded to the original question, this was a hard answer to hear, at odds with their underlying sense that their state of feeling *was* their point of orientation.

If Azzim could show flexibility in relation to everyday life, he was much stricter about the details of practice around prayer and fasting. The women found their encounter with this quite difficult as it revealed the accommodations they had got used to. Azzim was unimpressed by various examples that were brought of what were thought of as legitimate dispensations from prayer when travelling or unwell. They would argue with him, and complicated discussions ensued about journeys they had made or were going to make, about plane routes and prayer times, but Azzim made it clear that he planned his travel in order to ensure that he *could* pray at the right times, rather than finding himself in situations where he could not. Despite their increasing attentiveness to their religious practice over the period I knew them,[20] it emerged that this way of looking at the matter was quite contrary to how many of the women had seen their obligations. One asked, 'So you're saying that making sure you can pray should be the priority?'

In one class, a woman wanted to ask about 'when we forget *salat* (prayer)', apparently expecting to be told how to make up the omission: the class was shocked to learn that this was not possible. Azzim insisted that the only thing you could do was express regret and start to pray five times a day. This produced a sigh from some people who had thought prayer was like something you owed that could be made good later. Azzim was adamant that it was not a matter of making up for something not done. One had to accept responsibility for what had happened. Someone said that in Mauritius, people say that they will watch a movie and make up the prayer later, and as often happened, another person added, 'I used to do that'. Azzim again said, 'No, there is nothing like that. Prayer is for the appointed time'.

Following an explanation of something called 'corrective *sujuds*', extra pros-trations that needed to be undertaken when you became aware that you might have inadvertently missed something in your prayer, one of the women said she did not understand and, unusually, Azzim replied sharply, 'That's because you already have your own way of doing it'. Of course, all the women came with their own way of being Muslim, their own way of doing things, to which they felt an attachment. However, I thought Azzim was saying something more than this. Here he implied that something that could not be struggled with, however incompletely, reluctantly, and painfully became instead a concrete barrier to taking in something new.

During a discussion about prayer and the problem, outside of a mosque, of finding the correct direction in which to pray, one woman, whose job involves quite a lot of local travelling said that she worked out the direction for prayer in terms of where she was in relation to her cousin's house, but added some-what humorously,, 'Sometimes when I'm out somewhere like Chingford it gets complicated'. Azzim suggested prosaically that she buy a prayer mat with a spe-cial compass. Though the woman's remark was made with humour, her work involved her in the profoundly serious matter of visiting the dying at home, often at night. Her remark conveyed that despite all the compromises and approxima-tions of daily life and the mundane geography of family relations she nonetheless felt she was able to maintain her internal orientation as a Muslim. Though the class never challenged Azzim's radically transcendent theology, which it seemed that, at some level, many did not accept, they could, and did, retain a sense of their own lives and commitments as located in a world within which their reli-gion helped them to orientate (Baumann 1999: 78).

Moral development and the taking of responsibility

Azzim's knowledge and experience allowed him a freedom to think about the challenges posed by new situations that most of the women did not feel they had. For some, as their commitment to their religious practice grew, this predicament found a resolution in self-imposed solutions to the uncertainty in which they sometimes found themselves. What became visible at such moments was the internal conflict they experienced, the struggle to find a resolution and the price they were willing to pay. One young woman in the class said her parents had suggested she seek advice from Azzim about a situation that had arisen in her new job. There was to be a reception at which there would be alcohol. Her manager had said that soft drinks would also be available and that she need not come near the bar, but she was still unhappy about the event. Somewhat to her surprise, Azzim agreed with both the manager and her parents and could see no difficulty as long as she was not sitting down at a table with others to drink. In fact, there was an implication that he did not understand why she was so worried. However, we later heard that she had decided to stay away from the event altogether.

Another younger member of the class had spoken from time to time of wanting to marry a religiously observant young man. When this event occurred, several members of the class including myself were invited to the wedding in a mosque some distance away. A large hall was laid out with round tables and our group, together with children, joined those already seated. It slowly became clear that the wedding entailed complete gender segregation, with the women's celebration taking place in the hall of the mosque, away from the ceremony itself. This was a stricter interpretation of Islam than any of the other women in the class had expected or were accustomed to, and in this was unlike other Muslim weddings I had attended. The bride was led into the women's hall by female relatives; we never saw her with the bridegroom. As everyone crowded around with their cameras to greet her, it was explained that the bride's own strict religious obligations meant that no photographs should be taken of her. Talking to her much later, I understood that in organising her wedding in this way, she had gone beyond what was usual within her culture, beyond her deceased parents' religious practice and against the wishes of her married brothers and sisters (Rozario 2011). Though she regretted the upset her decision had caused, she felt that her new religious sensibilities demanded it and she was glad that she had managed to carry it through. Both these young women seemed to have felt an urgent need to adopt a stricter level of practice than that suggested by Azzim, their families, or the rest of the class. However, unlike the women that Mahmood writes of who, in such circumstances, sought stricter teachers, neither of these two young women left the class to go elsewhere, which suggests they continued to struggle with the gap between their religious ideals and the reality of ordinary lives.

Naila was a thoughtful member of the class. Though diligent in her religious practice, she was willing to admit openly to personal failure and difficulty. It was Naila who made comments to me such as, 'I used to do this' and 'I have always told my children that'. Yet she was actively engaged in her own development as a Muslim and her references to failure were not at all complacent. She expressed her opinions in the classes (Fadil 2011), but she also took opportunities to let me know, in private, of some of the conflictual situations in which she found herself – her feeling that she *should* go to a pub for a leaving party out of fellowship for those she worked with, or her decision to send her son to an Anglican secondary school rather than a private Muslim school in order that he would gain a broader understanding of the world he was living in: Naila felt that his religious education was sufficiently covered by his attendance at an after-school madrassa. If she found herself caught between different worlds, these were moral worlds and ethical dilemmas with which she felt herself to be actively engaged.

During my fieldwork, a tragedy befell Naila's extended family. There was a very painful discussion in the class about the need to accept what had happened as Allah's will, with many expressing their difficulty with this idea. As the group was breaking up, Naila looked at me and said with great feeling that now she understood something in a different way. 'We say that we accept the will of Allah, but now that this has happened and I must accept it, now I know what it means to be a servant of Allah'. This statement was accompanied by hand gesture as if taking something from the space in front of her down inside herself, suggesting the consumption of an invisible object. Her words and this gesture drew attention away from the acceptance of God's will, expressed perhaps rather too easily in ritualised speech, to the hidden internal effort such acceptance involved. Naila could acknowledge the presence of the natural inner resistance she felt to absorbing such a shocking experience as being the will of God. Though her words were also poignantly expressive, her gesture conveyed a sense that Naila herself was in a state for which language was insufficient and a bodily expression was needed. While it did not resolve her distress, her gesture depicted an embodied sense that the situation required her to take this painful experience inside herself. It also conveyed the hope that, if she did this, *something* would happen. This something could not be the undoing of the tragedy but might be a hoped-for transformation in which her pain could be experienced within the domain of Allah's will, that would lend it meaning. Her action suggested a bodily process like digestion that was able to effect such a transformation – a function that may re-establish what Crapanzano (2004: 104) calls a prayerful attitude that he suggests is akin to hope, as distinct from the concreteness of actual prayer that is *to* someone, or something, *for* something. In this example of an ethical intervention, I felt Naila was struggling for the resources to repair the wholeness of a moral domain that had been shattered by the tragedy and to re-establish a way of being within it – a Muslim life within God's creation – with a new sense of understanding gained painfully from experience (Bion 1962; Berliner and Sarro 2007).

Notes

1 For accounts of the complexity of religious ideas in which ordinary British Muslims find themselves and in which some are actively trying to negotiate a path, see Bowen (2015); Lewis and Hamid (2018); and Hamid (2018).

2 de Koning (2013) describes the perspective of individuals as they move in and between their engagement with Islamic institutions, and the Salafi ideas they encountered there, and their private lives as a dialectic in which individuals adapt a utopian vision to the everyday circumstances, and, paradoxically, create in the process a necessary bridge between these two poles of religious experience.

3 See note on 'learning from experience' in chapter 7.

4 This relational perspective on learning is in contrast to the essentially one-person model of self-development used by Mahmood (2005). In both the developmental and psychoanalytic models, the initial two-person relationship becomes a three-person world. Thus 'primary intersubjectivity' forms the matrix out of which 'secondary intersubjectivity' with its inclusion of a third person's perspective and the triangulated awareness of shared objects of interest, from which language emerges (Trevarthen 1998). See note 9.

5 Here the speaker uses the word God rather than Allah.

6 This refers to a soundly based account of the practice and sayings of the Prophet, but at other times, Azzim expressed more general reservations about the extent to which one should rely on hadith at all.

7 The long white religious garment worn by men.

8 This is, in a sense, a one-person cognitive perspective though the women were constantly drawn back into a felt relationship with God.

9 In the psychoanalytic model the 'triangulation' of mental space through the emergence of a third person perspective is a development that is unavoidably emotionally painful. The giving up of an exclusive relationship to the primary object of care for membership of a social world in which one may sometimes be only an observer of relationships from which one is excluded, and where one's own subjectivity is limited by the perspective of others, involves tolerating the anxieties this arouses (Britton 1989, 1998).

10 New members continued to arrive, generally only to disappear again after a few weeks, as if seeking something they did not find. However, despite Azzim's saying to new people that 'the sisters will help you catch up', by the second year, this was no longer possible, and the group became, in effect, closed, though one older Bangladeshi woman did manage to join late and became one of the most able in the group.

11 While this new consciousness may be the direct result of migration, there were indications that it was also fed by globalisation and parallel religious developments among those who had remained in Mauritius (Salvatore and Eickelman 2004).

12 Apart from one woman who worked in a private company, the group was mostly either working in the public sector or at home looking after children.

13 The slowness of this process was in contrast to Roy's emphasis on the need felt by some diaspora Muslims for a quick experience of religious transformation (2007).

14 While I knew nothing of Islamic theology and had to learn along with the class, I was able to read and understand Arabic sufficiently to be able to explain some of the grammar to others and this helped establish my place in the class.

15 Mourning has a particular place in the model of ethical development within psychoanalytic theory from Freud (1917) and Klein (1940) in that the capacity to acknowledge the reality of loss and damage, despite the anxieties associated with it, is the prerequisite for the development of the capacity to make reparation both externally and internally and the regaining of feelings of love and hope.

16 'Regained her capacity to think' because I am not suggesting that this individual lacked this under ordinary circumstances, only that under the pressure of the confusion in the class, it had been momentarily lost. Her intervention was an example of

triangulation (Rumsey 2010) in that it opened a mental space in which a new thought could occur, not as a once-and-for-all achievement but subject to vicissitudes, a space to be gained and lost.

17 The woman seemed to know from experience that the villagers saw the child as a dog to be thrown down a well while also finding within herself an awareness that they were all, in fact, in the presence of a child. She brought these two perceptions together in her minimal and, as it turned out, life-saving observation – 'She's not a dog after all'.

18 A saint – living or dead.

19 Laidlaw (2014) is critical of Mahmood's theorising of her interlocutors' experience as the exercise of ethical freedom since, in these terms, failures of religious practice can only indicate the need to try harder to bring yourself into conformity with the ideal rather than creating the possibility (and freedom) of reflection.

20 For example, I learnt from several of the women that they were now rising for dawn prayers and then going back to bed.

References

Baumann, G. (1999) *The Multicultural Riddle*. London: Routledge.

Berliner, D. and Sarro, R. (2007) 'On Learning Religion: An Introduction', in Berliner, D. and Sarro, R. (eds) *Learning Religion*. Oxford: Berghahn Books.

Bion, W. (1962) *Learning from Experience*. London: Heinemann.

Bowen, J. (2012) *A New Anthropology of Islam*. Cambridge: Cambridge University Press.

Bowen, I. (2015) *Medina in Birmingham, Najaf in Brent*. London: Hurst and company.

Britton, R. (1989) 'The Missing Link. Parental Sexuality in the Oedipus Complex', in Steiner, J. (ed) *The Oedipus Complex Today*. London Karnac.

Britton, R. (1998) 'Subjectivity, Objectivity and Triangular Space', in *Belief and Imagination*. London: Routledge.

Crapanzano, V. (2004) *Imaginative Horizons*. Chicago: Chicago University Press.

Das, V. (2013) 'Cohabiting an Interreligious Milieu: Reflections on Religious Diversity', in Lambek, M. and Boddy, J. (eds) *A Companion to Anthropology of Religion*. Chichester: John Wiley and Sons.

de Koning, M. (2013) 'The moral maze: Dutch Salafis and the construction of a moral community of the faithful', *Contemporary Islam* 7: 71–84.

Fadil, N. (2011) 'Not-/unveiling as an ethical practice', *Feminist Review* 98: 83–109.

Fadil, N. (2013) 'Performing the salat at work: Secular and pious Muslims negotiating the contours of the public in Belgium', *Ethnicities* 13(6): 729–750.

Freud, S. (1917) 'Mourning and Melancholia', in Strachey, J. (ed) *The Standard Edition of the Complete Psychological Works of Sigmond Freud*, 14: 237–258. London: Hogarth Press.

Hamid, S. (2018) *Sufis, Salafis and Islamists*. London: I.B. Tauris.

Huq, M. (2008) 'Reading the Qur'an in Bangladesh: The politics of belief among Islamist women', *Modern Asian Studies* 48(2/3): 457–488.

Jeldtoft, N. (2011) 'Lived Islam: Religious identity with "non-organized" Muslim minorities', *Ethnic and Racial Studies* 34(7): 1134–1151.

Keane, W. (2014) 'Affordances and reflexivity in ethical life: An ethnographic stance', *Anthropological Theory* 14(1): 3–26.

Klein, M. (1940) 'Mourning and its relation to manic depressive states', *International Journal of Psychoanalysis* 21: 125–153.

Laidlaw, J. (2014) *The Subject of Virtue: An Anthropology of Ethics and Freedom*. Cambridge: Cambridge University Press.

Lambek, M. (2002) 'Fantasy in Practice: Projection and Introjection, or the Witch and Spirit-Medium', in Kapferer, B. (ed) *Beyond Rationalism*. Oxford: Berghahn Books.

Lambek, M. (2007) 'On Catching Up with Oneself: Learning to Know that One Means What One Does', in Berliner, D. and Sarro, R. (eds) *Learning Religion*. Oxford: Berghahn.

Lewis, P. and Hamid, S. (2018) *British Muslims: New Directions in Islamic Thought, Creativity and Activism*. Edinburgh: Edinburgh University Press.

Liboratore, G. (2013) 'Doubt as a Double Edged Sword: Unanswerable Questions and Practical Solutions among Newly Practising Somali Muslims in London', in Pelkmans M. E. (ed) *Ethnographies of Doubt*. London: Tauris and Company.

Mahmood, S. (2005) *The Politics of Piety*. Princeton: Princeton University Press.

Mandaville, P. (2007) 'Globalization and the politics of religious knowledge; pluralising authority in the Muslim World', *Theory, Culture and Society* 24(2): 101–115.

Marchand, T. H. J. (2010) 'Making knowledge explorations of the indissoluble relation between minds bodies and environment', *Journal of the Royal Anthropological Institute* 16(S1): 1–21.

Marsden, M. (2008) 'Women, politics and Islamism in Northern Pakistan', *Modern Asian Studies* 42(2/3): 405–429.

Osella, F. and Soares, B. (2010) *Islam, Politics and Anthropology*. Chichester: Wiley–Blackwell.

Parkin, D. (2007) 'The Accidental in Religious Instruction', in Berliner, D. and Sarro, R. (eds) *Learning Religion*. Oxford: Berghahn Books.

Roy, O. (2004) *Globalised Islam: The Search for a New Ummah*. London: Hurst and Co.

Roy, O. (2007) *Secularism Confronts Islam*. New York: Columbia University Press.

Rozario, S. (2011) 'Islamic piety against the family: From "traditional" to "pure" Islam', *Contemporary Islam* 5(3): 285–308.

Rumsey, A. (2010). 'Ethics, Language and Human Sociality', in Lambek, M. (ed) *Ordinary Ethics*. New York: Fordham University Press.

Salvatore, A. and Eickelman, D. F. (2004) *Public Islam and the Common Good*. Leiden: Brill.

Schielke, S. (2009) 'Ambivalent commitments: Troubles of morality, religiosity and aspiration among young Egyptians', *Journal of Religion in Africa* 39(2): 158–185.

Shannahan, D. S. (2014) 'Gender, inclusivity and UK mosque experience', *Contemporary Islam* 8: 1–16.

Shively, K. (2014) 'Entangled ethics: Piety and agency in Turkey', *Anthropological Theory* 14(4): 462–480.

Shuttleworth, J. (2010) 'Faith and culture: Community life and the creation of a shared psychic reality', *Infant Observation* 13(1): 45–58.

Toren, C. (1993) 'Making history: The significance of childhood cognition for a comparative anthropology of the mind'. *Man* 28(3): 461–478.

Trevarthen, C. (1998) 'The Concept and Foundations of Infant Intersubjectivity', in Braten, S. (ed) *Intersubjective Communication and Emotion in Early Ontogeny*. Cambridge: Cambridge University Press.

Woodhead, L. ([2013] 2016) 'Tactical and Strategic Religion', in Dessing, N. et al (eds) *Everyday Lived Islam in Europe*. London: Routledge.

Zigon, J. (2007) 'Moral breakdown and the ethical demand', *Anthropological Theory* 7(1): 131–150.

9

PEDAGOGY, SOCIALISATION, AND THE TRANSMISSION OF A MORAL SENSIBILITY

The formation of ethical capacity has been linked to the nature of the pedagogic process and to socialisation more generally (Faubion 2001, 2011; Laidlaw 2014). The development of ethical capacity, Laidlaw (2014) argues, requires a different kind of pedagogic process from the discipline of pious self-fashioning described by Mahmood (2005), which may be initially freely chosen but, in so far as it is an ideal form of selfhood that is sought, the space of reflective freedom, essential to the exercise of ethical capacity, is reduced. Laidlaw suggests that what is required is a relationship between teacher and pupil that promotes maturation and sustains an openness to the complexity and contradictions of external reality and to the internal states of ambivalence that this stirs up. In this chapter, I will describe a children's class taught by one of the mosque imams and explore the stance he takes towards the children and what this conveys about his own attitude towards the contradictions and difficulties of life. To highlight the nature of what was being communicated, I will refer to an earlier contact I had with a traditional girls' madrassa class as a point of comparison (Shuttleworth 2008).

Bilal was a young man in his mid-twenties. He preached on Fridays at a local mental health unit and occasionally at the mosque, took weddings and funerals, and led prayers during the week. In addition to the children's class, he took another for young men and represented the mosque at various community events, including the borough commemoration of Remembrance Sunday.[1] Bilal had been chosen by the mosque trustees as being sympathetically responsive to Guyanese views and his presence within the class reflected this, which is not to say that there were no differences between him and those who ran the mosque. There were times when one saw him as just a young man siding with other young men such as an occasion when Mr Rahman had forbidden chairs being moved from one room to another and Bilal, expressing his exasperation with Mr Rahman openly, got up to help them carry chairs from his class to theirs.

DOI: 10.4324/9781003080008-9

Like the senior mosque imam Bilal was from a Bangladeshi background and his religious stance bridged at least some of the gaps between the expectations of the various cultural traditions within the congregation, and that between the formal rituals held in common within the congregation and those sought by of the Guyanese. His way of conducting himself in public conveyed both the living of a committed and knowledgeable Muslim life and a thoughtful engagement with the emotionally complicated experience of doing so.

I got to know Bilal because he was willing to let me sit in on a gender-mixed children's class for about 10–12 children aged between about 4 and 10 years old, which met on Saturdays. When I first attended, it was explained to me that the children were from second-generation Guyanese and Mauritian families who had not really practised their religion and that the children, therefore, lacked a background familiarity with Islam.[2] On later visits, it seemed that this demographic had started to change, and a wider spread of children was now present, including the daughter of one of the women in the Saturday class I attended. Bilal offered a view of Islam that was in marked contrast to that in the traditional, gender-segregated class for girls I had observed during a previous short fieldwork project. Not formally part of the mosque, the girls' class took place daily after school in a section of the old hall screened off from an equivalent boys' class. It was used mainly by more recently arrived East African families; the girls were all dressed in black *jilbab* and *hijab*. The class was taken by women from Uganda and Somalia, who followed a traditional style of Islamic pedagogy (Eickelman 1978) teaching Quran recitation through the rote learning of small sections of the Quran, with little, or no explicit discussion of its meaning or explanation of religious ideas. They tended to avert their attention from questions the girls sometimes raised about their lives as pupils of mainstream borough schools. One young girl asked about listening to music during school music lessons and was left looking troubled and uncomfortable by the firm reply that music was forbidden because it filled the heart and left no space for God.

Though the bulk of the time in Bilal's class was also spent in learning to read Arabic and to recite short sections of the Quran, though not from memory, his style of teaching and manner towards the children drew on a different conception of the role of a teacher. It also conveyed a different conception of Islam. Particularly striking was Bilal's willingness to acknowledge the children's involvement in secular activities and Christian festivals like Christmas because, as he explained in conversation with me, he wanted to dispel the conflict they might otherwise feel existed between Islam at the mosque and the world outside that both the children, and he himself, inhabited. Bilal conveyed that he saw his role as helping the children to manage the complications of their lives in a non-Muslim majority society and this was accomplished, in part, by the way, he himself managed moments of potential perturbation when they emerged in the class – moments that might otherwise have constituted a 'moral breakdown' (Zigon 2007) as the question about listening to music had been in the other class. On various occasions when children were absent, he would enquire if anyone knew where they were. Other children, who were related, or who went to the same school, would then supply the information that the absent child was participating in some kind of performance or was at a party. Bilal would make gently joking comments about these activities – 'Another party?' – but he conveyed an acceptance that, if a class takes place on a Saturday, such absences will happen. The religious responsibilities of the parents in such matters, that might also have been a source of tension in these situations, were, tactfully, not mentioned. He used humour to ease those situations where different aspects of the children's lives collided. When a boy dropped a children's book on Islam in the bath so that it dried with the pages stuck together and could no longer be read, Bilal took it from him and carefully peeled the pages apart while, at the same time, enquiring whether the book had jumped or was pushed. His way of responding to the children can be understood as both a conscious stance, which he could explain and justify, *and* as emerging from his way of 'being in the world' (Zigon 2007), an on-going way of comporting himself that extended beyond self-awareness into patterns of response that were the embodied outcome of his own life experiences and identifications. While such patterns emerge from within a lifeworld, this does not imply conformity to a single, coherent model. The self-consistency sought by the women in Mahmood's study was the conscious outcome of their response to an Islamic tradition and the claims of orthodoxy within that discourse (Mahmood 2005). Bilal managed the contradictions and difficulties that emerged in the class in different ways – what he said, how he conducted himself, and how he responded to the children all conveyed both a seriousness and a sense of coherence and balance between the mosque and the outside world. Since he has undergone a theological training and is practicing the obligations of Islam as an imam, the contrast with the accounts of the piety movement is not with respect to religious knowledge and commitment but rather reflects a different response to Islam, the non-Muslim world in which he grew up and the cultural traditions of the Guyanese and Mauritians. His presence as a teacher and his way of teaching drew on these experiences.

Bilal seemed comfortable with my presence and, on occasions when he was called out to deal with something elsewhere in the mosque, would say, 'Judy is in charge and she will help you with your homework if you ask her', which some of the youngest ones did. This was because he knew that I could read Arabic, but it was also indicative of his relaxed response to my presence as a non-Muslim undertaking research on ordinary Muslim practice. While this was consonant with the way he presided over the classes and no doubt reflected aspects of Bilal's personality, it also indicated a tolerance of uncertainty and difference that links to qualities in his religious stance. He conveyed a sense of someone who felt able to use his intellectual and emotional capacities freely.

Whether one can gain access to the lives of others in fieldwork may be in part a matter of how one introduces and positions oneself, as Dessing (2013) suggests, and on 'the researcher's ability to negotiate an identity that is betwixt and between' (Lukens-Bull 2007) but it also depends on whether there is a place in the lifeworld of those we wish to study that an ethnographer can meaningfully occupy. The availability of such a place depends, in turn, on the presence among those whose world we seek to understand of an idea of an unknown other whose wish to understand through observation is felt to be a mutually beneficial activity rather than a source of threat. This, in turn, reflects a conception of what the process of getting to know something or somebody involves. Bilal, like Azzim, offered me such a space as did the Guyanese and the group that had formed around them.

Bilal generally wore religious dress, a long white *thobe* and lace cap which marked out his role, but he sometimes arrived in ordinary clothes. On one occasion, he arrived limping in a tracksuit, telling the class that he had injured his leg playing football. The children were well aware that he was an enthusiastic Sunday footballer – 'as long as there isn't a funeral or wedding, I have to take at the mosque'. During the class, he sat on the floor surrounded by a circle of children. Most of the children wore ordinary clothes, with all-in-one *hijabs* for the girls. At the start of the lesson, they handed him envelopes with the payment for the class or explained that they had forgotten it. News of a new baby at home or a grandmother visiting from the family's home country would be offered while he took the envelopes – 'Oh, a used envelope – recycling, that's good, isn't it?' He set a low bookstand in front of him for the children to put their books on when they read to him and placed his phone at his side, answering some calls but just glancing across at the screen in response to others. There was a large ability range within the class – some struggled to recognise the letter sounds of Arabic, while a few were learning to read brief passages of the Quran. Children were called up to read to him the pieces they had prepared during the week while the rest of the group practiced, chatted, or fooled around quietly. Most of the children were eager to read and formed up like a line of twittering birds, whispering to each other while waiting their turn. However, on one occasion, a little girl burst into tears at the prospect, causing the others around her to laugh. Bilal hushed them, explaining her distress by saying, 'She is a passionate girl who wants to do well'. His attentiveness to the children in correcting their mistakes and in encouraging and congratulating their efforts conveyed an awareness of their feelings and a willingness to help the class as a whole to manage what individuals might find difficult. This was accomplished in a way that addressed both the overt task in hand *and* facilitated those processes, taking place out of, or on the edge of, awareness, by which the children might come to identify with the moral qualities and ethical potential in what was happening.

An element in the transmission of an ethical capacity was Bilal's willingness to accept the children's way of being, not only by responding to their questions but by managing what it was that was happening in the room, in part by absorbing potentially disruptive currents of feeling within the class.[3] Through this, the children were gaining experience of learning alongside each other within a Muslim space over which Bilal, as a reliable Muslim adult, was presiding. Sometimes his responses took a verbal form – an enquiry, a joke, a protective remark – that acknowledged a child's particular situation or their shared task of learning to be Muslim. The response could have been otherwise, as it was in the example of the girl in the traditional madrassa who asked about listening to music in school. Both teachers are in the middle of an on-going situation and both kinds of response carry the potential for a moral rather than a physiological account ('I can't hear you') or a simple rebuff ('I don't understand you'). By saying 'music fills the heart' the traditional woman teacher responded in a way that conveyed, unambiguously, her view that music was incompatible with Islam, and her manner embodied that view. Bilal, on the other hand, seemed to feel he also needed to enable the children to live as Muslims in a moral world in which musical performances and parties existed. His response is, in part, his considered judgement as an adult as to what is best in the circumstances, but it is also of a piece with his attuned responsiveness to the children. If in Zigon's terms, Bilal's presence and comportment were part of a continuing moral background, his ethical interventions, in choosing to interpret absence for a party in a light-hearted manner or in protecting the crying child by attributing her tears to her strong feelings, would also draw on his own internal background identifications and the understandings they engendered within him. His relaxed manner conveyed that these perturbations did not overwhelm him, that reparative interventions were well within his capacity as their teacher and as a Muslim adult and that managing these situations was a task he took responsibility for on behalf of the children.

By contrast, within the religious framework of the teacher of the girl who listened to music, the response to the disruption caused by her question was to ensure that the child understood the implications of a heart with no space left for God. The teacher did not appear to absorb the tension or to assist the child in managing the situation. The dilemma was left for the girl to address. Though there was a verbal interaction between them, it did not offer a shared language (Liberatore 2013) in which to encompass the experience in a context of 'mutual intelligibilty' (Rasanayagam 2013). It may be that this example had as much to do with the teacher as an individual as the demands of the religious stance she adopted, but it was consistent with the absolute nature of the ban on music that she felt it was her obligation to communicate. If in your view, something is absolutely forbidden, you do not have the space to be pragmatic that others may feel they have.[4]

Faubion (2011: 85) argues that Zigon's (2007) distinction between the moral and the ethical, as non-conscious and conscious responses, respectively, indicates a break in the continuity between these states. His argument is that both may be said to be rooted in, and emerge from, the same bodily-affective registers of unconscious intersubjectivity. The subtle attunements that emerge out of the direct bodily sensing (and the imaginative elaboration) of another's physical and mental state makes 'keeping going' possible but also feeds into that explicit, reflective, understanding of relationships that informs ethical judgement. Both Bilal's and the traditional teacher's ways of being with the children created their own continuity of atmospheres and expectations. From this perspective, the apparent randomness of everyday life becomes the medium in which significant social formations and collective ideas are carried and out of which the awareness of inhabiting a moral world alongside others may emerge. The nature of the relationship between these 'mutually constituting registers' (Eisenlohr 2006) may be such that moral reflectiveness and creative thought emerges, but not necessarily. Moral reflectiveness implies the taking of responsibility for thinking about what is experienced emotionally, and this involves managing an inherent tension between verbal thought and emotions (Marsden 2005: 247).[5]

Though Bilal maintained an approach that must have been familiar to the children from their primary schools, he became serious at prayer time. After a lesson about praying five times a day, the children had been asked to memorise, at home, the names of the prayers and the time periods within which the different prayers should be performed. When, the following week, he asked one of the boys about the homework, the boy read out the names of the prayers and times as pairs of numbers. Bilal joked that he had made it sound like they were football scores but when, shortly after, the call to prayer sounded, he told the children to listen carefully to the words of response to the *adhan* and then withdrew his attention from them to recite the words quietly. As the children left the room to pray, he reminded the girls, who went through to the balcony on their own, to pay proper attention rather than chatting. There was often at least one adult woman on the balcony who, even if unknown to any of the children, would assume responsibility for shepherding the girls into a line. On other occasions, my accompanying them may have kept Bilal's presence in mind so that the girls were able to organise themselves. Only once did I feel I had to intervene actively and that was when there had been a delay to the start of prayer, during which the girls began an absorbing game of running along the chairs at the back of the balcony. Bilal went downstairs with the boys to the men's prayer hall to take on the role of imam. On these occasions, I sometimes stood near the balcony railing from where I could watch him lead the boys, and any men present, in the afternoon prayer and so witnessed a further transformation, which the girls, like the women on the balcony, did not see directly in the way the men and boys did. Though there were opportunities to see something of this transformation at other times, this was a gendered divide that remained even for the Guyanese. Bilal, the young man, keen footballer, and friendly teacher, became an adult performing his own religious obligations with seriousness and an imam leading other adults in the worship of God.

To see an adult withdraw themselves from an ordinary engagement with the world into prayer, as happened with the infants and their mothers on the balcony, brings the religious domain into focus in a different way from the more continuously disciplined demeanour of the traditional teachers of the girls' after-school class. The reverse of a 'moral breakdown' (Zigon 2007), such moments of heightened moral sensibility stood out from the background way in which Bilal conducted himself, attentive to the children but also aware of and, like his phone, accessible to the other concerns of his life. This conscious withdrawing to an internal focus, emerging as it did out of a background of attentive attuning to what was going on around him, lent a distinctive quality to his presence – that of a man with a religious life of his own, who recognised and could speak of strong feelings in the children as well as a being able to interact with them in a playful way. The classes offered the children not only an opportunity to learn about Islam and to learn to read Arabic but an experience of being with someone with an engaged moral sensibility, who wanted them to learn how to be Muslim as a form of moral life, and with whom they might come to identify.

Bilal's Saturday afternoon class and the traditional girls' after-school class offered contrasting versions of the pedagogic process. Both offered the opportunity to learn religious skills and to assimilate and identify with a way of being in the world. Whatever may have been their private religious experience, the women teachers in the traditional class sought to present a model of self-contained, bodily comportment rooted in compliance to their understanding of the obligations of Islam and the avoidance of that which was deemed religiously inappropriate. Bilal, on the other hand, communicated a view of Islam as embedded in the world and in the local community. Yet his religious practice also suggested the capacity to withdraw temporarily to an internal focus, to a mindfulness of God. This constituted a coherent way of 'being in the world', but a sense of coherence that emerges through the effort of holding together the different aspects of human being is qualitatively different from that sought by those in the piety movement, based as it is on the exclusion of human contradiction. Yet the former mode of coherence does not only indicate pragmatic, improvisational qualities. It may rather be based on the moral qualities inherent in sustained identifications with internalised relationships through which an individual grows and develops. In Bilal's case, in addition to his identification with a friendly primary school teacher, his internal relationship to God seemed central to what he brought to the class and to the sermons I heard him give.

Faubion writes of the capacity to tolerate complexity required for *autopoiesis* as gained through experience over the course of development: 'Individual human beings typically display such complexity yet do so only after a considerable course of socialisation has taken place, only after a considerable dose of the intersubjective has already been incorporated into the self (and hence are never individuals in their pure individuality)' (2011: 119–120). The transmission of ethical capacities in a pedagogic relationship which supports maturation (Laidlaw 2014) and that which occurs in socialisation through prolonged but unplanned experiences of attuning intersubjectively to the states of others in everyday life are accomplished through the internalisation of relatedness to adults who have themselves developed their own capacity for openness to complexity and contradiction. This view of pedagogy and socialisation includes not only the sharing of a cognitive, language-mediated engagement with a body of knowledge but a foundation in the immediacy in which bodily-affective states are communicated, not only in infancy but throughout life. I have drawn attention to these processes as they were strikingly present within Bilal's class and because it is in these registers that the qualities of another person's presence are first and most profoundly communicated.

Bilal was able to tolerate the gap between the perfection of divine revelation and the weaknesses of the human condition; in the children's class, this was manifest in his assumption that the children needed his adult presence to help them to manage this gap. By being attentive to the children's experience, he was modifying the difficulties these situations presented for them and helping them to develop, through identification, the capacity to undertake this task for themselves. Though there were many indications that he did not think it helpful to undertake such moral work on behalf of adults as he did for the children, some did not respond to his prompting to take responsibility for themselves. Over time I became aware of Bilal's involvement as a giver of religious advice by text and telephone to young men who were constantly presenting him with questions about what was and was not permissible. Many such enquiries concerned football and clashes between prayer and match time. Though his advice was sometimes given in a rather light-hearted way, Bilal explained to me that there was a problem with the way people sometimes asked these questions and that it was necessary to prompt people to think for themselves rather than simply giving them an answer. Though he rarely preached at the mosque on Fridays, on one occasion during Ramadan, Bilal described it as a time of forgiveness. He complained that some people asked the imam to say prayers for forgiveness for them. 'And I say to them, your sorrow has to be your own. I can be sorry for my sins, but I can't be sorry for yours'.

Notes

1 It was clear that he did not think it would be possible for me to sit in on the class he taught for young men on a weekday evening.
2 Although on their arrival in London, the Guyanese had taken a relaxed view of such matters, the Trustees had moved towards encouraging formal religious education for children within the mosque. A dedicated space for teaching was planned in the new extension that was built after the end of my fieldwork.
3 In a paper explicitly concerned with the relevance of psychoanalytic ideas to anthropology, Lambek (2002: 200) distinguishes between processes of introjection (the taking in by an individual of feeling states from others in the outside world), which he argues could be usefully taken up by anthropology, and projection. The latter describes a process by which an individual may rid themselves of the awareness of feelings, often by provoking them in others, which Lambek suggests belongs to the domain of psychopathology. Though projection may be a necessary means of maintaining emotional equilibrium that, taken to extremes, constitutes a pathological process, it is possible to see the projection of somato-affective states as the original form of embodied communication in infancy that continues to be active throughout life. As a clinical concept, projective identification has had a complex developmental history of its own since Klein (1955). For a summary of post-Kleinian developments, see Spillius (2012).
4 Azzim argued that whereas everything that is permitted in worship is made clear in the Quran and sunnah only those things explicitly designated *haram* are forbidden and music, in his view, is not so specified.
5 Ethical development is a never completed task. Marsden's description of the Chitrali as sometimes exercising a robust moral capacity while, at other times, fearing the consequences of the integration of intellectual and emotional experience, implies an irresolvable and uncomfortable alternation that nonetheless sustains the living of a mindful life (Marsden 2005: 256).

References

Dessing, N. ([2013] 2016). How to Study Everyday Islam. In Dessing, N. et al (eds) *Eslam in Europe*. London: Routledge.

Eickelman, D. F. (1978) 'The art of memory: Islamic Education and its social reproduction', *Comparative Studies in Society and History* 20(4): 485–516.

Eisenlohr, P. (2006) *Little India: Diaspora, Time and Ethnolinguistic Belonging in Hindu Mauritius*. London: University of California Press.

Faubion, J. D. (2001) 'Toward an anthropology of Ethics: Foucault and the pedagogies of autopoiesis', *Representations* 74(1): 83–104.

Faubion, J. D. (2011) *An Anthropology of Ethics*. Cambridge: Cambridge University Press.

Klein, M. (1955) 'On Identification', in Money-Kyrle, R. (ed) *Writings of Melanie Klein 1975*, Volume 3, 141–175. London: Hogarth Press and International Library of Psychoanalysis [Reprinted London: Vintage 1997].

Laidlaw, J. (2014) *The Subject of Virtue: An Anthropology of Ethics and Freedom*. Cambridge: Cambridge University Press.

Lambek, M. (2002) 'Fantasy in Practice: Projection and Introjection, or the Witch and Spirit-Medium', in Kapferer, B. (ed) *Beyond Rationalism*. Oxford: Berghahn Books.

Liberatore, G. (2013) 'Doubt as a Double-Edged Sword: Unanswerable Questions and Practical Solutions among Newly Practicing Somali Muslims in London', in Pelkmans, M. (ed) *Ethnographies of Doubt*. London: Tauris and Company.

Lukens-Bull, R. (2007) 'Lost in the sea of subjectivity: The subject position of the researcher in the anthropology of Islam', *Contemporary Islam* 1: 173–192.

Mahmood, S. (2005) *The Politics of Piety*. Princeton: Princeton University Press.

Marsden, M. (2005) *Living Islam: Muslim Religious Experience in Pakistan's North-West Frontier*. Cambridge: Cambridge University Press.

Shuttleworth, J. (2008) 'Creating religious experience in contemporary society', *Infant Observation* 11(1): 17–28.

Spillius, E. B. (2012) 'Developments by Kleinian analysts', in Spillius, E. B. and O'Shaughnessy, E. (eds) *Projective Identification: The Fate of a Concept*, 49–60. Hove: Routledge.

Zigon, J. (2007) 'Moral breakdown and the ethical demand', *Anthropological Theory* 7(1): 131–150.

10
CONCLUSION

At the time of my fieldwork, the generation who came to London in the 1960s was still active in the running of the mosque together with some from the next generation, now in middle age. Young adults and adolescents were also much in evidence at communal events. This echoes Roy's description of the concrete re-establishing of a post-migration Muslim community where the original 'solidarity group' puts down roots and functions as a 'business network', builds a mosque and makes links to the structures of power within a local area and on this basis, retains contact with younger generations (Roy 2004: 119). Though there was a sense of impending change, the congregation was continuing to grow and there were plans, later completed, for a new building on the site of the old hall that was to include an education area and a large space for meals and for meetings with others from the wider non-Muslim community that was separate from that used for prayer so that it would not be necessary to remove shoes.

After the difficulties and false starts of the early years, the Guyanese built their mosque and their place in the local community, but it was a slow, step-by-step process that had meant having sufficient moral and material resources and trust in each other to keep going through the uncertainties as to how it would turn out. The regular practice of communal prayer that took place first in private homes and then in the old hall before the mosque was built enabled this otherwise fragile endeavour to be experienced as taking place within an enduring religious tradition and a timescale that outlasts the doubts and failures of an individual lifespan. The variations in practice and commitment of ordinary Muslims have found their place within the anthropology of everyday Islam, and for some of those I got to know the presence of a mosque on the corner of a nearby street and a congregation among whom were familiar faces, was an accessible place to turn to in times of need, to celebrate *eid* or to lend a hand at some communal event.

DOI: 10.4324/9781003080008-10

The Guyanese brought with them to London a way of living a Muslim life that was embedded in the idea of Guyana as multi-ethnic, multi-faith society in which relations of mutual recognition and participation had grown up between different religious traditions. The mosque they built in London encapsulated the values of this world by creating a religious space for Guyanese and non-Guyanese Muslims that could also include non-Muslim family members and friends of the Guyanese and, on occasion, the wider community beyond. With this heritage came a sense among the older generation of indebtedness to forebears who had 'kept the lamp burning' and a continuing sense of responsibility among younger members of the congregation for keeping alive these qualities and commitments through participating in the care of the mosque and the shop and in the serving of meals. Over time, the mosque attracted an increasingly diverse congregation and though some of this larger group restricted their attendance to core rituals, others participated in communal events, identified with the Guyanese, and spoke of 'their mosque'.

The values that the Guyanese located in an idea of 'Guyana' lived on in styles of speech and sociability and a confidence in addressing challenges. Through this, as Rasanayagam suggests, ordinary social relationships become a medium of moral experience and the source of that 'mutual intelligibility' which people find in living alongside each other – 'an intelligibility that extends beyond specifically Muslim self-understandings' (Rasanayagam 2013). While this intelligibility may be transmitted through day-to-day activities, verbal responses to disruptions and challenges made explicit how the past underpinned their understanding of what it was to live a Muslim life.

Living with the gap between an ideal and reality

From the perspective of many of those described in studies of Muslim renewal, Guyanese religious practice, and even the practice of some in the Saturday women's class, would be regarded as failing – as being deficient in both textual knowledge and practice, and as not observing gender-separation or appropriate distancing from non-Muslims. Yet the Guyanese set a positive religious and moral value on gender-mixed sociality and on the accommodation of other faith traditions, as they did on the prayerful framing of social occasions and life-cycle events. The tension between the different ways of being Muslim that was sometimes present within the mosque reflected different attitudes to the inevitable gap between the 'messiness of the human world and the perfection of Islam' (Simon 2009: 258) and the painful awareness of the contradictions, ambivalence, and failures of ordinary life that this brought. This gap was managed in different ways. While some, like the young woman who wanted to be a religiously correct Muslim bride, sought to bring themselves into more complete conformity with their view of God's will, others seemed content to protect the formalities of ritual without necessarily feeling that ritual obligations should extend out into the everyday world. Maintaining a sharp distinction between the unchanging nature of the divine on the one hand and the changeable unpredictability of the human, on the other is not of critical significance if, as among the Guyanese, you see being Muslim as, at least in part, instantiated in a way of living in the world as it is that you understand as a complicated human inheritance.

For many Guyanese and Mauritians, and others at the mosque, being Muslim was not just inevitably, but *properly* lived out collectively within and through the acknowledgment of diversity and the contradictions of human culture, in which both men and women participate. At various points, individual Guyanese voiced their thoughts on the religious and social values of their world – a relationship to that moral world that cannot be understood only on the model of conformity to a religious tradition or as a passive immersion in an unreflective form of traditional practice but rather as actively created through an acknowledged dependence on, and active use of, the moral resources handed on by others.[1] It is not that the Guyanese necessarily lived lives that were always consistent with these ideas, but that these were the values those I got to know had recourse to in moments of difficulty. The balancing of the claims of different perspectives was a matter of active engagement in the lived moment, something accomplished in and through the inherent unpredictability of encounters with others. How this moral inheritance is carried forward is unpredictable. As Simon (2014) puts it, the moral subjectivity of ordinary Muslims cannot be understood as determined by adherence to the norms of Islam as an ideal social order, rather they draw, in unpredictable ways, on both individual experience *and* a shared background of intersubjective currents within the life of a community and its traditions. If the efforts of ordinary people, whether Muslim or otherwise, to lead more or less good lives points to moments of courage and creativity in the exercise of ethical capacity it also involves facing the ambiguity of everyday experience and the inevitable failure to live up to the ideal. This may, in turn, lead to further development through the need to revitalise a moral world.

While ethnographies of participation in religious renewal movements have concentrated for the most part on aspiration and achievement, Deeb (2006) concludes her ethnography of Shi'a piety in Lebanon with a chapter on those who found themselves unable, or unwilling, to fulfil its demands, and whose predicament was expressed in disclosures to the ethnographer that were private and painful. The loss of religious faith has become an object of study through the accounts of those who experienced the failure of disciplinary practices to produce the desired pious states and who, as a result, found it difficult to maintain their motivation to practice (Schielke 2009). Simon (2014) describes how his informants spoke of having ceased to pray and that there seemed to be nothing that they felt they could do to rescue themselves from their state of hopelessness. They could speak of their situation but, despite insisting that praying would restore them to calm, they found themselves unable to do so.

The vicissitudes of hope, doubt, and disillusionment and the fragility inherent in periods of enthusiastic commitment constitute an inevitable dynamic within an individual life and in collective human endeavours (Pelkmans 2017) that need to be survived if hope is to be rediscovered and such projects are to endure. There had been such crises within the congregation in the past – the split within the original group over whether to build a mosque or continue to pray in private houses, the dispute with the two Guyanese imams whose religious views were incompatible with those of the Guyanese congregation as well as the more diffuse challenge posed by the growth of radical Islam. And another crisis was pending in which a new generation, many born in London, would have to take over the project from their parents. That the mosque was both a material and moral object gave it a solidity and reliability. The mosque as a material structure was a focus of on-going participation in its care and maintenance; the life of the mosque generated a receptive human space within which the vicissitudes of religious practice could be contained and managed, whether through collective ritual, occasions that created a general sense of community or simply through the quality of continuity – by the mosque 'going on being' there.[2]

While the processes that sustained an on-going commitment to being Muslim and to attendance at the mosque were partly located in embodied experience, they were also reflected in different conscious religious conceptions shared among the Guyanese and Mauritians and others in the group around them. For them, it was through a relationship to God, on the model of intimate human relationships, and the emotional resources available within such a relationship that the gap between religious ideals and reality could be managed and the experience of failure repaired. It was this that my Bangladeshi friend referred to when going to the mosque to 'make her peace with God'. Similarly in his sermons, Bilal presented an image of God as desiring our requests to be forgiven and spoke of the enormity of God's capacity for forgiveness in comparison to our sins: we should not assume that we will not be forgiven, but neither should we just wait for *hajj* or old age. 'One should do it now ... one should be really sorry ... it is not just a matter of saying words'. While this style of sermon directs itself to private experience, it also creates a kind of communality through the assumption of a shared human need for forgiveness that is obstructed by our shared human weaknesses – our prevarications and our unwillingness to forgive others. The remedy he suggested for an inability to forgive someone else was to ask God to forgive both of you. However, such a relationship between the individual and God is not a perspective shared by all. Among some in the congregation, it was felt necessary for others to mediate with God, just as some people felt there was a need for others to be repositories of religious knowledge. Azzim never spoke of a direct emotional relationship with God; it would not have been consistent with his view of the radical otherness of God. It was striking, therefore, that the notion of an emotionally responsive imminent God kept surfacing as an elusive but persistent idea among the women in his classes.

The sustaining a congregation

Describing the pervasive presence of hope as necessary to the living of a life, Zigon quotes one of his interlocutors as saying, 'without hope we do not live, we merely exist' (2009: 268) – a remark that is reminiscent of the woman in the Saturday class saying that before she turned to her religion in London, she had been 'just living for the sake of living'. What is it that is introduced into a life in this way, by hope? If, as for Zigon, hope is the capacity to sustain a lifeworld, what would that sustaining of a world involve?

Crapanzano (2004: 99) suggests hope is a state in which the awaited outcome is uncertain and contingent on the agency of others and chance events. Though Zigon (2009) reads this as indicating passivity, the situation in Bilal's sermon is not one of passively waiting for some external event though it does involve recognising dependence on another. Here the individual must *do* something – in this case, they must forgive others and seek God's forgiveness. Moreover, repairing these relationships requires the prior recognition that something has in some way been damaged – failure has itself to become an object of awareness. As in the discussion in the women's class about 'missed prayers' that they discover cannot be made up for later, this recognition brings into focus the reality of conflicting commitments and the fact that what is past cannot simply be undone. The irreversibility of time creates the subtle nature of moral responsibility, demanding the capacity to accept and live with consequences that one could not necessarily have consciously anticipated Lambek (2010: 53).

Crapanzano (2004: 104) distinguishes between what he calls a 'prayerful' attitude towards an unknown and unreachable horizon and the concrete and instrumental nature of a prayer to someone and for something. The former supposes the fragility of awaiting the unfolding of something that is as yet unknown, akin to the stance that Keats describes as 'negative capability'[3]; the latter is focused on the attainment of an objective. If, at one level, the mosque was such a concrete desired goal, continuing the work of earlier generations of Guyanese Muslims in a new context and into an unknown future involved keeping alive a communal state of hopeful expectancy. Does the turning to God for forgiveness that Bilal speaks of necessarily involve the concrete demands of instrumental prayer or could 'making one's peace with God' return the individual to that pervasive, open-ended, trusting moral stance towards life that Crapanzano calls 'the prayerful'? Certainly, as Dahlgren and Schielke (2013) argue, the elusive nature of what it is 'to strive for a morally sound life' cannot be grasped simply by recourse to a designation such as 'Muslim'. As they put it, 'if we want to understand what it means to live a Muslim life, we need a theory about what it means to live a life more urgently than we need a theory of Islam' (Dahlgren and Schielke 2013: 11). They argue that an experience of 'wholeness and trust' has something to do with the capacity to maintain a sense of direction and that this has its source in 'the intersection of the individual and the intimate with the social and the communal' (Dahlgren and Schielke 2013: 12). This suggests that such an intersection creates a space in which the fluidity of ordinary lives can find a shared public form that is felt to be whole and to which a relationship of hopeful trust can be anchored.[4] The woman who spoke in the class about the difficulty of finding the correct geographical orientation for prayer when she was working far from home was indicating a trust in her internal religious orientation in finding her way within a wider world.

When they were challenged, the Guyanese often felt that what they valued in multi-faith and gender-mixed relationships was at stake. For Ali it was not just permitted to attend the funeral rituals of non-Muslim friends and relatives, it was important to affirm the positive moral value he felt such relationships had had in the living of his life. That he reflected upon his experience from this standpoint suggests both an individual mind and a form of shared Muslim space within which the messiness of human experience could be accommodated rather than needing to be kept at bay to protect an ideal. Though Azzim[5] saw 'a thinking mind' as divinely given for the study and understanding of God's revelation in the Quran and of creation through natural science, it was also what he drew on to recognise the implications of unpalatable aspects of the human world – the urge among Muslims to form exclusive groups who feel that only they are right or the evasion of human responsibility for impulses that became located in the *jinn*. Despite Azzim's insistence on the obligations of Islam and the need for the women in the class to develop their textual understanding, the idea of a 'thinking mind' gave expression to the need for the time and space for a process of thinking to occur. Yet there were moments when that space disappeared – when the implications of Azzim's teaching were not only too demanding for the women to meet but too difficult even to recognise.

The life of the mosque as an on-going communal responsibility

The moral qualities of a shared world, created through our embodied capacity to attune to others, generates both the motivation and sensibility needed to maintain that world. Like the familiarity with the bodily movements and music of collective prayer at the mosque in a language that most do not understand, ordinary social life also proceeds on the basis of our bodily capacity to attune to one another and to sense the embodied state of others. This state of others, and that of a world shared with them, refers not only to external circumstances, though ruptures at this level are most clearly observable. It also refers to the felt vitality and viability of those commitments and that world amid the inevitable fluctuation in those relationships (Stern 2012). The scenes in and around the kitchen during Ramadan expressed the state of life within their community's commitment to a way of being Muslim, while the ritual for the sick sister carried currents of anxiety and vulnerability in the face of the task of 'maintaining the world' as Zigon (2009) puts it. A moral world inhabited with others extends the practice of virtue from the personal to include what Faubion (2011: 72) calls 'other-regarding virtues' such that others are not simply the means to a care of the self but become, themselves, objects of care. As he puts it, '[G]reek ethics is indeed personal, but unlike ethics grounded in a metaphysics of autonomy, of a radical and absolute freedom, it places ethical practice in the encompassing web of the house and polis' (ibid: 75). The mosque is a manifestation of such a concern with the collective and the practical demands that must be met for an imagined world to find a shared public form, in this case, a building standing on a busy street in London.

The gender-mixed and multi-faith aspects of mosque events were the most striking features of this Guyanese-oriented world, marking it out from other Muslim traditions that were also present at times within the mosque. Yet the importance of gender-mixed events went beyond resisting the divisions and exclusions that some other Muslim traditions required between men and women as between those of other faiths and none. Though no one ever said it in this way, the lively gathering of men and women in the kitchen, the jokes in the shop, and the freedom to socialise accorded to the younger generation, suggest that such relationships between men and women were a source of vitality and sense of moral life for the community – just as relationships with those of other faiths were positively valued as a resource to be drawn on. This embracing of difference generated a robust sense of managing the challenges of life. Though both kinds of mixing would be at odds with the religious practice of some within the congregation, Guyanese sociality at the mosque had, nonetheless, a Muslim framing. It took place in relation to Ramadan, religious festivals and rituals that were prompted by the human need to turn to God, and the imam or one of the Trustees said prayers before and at the close of such occasions. What may have begun in the loss of India among a group of migrants from the sub-continent had become, through the emergence in Guyana of a new idea of Muslim Indianness, and a subsequent migration to the UK, something distinctive and valued that the Guyanese wished to protect. Yet the mosque not only reproduced the familiar customs of a Guyanese past: it also created a live on-going situation in the present in which this heritage was inevitably and inexorably being re-cast in new terms, as was happening in Bilal's class. The inclusion of both genders and the encompassing of other faith traditions were felt by the Guyanese as a source of strength, but this was not without its risks since relaxed gender-mixed sociability gives that freedom to the young that makes marrying out into other ethnic and faith groups more likely. Whether that generation will still look to the mosque as a source of religious and communal meaning is an open question though judging by the presence, at some communal events, of a scattering of elderly, white British widows in ordinary clothes and with heads uncovered, this is not an entirely new feature of Guyanese life.

Notes

1 This sense of dependence on what has been received from others was a central element in Klein's model of development. Rather than an individual in isolation, it is from an individual's dependence on others in infancy and, in time, the recognition and acceptance of that dependence, that the capacity for relationships both to others and to the internalised moral qualities of a shared world emerges (Klein 1959).

2 From a developmental perspective, Winnicott (1960) argues that it is through the continuity of the human environment of parental care, that the infant personality gains coherence.

3 A phrase first used by Keats to describe the ability of great writers such as Shakespeare to tolerate 'uncertainty and doubt' (Rollins 1958). Keat's phrase was taken up by the psychoanalyst Wilfred Bion to refer to the importance of an attitude of open-mindedness and the capacity to bear the pain of not knowing in the analytic setting (Bion 1962).
4 What Dahlgren and Schielke suggest is akin to what Winnicott (1953), a paediatrician and psychoanalyst, called 'transitional space', that between the infant and the adult caregiver within which the infant's encounter with a cultural world first takes place.
5 Azzim, a freelance religious teacher, is described in Chapters 2, 7, and 8.

References

Bion, W. (1962) *Learning from Experience*. London: Heinemann.

Crapanzano, V. (2004) *Imaginative Horizons*. Chicago: Chicago University Press.

Dahlgren, S. and Schielke, S. (2013) 'Introduction', *Contemporary Islam* 7(1): 1–13.

Deeb, L. (2006) *An Enchanted Modern: Gender and Public Piety in Shi'a Lebanon*. Princeton: Princeton University Press.

Faubion, J. (2011) *An Anthropology of Ethics*. Cambridge: Cambridge University Press.

Klein, M. (1959) 'Our adult world and its roots in infancy', *Human Relations* 12: 201–303. Republished in *The Writings of Melanie Klein*, Volume 3. London: Hogarth Press.

Lambek, M. (ed) (2010) *Ordinary Ethics*. New York: Fordham University Press.

Pelkmans, M. E. (2017) *Fragile Convictions*. New York: Cornell University Press.

Rasanayagam, J. (2013) 'Beyond Islam: Tradition and the Intelligibility of Experience', in Marsden, M. and Retsikas, K. (eds) *Articulating Islam: Anthropological Approaches to Muslim Worlds*. London: Springer.

Rollins, H. E. (ed) (1958) *Letters of John Keats*. Cambridge: CUP, pp. 193–194.

Roy, O. (2004) *Globalised Islam: The Search for a New Ummah*. London: Hurst and Co.

Schielke, S. (2009) 'Ambivalent commitments: Troubles of morality, religiosity and aspiration among young Egyptians', *Journal of Religion in Africa* 39(2): 158–185.

Simon, G. M. (2009) 'The soul freed of cares', *American Ethnologist* 36(2): 258–275.

Simon, G. M. (2014) *Caged in on the Outside: Moral Subjectivity, Selfhood, and Islam in Minangkabau, Indonesia*. Honolulu: University of Hawai'i Press.

Stern, D. (2012) *Forms of Vitality*. Oxford: Oxford University Press.

Winnicott, D. W. (1953) 'Transitional objects and transitional phenomena', *International Journal of Psychoanalysis* 34: 89–97, also in *Collected Papers: Through Paediatrics to Psychoanalysis*. London: Hogarth Press/Institute of Psychoanalysis.

Winnicott, D. W. (1960) 'The Theory of Parent–Infant Relationship', in Khan, M. M (ed) *Maturational Processes and the Facilitating Environment*. London: Hogarth.

Zigon, J. (2009) 'Hope dies last'. *Anthropological Theory* 9(3): 253–271.

REFERENCES

Austin, J. L. ([1962] 1975) *How to Do Things with Words*. Cambridge: Harvard University Press.

Baumann, G. (1996) *Contesting Cultures: Discourses of Identity in Multi-Ethnic London*. Cambridge: Cambridge University Press.

Baumann, G. (1999) *The Multicultural Riddle*. London: Routledge.

Berliner, D. and Sarro, R (2007) 'On Learning Religion: An Introduction', in Berliner, D. and Sarro, R. (eds) *Learning Religion*. Oxford: Berghahn Books.

Bion, W. (1961) *Experiences in Groups*. New York: Basic Books.

Bion, W. (1962) *Learning from Experience*. London: Heinemann.

Bowen, I. (2015) *Medina in Birmingham, Najaf in Brent*. London: Hurst and Company.

Bowen, J. (1989) 'Salat in Indonesia: The social meanings of an Islamic ritual', *Man* 24(4): 600–619.

Bowen, J. (2007) *Why the French don't like Headscarves: Islam, the State and Public Space*. Princeton: Princeton University Press.

Bowen, J. (2010) *Can Islam Be French? Pluralism and Pragmatism in a Secularist State*. Princeton: Princeton University Press.

Bowen, J. (2012) *A New Anthropology of Islam*. Cambridge: Cambridge University Press.

Boyle, H. (2006) 'Memorization and learning in Islamic schools', *Comparative Education Review* 50(3): 478–495.

Britton, R. (1989) 'The Missing Link. Parental Sexuality in the Oedipus Complex', in Steiner, J. (ed) *The Oedipus Complex Today*. London: Karnac.

Britton, R. (1998) 'Subjectivity, Objectivity and Triangular Space', in Britton, R. (ed) *Belief and Imagination*. London: Routledge.

Britton, R. (2001) 'Beyond the Depressive Position: Ps (n+1)', in Bronstein, C. (ed) *Kleinian Theory: A Contemporary Perspective*. London: Whurr.

Caper, R. (2020) *Bion and Thought Too Deep for Words*. Abingdon: Routledge.

Cenker, M. (2015) 'Ummah in the translocal imaginations of migrant Muslims in Slovakia', *Contemporary Islam* 29(2): 149–169.

Chickrie, R. (1999) 'Muslims in Guyana: History, traditions, conflict and Change', *Journal of Muslim Minority Affairs* 19(2): 181–195.

Chickrie, R. (2007) 'Islamic organisations in Guyana: Seventy years of history and politics, 1936–2006', *Journal of Muslim Minority Affairs* 27(3): 401–428.

Chickrie, R. and Khanam, B. (2016) 'Hindustani Muslims in Guyana: Tradition, Conflict and Change, 1838 to the Present', in Hassankhan, M. S. and Goolam, V. (eds) *Indentured Muslims in the Diaspora*. New Delhi: Manhar.

Clarke, M. (2013) 'Integrity and Commitment in the Anthropology of Islam', in Marsden, M. and Konstantinos, R. (eds) *Articulating Islam: Anthropological Approaches to Muslim Worlds*. London: Springe.

Condon, W. S. and Sander. L. W. (1974) 'Synchrony demonstrated between movements of the neonate and adult speech', *Child Development* 45(2): 456–462.

Connolly, W. (2006) 'Europe. A Minor Tradition', in Scott, D. and Hirschkind, C. (eds) *Powers of the Secular Modern*. Stanford: Stanford University Press.

Crapanzano, V. (2004) *Imaginative Horizons*. Chicago: Chicago University Press.

Dahlgren, S. and Schielke S. (2013) 'Introduction', *Contemporary Islam* 7(1): 1–13.

Damasio, A. (1999) *The Feeling of What Happens*. London: Heinemann.

Das, V. (2013) 'Cohabiting an Interreligious Milieu: Reflections on Religious Diversity', in Lambek, M. and Boddy, J. (eds) *A Companion to Anthropology of Religion*. Chichester: John Wiley and Sons.

Deeb, L. (2006) *An Enchanted Modern: Gender and Public Piety in Shi'a Lebanon*. Princeton: Princeton University Press.

Deeb, L. (2009) 'Emulating and/or embodying the ideal: The gendering of temporal frameworks and Islamic roles models in Shi'a Lebanon', *American Ethnologist* 36(2): 242–257.

de Koning, M. (2013) 'The moral maze: Dutch Salafis and the construction of a moral community of the faithful', *Contemporary Islam* 7: 71–84.

de Kruijf, J. (2007) 'Muslim transnationalism in Indo-Guyana: Localized globalization and battles over a cultural Islam', *European Journal of Anthropology* 50: 102–124.

Dessing N. ([2013] 2016). 'How to Study Everyday Islam', in Dessing, N. et al (eds) *Everyday Lived Islam in Europe*. London: Routledge.

Eade, J. (1996) 'Nationalism, Community, the Islamization of Space in London', in Metcalf, B. D. (ed) *Making Muslim Space in North America and Europe*. Berkeley: University of California.

Eickelman, D. F. (1978) 'The art of memory: Islamic education and its social reproduction', *Comparative Studies in Society and History* 20(4): 485–516.

Eickelman, D. F. (1992) 'Mass higher education and the religious imagination in contemporary Arab societies', *American Ethnologist* 19(4): 643–655.

Eickelman, D. F. (2000) 'Islam and the languages of modernity', *Daedalus* 129(1): 119–135.

Eisenlohr, P. (2006) *Little India: Diaspora, Time and Ethnolinguistic Belonging in Hindu Mauritius*. London: University of California Press.

Eisenlohr, P. (2011) 'Religious media, devotional Islam and the morality of ethnic pluralism', *World Development* 39(2): 261–269.

Eisenlohr, P. (2013) 'Mediality and materiality in religious performance: Religion as heritage in Mauritius', *Material Religion* 9(3): 328–348.

Eisenlohr, P. (2015) 'Mediating junctures of time: ancestral chronotypes in ritual and media practices' *Anthropological Quarterly* 88 (2) 281–304.

Elster, J. (1999) *Strong Feelings*. Cambridge, MA: The MIT Press.

Fadil, N. (2011) 'Not-/unveiling as an ethical practice', *Feminist Review* 98: 83–109.

Fadil, N. (2013) 'Performing the salat at work: Secular and pious Muslims negotiating the contours of the public in Belgium', *Ethnicities* 13(6): 729–750.

Fadil, N. (2019) 'The anthropology of Islam in Europe. A double epistemological impasse', *Annual Review of Anthropology* 48: 117–132.

Fadil, N. and Fernando, M. (2015) 'Rediscovering the "everyday" Muslim: Notes on an anthropological divide', *Journal of Ethnographic Theory* 5(2): 59–88.

Faubion, J. D. (2001) 'Towards an anthropology of ethics: Foucault and the pedagogies of autopoiesis', *Representations* 74(1): 83–104.

Faubion, J. D. (2011) *An Anthropology of Ethics*. Cambridge: Cambridge University Press.

Freud, S. 1917. 'Mourning and Melancholia', in Strachey, J. (ed) *The Standard Edition of the Complete Psychological Works of Sigmond Freud*, 14: 237–258. London: Hogarth Press.

Ghannam, F. (2011) 'Mobility, liminality and embodiment in urban Egypt', *American Ethnologist* 38(4): 790–800.

Halstead, M. (2004) 'An Islamic concept of education', *Comparative Education* 40(4): 517–529.

Halstead, N. (2008) 'Violence, past and present: "Mati" and "non-Mati" people', *History and Anthropology* 19(2): 115–129.

Haidar, G. (1996) 'Muslim Space and the Practice of Architecture: A Personal Odyssey' in Metcalf, B. D. (ed) *Making Muslim Space in North America and Europe*. Berkeley: University of California.

Hamid, S. (2018) *Sufis, Salafis and Islamists*. London: I.B. Tauris.

Hellyer, H. A. (2009) *Muslims of Europe: The 'Other' Europeans*. Edinburgh: Edinburgh University Press.

Henkel, H. (2005) 'Between belief and unbelief lies the performance of *salat*: Meaning and the efficacy of Muslim ritual', *Journal of Royal Anthropological Institute* 11: 487–507.

Hinshelwood, R. (2003) 'Group Mentality and "Having a Mind"', in Lipgar, R. M. and Pines, M. (eds) *Building on Bion: Roots*. London: Jessica Kingsley.

Hirschkind, C. (2006) *Ethical Soundscapes*. New York: Columbia University Press.

Hobson, P. (1998) 'The Inter-Subjective Foundations of Thought', in Braten, S. (ed) *Intersubjective Communication and Emotion in Early Ontogeny*. Cambridge: Cambridge University Press.

Hobson, P. (2002) *The Cradle of Thought*. London: Pan Macmillan.

Hounet, Y. (2012) 'The Ma'ruf: an Ethnography of Ritual (South Algeria)', in Dupret, B., Pierret, T., Pinto, P. and Spellman-Poots, K. (eds) *Ethnographies in Islam*. Edinburgh: Edinburgh University Press.

Huq, M. (2008) 'Reading the Qur'an in Bangladesh: The politics of belief among Islamist women', *Modern Asian Studies* 48(2/3): 457–488.

Isaacs, S. (1952) 'The nature and function of phantasy', *International Journal of Psychoanalysis* 29(2): 558–566.

Jayawardena, C. (1963) *Conflict and Solidarity on a Guyanese Plantation*. London: Athlone Press.

Jayawardena, C. (1966) 'Religious belief and social change: Aspects of the development of Hinduism in British Guiana', *Comparative Studies in Society and History* 8: 211–240.

Jayawardena, C. (1968) 'Ideology and conflict in lower class communities', *Comparative Studies in Society and History* 10: 413–446.

Jayawardena, C. (1980) 'Culture and ethnicity in Guyana and Fiji', *Man* 15(3): 430–450.

Jeldtoft, N. (2011) 'Lived Islam: Religious identity with 'non-organized' Muslim minorities', *Ethnic and Racial Studies* 34(7): 1134–1151.

Jouili, J. S. (2015) *Pious Practice and Secular Constraints*. Stanford: Stanford University Press.

Jousse, M. ([1925] 1990) *The Oral Style*. New York: Garland Publishing Inc.

Keane, W. (2007) *Christian Moderns: Freedom and Fetish on the Mission Encounter*. Berkeley: University of California Press.

Keane, W. (2010) 'Minds, Surfaces and Reasons in the Anthropology of Ethics', in Lambek, M. (ed) *Ordinary Ethics*. New York: Fordham University Press.

Keane, W. (2013) 'On spirit writing: Materialities of language and the religious work of transduction', *Journal of the Royal Anthropological Institute* 19: 1–17.

Keane, W. (2014) 'Affordances and reflexivity in ethical life: An ethnographic stance', *Anthropological Theory* 14(1): 3–26.

Keane, W. (2016) *Ethical Life: Its Natural and Social Histories*. Princeton: Princeton University Press.

Khan, A. (1997) 'Migration narratives and moral imperatives: Local and global in the Muslim Caribbean', *Comparative Studies of South Asia, Africa and the Middle East* 17(1): 127 114.

Khan, A. (2004) 'Sacred subversions? Syncretic Creoles, the Indo-Caribbean, and "Cultures in-between"', *Radical History Review* 89: 165–184.

Khanam, B. and Chickrie, R. (2009) '170th anniversary of the arrival of the first Hindustani Muslims from India to British Guiana', *Journal of Muslim Minority Affairs* 29(2): 195–222.

Klein, M. (1937) 'Love Guilt and Reparation', in Money-Kyrle, R *The Writings of Melanie Klein* 1975 Volume 1. London: Hogarth Press and International Library of Psychoanalysis 103 [Reprinted London: Vintage 1988].

Klein, M. (1940) 'Mourning and its relation to manic depressive states', *International Journal of Psychoanalysis* 21: 125–153.

Klein, M. (1952) 'On Observing the Behaviour of Young Children', in Money-Kyrle, R (ed) *The Writings of Melanie Klein* 1975 Volume 3. London: Hogarth Press and International Library of Psychoanalysis 104 [Reprinted London; Vintage 1997].

Klein, M. (1955) 'On Identification', in Money-Kyrle, R. (ed) *The Writings of Melanie Klein* 1975, Volume 3, 141–175. London: Hogarth Press and International Library of Psychoanalysis [Reprinted 1997 London: Vintage].

Klein, M. (1959) 'Our Adult World and Its Roots in Infancy', in Money-Kyrle, R. (ed) *The Writings of Melanie Klein* 1975 Volume 3. London: Hogarth Press and International Library of Psychoanalysis 104 [Reprinted London; Vintage 1997].

Kresse, K. (2013) 'On the Skills to Navigate the World, and Religion, for Coastal Muslims in Kenya', in Marsden, M. and Retsikas, K (eds) *Articulating Islam: Anthropological Approaches to Muslim Worlds*. London: Springer.

Laidlaw, J. (2002) 'For an anthropology of ethics and freedom', *Journal of the Royal Anthropological Institute* 8: 311–332.

Laidlaw, J. (2014) *The Subject of Virtue: An Anthropology of Ethics and Freedom*. Cambridge: Cambridge University Press.

Lal, B. V. (2018) 'Indian Indenture: Experiment and Experience', in Chatterji, J. and Washbrook, D. (eds) *Routledge Handbook of the South Asian Diaspora*. London: Routledge.

Lambek, M. (2000) 'The anthropology of religion and the quarrel between poetry and philosophy', *Current Anthropology* 41: 3.

Lambek, M. (2002) 'Fantasy in Practice: Projection and Introjection, or the Witch and Spirit-Medium', in Kapferer, B. (ed.) *Beyond Rationalism*. Oxford: Berghahn Books.

Lambek, M. (2007) 'On Catching Up with Oneself: Learning to Know That One Means What One Does', in Berliner, D. and Sarro, R. (eds) *Learning Religion*. Oxford: Berghahn.

Lambek, M. (2010) 'Introduction', in Lambek, M. (ed) *Ordinary Ethics*. New York: Fordham University Press.

Lambek, M. (2013) 'What Is "Religion" for Anthropology? And What Has Anthropology Brought to "Religion"?', in Lambek, M. and Boddy, J. (eds) *A Companion to Anthropology of Religion*. Oxford: Wiley Blackwell.

Laughlin, C., McManus. J, and d'Aquili, E. (1990) *Brain, Symbol and Experience: Towards a Neuro-Phenomenology of Human Consciousness.* Boston: New Science Library.

Lear, J. (2006) *Radical Hope: Ethics in the Face of Cultural Devastation.* London: Harvard University Press.

Leonard, K. (2018) 'Indians Abroad: Mixing It Up', in Chatterji, J. and Washbrook, D. (eds) *Routledge Handbook of the South Asian Diaspora.* London: Routledge.

Lewis, P. and Hamid, S. (2018) *British Muslims: New Directions in Islamic Thought, Creativity and Activism.* Edinburgh: Edinburgh University Press.

Liberatore, G. (2013) 'Doubt as a Double-Edged Sword: Unanswerable Questions and Practical Solutions among Newly Practicing Somali Muslims in London', in Pelkmans, M. E. (ed) *Ethnographies of Doubt.* London: Tauris and Company.

Lukens-Bull, R. (2007) 'Lost in the sea of subjectivity: The subject position of the researcher in the anthropology of Islam', *Contemporary Islam* 1: 173–192.

MacIntyre, A. (1981) *After Virtue.* London: Duckworth.

Mahmood, S. (2005) *The Politics of Piety.* Princeton: Princeton University Press.

Makris, G. P. (2007) *Islam in the Middle East: A Living Tradition.* Oxford: Blackwell.

Malloch, S. and Trevarthen, C. (2009) *Communicative Musicality.* Oxford: Oxford University Press.

Mandaville, P. (2007) 'Globalization and the politics of religious knowledge; pluralising authority in the Muslim World', *Theory, Culture and Society* 24(2): 101–115.

Mandel, R. (2008) *Cosmopolitan Anxieties: Turkish Challenges to Citizenship and Belonging in Germany.* London: Duke University Press.

Marchand, T. (2010) 'Making knowledge: Explorations of the indissoluble relation between minds bodies and environment', *Journal of the Royal Anthropological Institute* 16(special issue): 1–21.

Marsden, M. (2005) *Living Islam: Muslim Religious Experience in Pakistan's North-West Frontier.* Cambridge: Cambridge University Press.

Marsden, M. (2008) 'Women, politics and Islamism in Northern Pakistan', *Modern Asian Studies* 42(2/3): 405–429.

Marsden, M. and Retsikas, K. (eds) (2013) *Articulating Islam: Anthropological Approaches to Muslim Worlds.* London: Springer.

Martin, E. (2013) 'The potentiality of ethnography and the limits of affect theory', *Current Anthropology* 54(S7): S149–S158.

Massumi, B. (2002) *Parables of the Virtual.* London: Duke University.

Mattingly, C. (2012) 'Two virtue ethics and the anthropology of morality', *Anthropology Theory* 12(12): 161–184.

McGilchrist, I. (2010) *The Master and His Emissary: The Divided Brain and the Making of the Western World.* New Haven: Yale University Press.

Melter, D. (1986) *Studies in Extended Metapsychology: Clinical Applications of Bion's Ideas.* Pethshire: Clunie Press.

Miller, L., Rustin, M. E., Rustin, M. J. and Shuttleworth, J. (1989) *Closely Observed Infants.* London: Routledge.

Mohapatra, P. (2006) '"Following custom?" Representations of community among Indian labour in the West Indies, 1880–1920', *International Review of Social History* 51: 173–202.

Nussbaum, M. (1997) *Cultivating Humanity: A Classical Defence of Reform in Liberal Education.* Cambridge, MA: Harvard University Press.

Orsi, R. A. (2012) 'Afterward: Everyday Religion and the Contemporary World', in Osella, F. and Soares, B. (eds) *Islam, Politics and Anthropology.* Chichester: Wiley-Blackwell.

Osella, F. and Soares, B. (2010) *Islam, Politics and Anthropology.* Chichester: Wiley-Blackwell.

Pandian, A. and Ali D. (2010) *Ethical Life in South Asia.* Indianapolis: Indiana University Press.

Parkin, David. 2007. 'The Accidental in Religious Instruction', in Berliner, D. and Sarro, R. (eds) *Learning Religion*. Oxford: Berghahn Books.

Paul, K. (2018) 'Mourning and the Development of Internal Objects', in Garvey, P. and Long, K. (eds) *The Klein Tradition*. London: Routledge.

Pedersen, M. H. (2015) 'Islam in the Family: The Religious Socialisation of Children in a Danish Provincial Town', in Sedgwick, M. (ed) *Making European Muslims*. Abingdon: Routledge.

Pelkmans, M.E. (2013) *Ethnographies of Doubt*. New York: I.B. Tauris and Co Ltd.

Pelkmans, M. E. (2017) *Fragile Convictions*. New York: Cornell University Press.

Qureshi, R. (1996) 'Transcending Space: Recitation and Community among South Asian Muslims in Canada', in Metcalfe, B. D. (ed) *Making Muslim Space in North America and Europe*. Berkeley: University of California Press.

Rappaport, R. (1999) *Ritual and Religion in the Making of Humanity*. Cambridge: Cambridge University Press.

Rauf, M. A. (1974) *Indian Village in Guiana: A Study of Cultural Change and Ethnic Identity*. Leiden: Brill.

Rasanayagam, J. (2011) *Islam in Post-Soviet Uzbekistan*. Cambridge: Cambridge University Press.

Rasanayagam, J. (2013) 'Beyond Islam: Tradition and the Intelligibility of Experience', in Marsden, M. and Retsikas, K. (eds) *Articulating Islam: Anthropological Approaches to Muslim Worlds*. London: Springer.

Rasanayagam, J. (2018) 'Anthropology in conversation with an Islamic tradition: Emmanuel Levinas and the practice of critique', *Journal of the Royal Anthropological Institute* 24(1): 90–106.

Rissanen, I. (2015) 'Negotiating Identity, Difference and Citizenship in Finnish Islamic Education', in Sedgwick, M. (ed) *Making European Muslims*. Abingdon: Routledge.

Robinson, K. (2006) 'Idioms of vernacular humanism: The West and the East', *Anthropological Forum* 16(3): 241–255.

Rollins, H. E. (ed) (1958) *Letters of John Keats*. Cambridge: Cambridge University Press.

Roy, O. (2004) *Globalised Islam: The Search for a New Ummah*. London: Hurst and Co.

Roy, O. (2007) *Secularism Confronts Islam*. New York: Columbia University Press.

Rozario, S. (2011) 'Islamic piety against the family: From "traditional" to "pure" Islam', *Contemporary Islam* 5(3): 285–308.

Rumsey, A. (2010) 'Ethics, Language and Human Sociality', in Lambek, M. (ed) *Ordinary Ethics*. New York: Fordham University Press.

Rustin, M. J. (2006) 'Infant observation research. What have we learnt so far?', *Infant Observation* 9(1): 35–52.

Rustin, M. J. (2012) 'Infant Observation as a Method of Research', in Urwin, C. and Sternberg, J. (eds) *Infant Observation and Research*. Hove: Routledge.

Rustin, M. E. and Rustin, M. J. (2017) *Reading Klein*. New York: Routledge.

Salvatore, A and Eickelman, D. F. (2004) *Public Islam and the Common Good*. Leiden: Brill.

Sayyid, S. (2006) 'Islam and knowledge', *Theory, Culture and Society* 23(2–3): 177–179.

Schielke, S. (2009) 'Ambivalent commitments: Troubles of morality, religiosity and aspiration among young Egyptians', *Journal of Religion in Africa* 39(2): 158–185.

Schielke, S. (2010) 'Being Good in Ramadan: Ambivalence, Fragmentation, and the Moral Self in the Lives of Young Egyptians', in Osella, F. and Soares, B. (eds) *Islam, Politics and Anthropology*. Chichester: Wiley-Blackwell.

Schielke, S. and Debevec L. (2012) 'Introduction', in Schielke, S. and Debevec, L. (eds) *Ordinary Lives and Grand Schemas: An Anthropology of Everyday Religion*. Oxford: Berghahn Books.

Shannahan, D. S. (2014) 'Gender, inclusivity and UK mosque experience', *Contemporary Islam* 8: 1–16.

Shively, K. (2014) 'Entangled ethics: Piety and agency in Turkey', *Anthropological Theory* 14(4): 462–480.

Shukla, S. (2001) 'Locations for South Asian diasporas', *Annual Review of Anthropology* 30: 551–572.

Shuttleworth, J. (1989) 'Psychoanalytic Theory and Infant Development', in Miller, L. Rustin, M. E., Rustin, M. J. and Shuttleworth, J. (eds) *Closely Observed Infants.* London: Routledge.

Shuttleworth, J. (2008) 'Creating religious experience in contemporary society', *Infant Observation* 11(1): 17–28.

Shuttleworth, J. (2010) 'Faith and culture: Community life and the creation of a shared psychic reality', *Infant Observation* 13(1): 45–58.

Shuttleworth, J. (2017) 'Reading Klein; review article' *Infant Observation* 20(2–3): 196–198.

Shuttleworth, J. Britton, J. Keenan, A. and Thomaidis-Zades, K. et al (2017) 'Thinking Psychoanalytically about Mental Health Services for Children, Adolescents and Their Parents', in Vaspe, A. (ed) *Psychoanalysis, the NHS, and Mental Health Work Today,* London: Karnac.

Simon, G. M. (2009) 'The soul freed of cares', *American Ethnologist* 36(2): 258–275.

Simon, G. M. (2014) *Caged in on the Outside: Moral Subjectivity, Selfhood, and Islam in Minangkabau, Indonesia,* Honolulu: University of Hawai'i Press.

Soares, B. and Osella, F. ([2009 2010). 'Islam, Politics, Anthropology', in Osella, F. and Soares B. (eds) *Islam, Politics, Anthropology.* Chichester: John Wiley and Sons.

Sovik, M. (2015) 'Religion and Citizenship in France and Germany: Models of Integration and the Presence of Islam in Public Schools', in Sedgwick, M. (ed) *Making European Muslims.* Abingdon: Routledge.

Spillius, E. B. (2005) 'Anthropology and psychoanalysis: A personal concordance', *The Sociological Review* 53(4): 658–671.

Spillius, E. B. (2012) 'Developments by Kleinian Analysts', in Spillius, E. B. and O'Shaughnessy, E. (eds) *Projective Identification: The Fate of a Concept,* 49–60. Hove: Routledge.

Stafford, C. (2007) 'What Is Interesting about Chinese Religion', in Berliner, D. and Sarro, R (eds) *Learning Religion.* Oxford: Berghahn.

Stern, D. (1985) *The Interpersonal World of the Infant: A View from Psychoanalysis and Developmental Psychology.* New York: Basic Books.

Stern, D. (2012) *Forms of Vitality.* Oxford: Oxford University Press.

Tarlo, E. (2005) 'Reconsidering stereotypes: Anthropological reflections on the jilbab controversy', *Anthropology Today* 21(6): 13–17.

Tarlo, E. (2010) *Visibly Muslim: Bodies of Faith: Fashion, Politics, Faith.* Oxford: Berg.

Tarlo, E. (2018) 'Dress and the South Asian Diaspora', in Chatterji, J. and Washbrook, D. (eds) *Routledge Handbook of the South Asian Diaspora.* London: Routledge.

Timimi, S. (2015) 'Children and young people's improving access to psychological therapies: Inspiring innovation or more of the same?' *British Journal of Psychiatry Bulletin* 39: 57–60.

Tomasello, M. (1999) *The Cultural Origins of Human Cognition.* Cambridge: Cambridge University Press.

Toren, C. (1993) 'Making history: The significance of childhood cognition for a comparative anthropology of the mind', *Man* 28(3): 461–478.

Trevarthen, C. (1979) 'Communication and Co-Operation in Early Infancy: The Origins of Primary Inter-Subjectivity', in Bullowa, M. (ed) *Before Speech*. Cambridge: Cambridge University Press.

Trevarthen, C. (1998) 'The Concept and Foundations of Infant Intersubjectivity', in Braten, S. (ed) *Intersubjective Communication and Emotion in Early Ontogeny*. Cambridge: Cambridge University Press.

Trevarthen, C. and Aitkins, K. (2001) 'Infant intersubjectivity: Research, theory and clinical applications', *Journal of Child Psychology and Psychiatry* 42: 3–48.

Tronick, E. (2007) *The Neurobehavioural and Social-Emotional Developments of Infants and Children*. London: W.W. Norton.

Turner, V. (1969) *The Ritual Process*. Chicago: Aldine.

Urwin, C. and Sternberg, J. (eds) (2012) *Infant Observation and Research*. Hove: Routledge.

Verkaaik, O. (2012) 'Designing the 'anti-mosque': Identity, religion, and affect in contemporary European mosque design', *Social Anthropology* 20(2): 161–176.

Vertovec, S. (1994) '"Official" and "popular" Hinduism in diaspora: Historical and contemporary trends in Surinam, Trinidad and Guyana', *Contributions to Indian Sociology* 28(1): 123–147.

Vertovec, S. (2000) *The Hindu Diaspora*. London: Routledge.

Vertovec, S. (2002) 'Islamophobia and Muslim Recognition in Britain', in Haddad, Y. (ed) *Muslims in the West: From Sojourners to Citizens*. Oxford: Oxford University Press.

Waddell, M. (2006) 'Infant observation in Britain: A Tavistock approach', *International Journal of Psychoanalysis* 87(4): 4–22.

Waddell, M. (2019) '"All the light we cannot see": Psychoanalytic and poetic reflections on the nature of hope', *International Journal of Psychoanalysis* 100(6): 1405–1421.

Werbner, P. (2002) *Imagined Diasporas among Manchester Muslims*. Santa Fe: School of American Research Press.

Werbner, P. (2018) 'Ritual, Religion and Aesthetics in the Pakistani and South Asian diaspora', in Chatterji, J. and Washbrook, D. (eds) *Routledge Handbook of the South Asian Diaspora*. London: Routledge.

Wesselhoeft, K. (2010) 'Making Muslim minds: Question and answers as a genre of moral reasoning in an urban French mosque', *Journal of the American Academy of Religion* 78(3): 790–823.

Williams, B. F. (1991) *Stains on My Name, War in My Veins: Guyana and the Politics of the Cultural Struggle*. London: Duke University Press.

Winnicott, D. W. (1953) '"Transitional objects and transitional Phenomena', *International Journal of Psychoanalysis* 34: 89–97, also in Through Paediatrics to Psychoanalysis. New York: Basic Books.

Winnicott, D. W. (1960) 'The Theory of Parent–Infant Relationship', in Khan, M.M. (ed) *Maturational Processes and the Facilitating Environment*. London: Hogarth.

Woodhead, L. ([2013] 2016) 'Tactical and Strategic Religion', in Dessing, N. et al (eds) *Everyday Lived Islam in Europe*. London: Routledge.

Zigon, J. (2007) 'Moral breakdown and the ethical demand', *Anthropological Theory* 7(1): 131–150.

Zigon, J. (2009) 'Hope dies last', *Anthropological Theory* 9(3): 253–271.

Zigon, J. and Throop, J. (2014) 'Moral experience: Introduction', *Ethos* 42(1): 1–15.

INDEX

Note: Page numbers followed by "n" refer to notes.